JOHN GRIERSON AND THE NATIONAL FILM BOARD

Gary Evans

JOHN GRIERSON
and the
National
Film Board

THE POLITICS OF
WARTIME PROPAGANDA

UNIVERSITY OF TORONTO PRESS
Toronto Buffalo London

© University of Toronto Press 1984
Toronto Buffalo London
Printed in Canada

ISBN 0-8020-2519-6

Canadian Cataloguing in Publication Data

Evans, Gary, 1944–
  John Grierson and the National Film Board : the
  politics of wartime propaganda,
  Includes index.
  Bibliography: p.
  ISBN 0-8020-2519-6
  1. Grierson, John, 1898–1972. 2. World War, 1939–1945 –
  Canada – Propaganda. 3. Moving-pictures, Documentary –
  Canada – History. 4. Moving-pictures in propaganda.
  I. Title.
  D810.P7C2 1984   940.54′88971   C84-098405-7

This book has been published with the assistance of the Canada Council
and the Ontario Arts Council under their block grant programs.

To my parents, brothers Sheldon and Richard,
and my son Jesse

Contents

Acknowledgments

My thanks to the staff of the following institutions:

At the Public Archives of Canada, Ottawa, Dr W.I. Smith, the Dominion Archivist, who permitted me to see some files of the William Lyon Mackenzie King Papers when they were closed to the public. Also, J.F. Kidd, John Smart, David Smith, and James Whelan of the Post-Confederation Section, Government Documents and Manuscript Division.

At the Centre de Documentation Cinématographique, Bibliothèque Nationale, Montréal, Monsieur Pierre Allard, Director, who permitted me to see the uncatalogued Grierson Papers.

At the film archives of the National Film Board of Canada, Montreal, Madame Toni Lapointe, Director, who allowed me to set up makeshift screening facilities in the archives and who facilitated the film research.

The Film Board's Public Relations Information Officer, Sally Bochner, arranged for the reproduction of archival photographs.

The British Information Services, Ottawa, provided me with early documentary films and Grierson-related film material.

I have used the following libraries in Britain and Canada: the British Library; Centre de Documentation Cinématographique, Bibliothèque Nationale, Montréal; the Library of the National Film Board of Canada; McLennan Library of McGill University; the National Library of Canada. My thanks to them for permission to photocopy books, periodicals, documents, and other relevant material. Also, Mr David Jones of Dawson College Library, Montreal, was helpful in obtaining microfilms and articles which were not easily accessible.

I owe a great debt to Mr Tom Daly, Executive Producer at the National Film Board, whose prodigious memory of people, events, and films in 1940s Canada helped pinpoint details which added substantially to the work. He spent considerable time reading and criticizing the text and was an invaluable aid. His encouragement, guidance, and friendship over the years of this project will never be forgotten.

Thanks too to Professor Hugo McPherson, former Film Commissioner of the National Film Board, who presently is John Grierson Professor of Communications at McGill University, for his support, helpful comments, and enthusiasm.

To Peter Harcourt of Carlton University, Ottawa, and Peter Morris of Queen's University, Kingston, two of the most knowledgeable minds in Canadian film, I owe special thanks. They were very generous with their time and their criticisms were invaluable in the shaping of the text.

I was also most fortunate to have two of the early members of the first documentary school read the manuscript and then spend considerable time discussing it with me. Mr Stuart Legg, who in many ways remains an unsung eminence in the history of wartime film propaganda, was of great assistance. Not only does he have a great memory of people, facts, and details; his emphasis also sharpened the perspective and provided a useful counterpoint against which to measure my conclusions. Mr Basil Wright was helpful with his unique perspective on the documentary movement in Britain in the thirties and forties.

A special thanks to friends Ronald Blumer and Susan Schouten, whose interest in and knowledge of the subject in general and Grierson in particular encouraged me over the years of the project. In our many discussions before, during, and after the writing, their comments and criticisms were most helpful in giving cohesion to the whole.

There were numerous individuals and friends who encouraged this book. Rik Davidson of the University of Toronto Press, Piers Handling, Cheryl Buckman, Gertrude McFarlane, and Barbara Confino, Professor Peter Ohlin of McGill University, Professor Peter Marshall of the University of Manchester, England, and Dimmi Bourland deserve special acknowledgment in this regard. James A. Beveridge of York University and Stanley Hawes of Sydney, Australia, tried to assign credits to World in Action and Canada Carries On productions from memory.

My typist, Margaret Blevins, has once again displayed patience, boundless energy, and extreme accuracy in her work. Thank you.

To Canada Council Explorations Programme, my appreciation for subsidizing my leave of absence from college teaching duties at one point during this project. This book has been published with the help of a grant from the Social Science Federation of Canada, using funds provided by the Social Sciences and Humanities Research Council of Canada.

Traditionally the historian relies upon written documents to answer the questions he poses. In this book the films themselves serve as primary sources as do the principals who made the documents. I interviewed a number of these individuals after I had gathered information from print and film sources, either to substantiate what I had already found or to seek another perspective on the subject. Methodology still dictates that print and film documents, fixed and unaffected by emotions, distortions of memory, or the passage of time, are the best sources to reconstruct the story, even if they occasionally conflict with what living people think they remember. My apologies to them if I have misstated or misinterpreted what was said in personal interviews. Errors of omission or commission are mine. To recall the warning of Sir Walter Raleigh to writers of modern history, 'Whosoever, in writing a modern history shall follow truth too near the heels, it may haply strike out his teeth.' Raleigh ended his days on the executioner's block in the Tower of London.

My appreciation extends to the following people, listed alphabetically, whom I interviewed: Evelyn Spice Cherry, David Coplan, Lady Margaret Ann Elton, Guy Glover, H. Forsyth Hardy, Ross McLean, Gerald Noxon, J.W. Pickersgill, Paul Rotha, Walter Turnbull, Dan Wallace, and Helen Watson.

I am most indebted of all to the late John Grierson, whom I knew in his last years when he taught at McGill University, Montreal. I consider it to be something of an advantage to have approached this book as an outsider from another generation, whose main preoccupation is not film. Grierson allowed me to attend the majority of his lectures and seminars in 1970 and 1971 and to interview him on numerous occasions in the relaxed atmosphere of his residence. He was somewhat doubtful, though not discouraging, of this project, because of a fear that what might emerge would be a history of the man, rather than a history of the movement he founded and the idea for which it stood. I trust I have avoided that pitfall. The man could not be separated from the movement – he stood above it, a teacher, a master, a prophet and a colossus. His story is the story of a modern-day moral crusade which kept its optimism in this century of wars and contradictions. It was a message on behalf of and to the millions, that despite its self-destructive tendencies, the world will become a better place in which to live, because humanity wills it so.

Sawyerville and Montreal,
Quebec, Canada,
March 1982

Now I want you just to try to understand what we're endeavouring to do. You have to see the perspectives, the growing points behind what's going on up here on the Hill. A nation at war; but still bemused. Still half asleep. You have to search, to analyze, to articulate the potential of Canada and make it so compelling that people will want to plunge their hands into their own pockets. Their *own* pockets. You understand?

John Grierson, 1939

We are apt to think of art as something on the sidelines of life – pretty pictures on the walls, songs and music for relaxation reading – very occasional movies to while away the time on a dull night. But art is something deeper than that. If you must know the truth of art, think not of art itself but of will-power. Will-power, we know, is the strong stuff in the hearts of men that makes them fight. Will-power is the hope and the vision and the faith that makes them think that something is worth fighting for. And art – art is every song, every picture, every word that warms the faith, confirms the purpose and fires the heart. They tell us that art is a mirror – a mirror held up to nature. I think that is a false image, conceived by men in quiet unchanging times. In a society like ours, which is even now in the throes of a war of ideas and in a state of social revolution of the profoundest nature, art is not a mirror but a hammer. It is a weapon in our hands to see and to say what is right and good and beautiful and hammer it out as the mold and pattern of men's actions.

John Grierson, 'Art in Action,' 1940

The NFB wartime headquarters in a ramshackle former lumber mill on John Street, Ottawa. (NFB)

The Lighting Stores and Camera Department depot on Sparks Street was one of thirteen different buildings the NFB occupied in Ottawa. (NFB)

Using cramped facilities sometimes around the clock, busy NFB teams would assemble stock shots, edit, wade through the myriad details of each film, and check for overall accuracy in reporting. (NFB)

Sydney Newman and his *Canada Carries On* production staff in conference, 1945. (NFB)

JOHN GRIERSON AND THE NATIONAL FILM BOARD

Introduction

He was short, wiry, and sandy-haired, a firebrand of a personality whose wide blue eyes could rivet the person being addressed, while a staccato of phrases ranging from Calvin to Spinoza, from Marx to Gobineau, from Goya to Charlie Chaplin, from the greatest English poetry to the most vulgar epithets, peppered the mind like a machine-gun burst. Never at a loss for words or images, he hammered, cajoled, coaxed, demolished, then resuscitated those he chose to work for and with him. He believed he made it clear to his political masters he belonged to no man or party. From 1939 to 1945 Canada was in a world at war again and he was its propaganda maestro. No one ever called him by his first name; he was always Grierson.

Prime organizer of the documentary film movement and one of the single most important figures in documentary film in this century, John Grierson came to Canada to proselytize for the film movement he had begun; upon the outbreak of war, he found himself called upon to rally a depression-exhausted Canada to answer the fascist challenge to civilization. Grierson, who had made documentary portray peacetime with the same verve and excitement as would later portray wartime, was given the task of boosting national morale. The organization he had just helped to create, the National Film Board of Canada, was to become the national film propaganda agency.

The impact of Canada's film propaganda would be far-reaching and permanent because Grierson turned it into a crusade which to him had near-religious overtones. Grierson, propagandist, educator, mastermind, and high priest of totalitarian information, was planning to build a brave new world based on the changes he could see coming as a result of the new age and techniques of mass communications. The crusade was to change Canada's ideas about film, about propaganda, and perhaps even about the way it perceived itself as a nation. Wartime film propaganda forced Canadians to see themselves as individuals and as groups thrust on to the world stage. Every citizen was an actor in the great drama of world war. New world relationships like geopolitics and internationalism replaced old self-images of friendly tourist guides in a country of romantic natural wonders. On every level Grierson was making Canadians understand their roles as raw-material suppliers, as food producers and munitions makers, and as essential military components in the fight to save the democratic ideals which fascism wanted to crush. When he moved laterally into print propaganda, he intensified campaigns to urge Canadians to enlist, buy victory bonds, sacrifice, salvage, produce munitions and aircraft, cooperate with management, understand inflation, eat nutritionally, avoid loose talk, prepare for electrification, and perform a whole host of other communal activities whose purpose was to unite the nation.

Film propaganda was as bewildering as it was new, for it made a world war thousands of miles away urgent, immediate, and personal. The visual images which millions saw each week at Canadian theatres and in non-theatrical screenings brought them close to the crisis, imposed on them a kind of collective responsibility to act selflessly, and pointed to the great rewards to accrue in the postwar world of peace. War was the context of most films, with a constant messianic promise of peace.

Why does wartime film propaganda deserve of so much attention? Because in the pre-television age, the cinema was the common national entertainment medium. During the world crisis, theatre-owners voluntarily donated screen time and paid rental fees to screen official propaganda. These films reached millions on a regular basis both in Canada and in the United States. Until television, film was the most pervasive audio-visual means of reaching mass audiences, especially the young and less literate. Non-theatrical film circuits were expanded and millions more saw official propaganda films regularly. With such an available audience, the official propaganda film could and probably did make a substantial impact upon the population over six years of war. It is not possible to assess that impact exactly, but one may safely assume that regular exposure most certainly left an impression on national audiences. For Grierson, it was an opportunity to reach the population in a way that the British documentary movement never had. He was engaged in a totalitarian war for the population's minds, something which he fearlessly enunciated in a 1943 propaganda film called *The War for Men's Minds*.

This remarkable Scotsman's public career in Canada is the focal point of this book. He transplanted the documentary movement to Canada from Britain with characteristic energy, drive, and devotion. The crisis of war gave Grierson the freedom to reshape the propaganda film. It differed substantially from its First World War antecedents, and from the documentary films of 1930s Britain. Casually monitored by his busy superiors, he not only dominated the war propaganda machinery but also created an environment to protect the young filmmakers. Shielded by what he called a 'ring of steel,' they produced their propaganda almost unhampered by the political powers whose attention seemed fixed elsewhere. Grierson's brilliant British lieutenant, Stuart Legg, became the intellectual force behind the two theatrical series, *Canada Carries On* and *The World in Action*, and set standards for the next generation of Canadian filmmakers.

Grierson remains the focal character of this book though this is not intended to be a systematic chronology of what he did when and why. The official biography, *John Grierson: A Documentary Biography* by H. Forsyth Hardy, appeared when this book was in the manuscript stage and can provide the interested reader with a chronology, complete with dozens of personal anecdotes about Grierson by those who knew him. Hardy concentrates on the dynamic aspect of Grierson's public personality with near-hagiographical embellishments. But Grierson believed that the ideas he promoted were far more important to the future of film and communications that were the strengths and weaknesses of his personal character. When I first met Grierson in 1970 at McGill University, he pointed me constantly away from the biographical and always toward the idea, the material realities and the politics of his era. It was one way of demonstrating the Hegelian, Marxist, and Machiavellian influences on him. Also, he was trying to demonstrate that what documentary had done for the world was far more important than what he as a catalyst had done for documentary. We first met after I had spent weeks preparing for our encounter by reading everything I could about the documentary movement. Characteristically, he dis-

John Grierson (NFB)

Taking the cue from their political superiors, John Grierson and Stuart Legg (left) would lay out themes for the coming year's theatrical series. Grierson could spend up to $5,000 on the phone, which he called 'a wonderful lubricant with which to get things done.' (NFB)

Grierson insisted, 'You must forever go to where the people are.' Non-theatrical NFB films reached tens of thousands of Canadians monthly. (NFB)

missed me brusquely and told me to go read everything I could find about Goebbels. Not only was he testing the hopeful author's threshold of endurance; he was also saying that what Goebbels did for the Nazis Grierson and his movement were trying to do for democracy. After reading and digesting hundreds more pages of material, I slowly realized the the Second World War was at least on one level a chess game between the Goebbels and Grierson teams, a game whose winner would determine the alignment of loyalties and nations (perhaps) for centuries to come. The Canadian wartime propaganda film was part of the nascent communications revolution. It also was part of a crusade which tried to rationalize modern man's activities and consciousness.

The Italian Marxist, Antonio Gramsci, was also thinking and writing about communications issues as he pined away in an Italian prison in the thirties.[1] His major ideas on ideological hegemony and class struggle may be convenient reference points to analyse the conflict which was unfolding between fascism and democracy, and on a lesser level between Goebbels and Grierson. Though it is unlikely that Grierson had even heard of Gramsci, he was partly engaged in the process Gramsci was writing about, albeit from a different perspective. Gramsci was seeking to establish an organic unity between the intellectuals and the lower strata in an effort to lead the simple people to a higher conception of life. One of the most important ideas to filter down from the thirties and from Gramsci himself was the realization that the state now had the tools to use media to control and manipulate the population. This meant that the state could become more repressive than it had ever been: not only could it dominate its population by direct physical coercion, but it could also mystify power relations and public issues and events while wielding its power. The state used bureaucracy and technology as its source of cultural, intellectual, and ideological domination, thereby obscuring class and power relations. Grierson saw fascism abuse the power of the state and realized that the same abuses could happen in liberal democracy. He seized upon the documentary idea as being the vehicle for the democratic state to avoid abuse of power and to propagate new conceptions. War let him mobilize film to give the story of a great historical event. This would secure the present. To secure the future he wanted films to portray everyday things, the values and ideals that make life worth living. In this context he talked about educating people who shared the same manias. Grierson believed that the documentary idea, in shunning repression and mystification, could play the role of honest broker between the power of the state and the people, a kind of friendly medium in the service of two-way communication between the governors and the governed. Unlike Gramsci, Grierson and the documentary movement refused to consider the option of revolution in their attempt to communicate a higher conception of life. His documentary film of the 1930s and later the Canadian war propaganda film promised to change mass consciousness within the existing structures while providing the working class with a unified rather than fragmented consciousness. The Canadian war propaganda film would never tire of repeating its arguments and would work incessantly to raise the intellectual level of mass society.

The methodology or technique which documentary film employed was 'direct address'; that is, the viewer was aware of himself as the subject to whom the film was addressed. A narrator communicated with the viewer almost always as a voice of authority whose non-stop narration was unashamedly propositional, representing the point of view the film was trying to affirm.[2] This direct, authoritarian approach was not necessarily 'preachy' but in true classical style used synchronization of narration and visuals to interrelate elements whose internal structure was otherwise unspecified. Thus a library stock shot of a Chinese woman footbound and crawling toward the camera as a crowd of refugees streamed past her became analytically precise as the voice of authority insisted that 'with such proof of their own towering strength, the people of the earch march forward in their new age – march in the certainty that the gates of hell cannot prevail against them.' This sequence, predicting a brave new 'people's' postwar world, was the conclusion of the film Grierson thought was one of the Film Board's best, *The War for Men's Minds*. Theatrical wartime film propaganda continued the tradition of 'classical' expository cinema in which narrated sequences set in place a block of argumentation which the image track illustrated redundantly. It was one form of 'the creative interpretation of actuality,' Grierson's universal definition for documentary.

The approach to film was materialist, dealing with material and geopolitical factors which were affecting a world at war. But materialist factors or no, Grierson shunned Marxist dogma. Tom Daly, then an apprentice, explained how he understood the Grierson outlook: 'It was more an organic view of the world. It was not a political matter, but a human matter of correspondence. Grierson believed that democracy began with the manias people shared with each other. The manias created conviction and with conviction, a point of understanding begins.'

Documentary had not been associated with left labour causes; this meant of course that there were no political reservations about the expanded use of documentary at the beginning of the war. Prime Minister King knew what he wanted: not to have propaganda as that term was understood, but rather 'an interpretation of information using different media for the purpose.' He did not want public information to have two sides. His government was not seeking to mislead anyone, least of all to advertise itself. But the war effort had to be made better known. He nodded to Grierson.

That nod was interpreted by Grierson as a signal to undertake an evangelical mission. The mission soon extended further than film. In 1943 he would find himself in the unprecedented position of managing the government's information apparatus at the Wartime Information Board as well as continuing as film commissioner of the National Film Board. He became known as 'the propaganda maestro' as he orchestrated numerous national campaigns, in the belief he was advertising the country, not the government.

'Propaganda' is one of those Pavlovian words which more often than not sets people frothing, not salivating, at the mouth. Most liberal democracies have been very slow to use the medium of film propaganda to reach the masses other than in times of national crisis. This is probably because, in peacetime, liberal democratic governments have generally not been keen to elicit overtly positive and common responses from their citizens. While such governments this century have come to provide more and more social welfare for their citizens, there is still a strong incoherent belief that government ought to diminish its presence in the daily life of a society. Many people possess a deeply entrenched aversion to systematic government communication because of the fear that 'they' might manipulate 'us.'

From the First World War there grew a belief that propaganda was what the enemy started; that is, he was spreading ideas, facts, or allegations to further his cause and to damage the opposing side's cause. Hence the opposing side was obliged to do its part to offset this by spreading its own information from its own point of view. Propaganda from the other side came to be recognized as something one did not like and which was easily recognized for its mendacity. One's own side (the side of God) spread the truth in order to offset the enemy's lies. Of course, one's own propaganda was good and it furthered one's cause. From 1945, liberal democracies have ceased using the words 'information' and 'propaganda' interchangeably, preferring to use only 'information' in official titles. Today, most will accept the assertion that it is the others who use propaganda and one's own side which uses information. Propaganda continues to be 'what you don't like,' and the sophisticated world of advertising (goods and politics) works from the premise that contemporary society should not recognize information components as ideas, facts, or allegations for one's own cause but as values which everyone shares by common consent. These values are not controversial and do not try to convince. They only affirm. Most of us believe that advocacy of what we believe in is education and advocacy of what we do not believe in is propaganda.[3] Contemporary advertisers would be hard pressed to deny that they are engaged in promoting mass suggestion – and that is precisely what propaganda tries to achieve. This book hopes to show how Canadian government film propaganda during the Second World War was unashamedly propositional. Its purpose was to further national goals and institutions. The propaganda was educational, inspirational, and evocative. Grierson, who saw no distinction between propaganda and education, used film and print to promote a strange blend of mass suggestion and education. To him, education promoted a point of view while suppressing difficulties and objections. Traditionally in a liberal democracy education faces those difficulties and objections. But curiously, in times of national crisis, the population seems willing to accept the Grierson approach. Wartime Canada seemed eager to accept the unifying element of mass suggestion, which by virtue of its communal appeal helped ease the individual's fear of having to cope with the world crisis alone. Perhaps this is why in wartime Canada the propaganda film was welcomed so widely and developed in a *laisser-faire* atmosphere with practically no official opposition. There is no record of official complaint that the National Film Board avoided totally the divisive issue of conscription or that it covered up and failed to illuminate the disastrous Dieppe raid. Grierson was there to inspire, not question, and to promote hope over cynicism or despair.

The story of Grierson's promotion of Canadian film propaganda in the Second World War needs a historical foundation upon which to rest, or it might seem like philosophical 'news from nowhere' saying much but meaning little. For this reason I begin with a background chapter, general in its treatment of the subject of film propaganda and Grierson's documentary movement but essential to understanding later developments. It discusses how Canada had a flair for film propaganda both before and during the First World War. For all the belligerents, the 1914–18 conflict became totalitarian as the state pervaded nearly every aspect of national life. The propaganda film was one of several vehicles both the Canadian and British governments used to reach their citizens. Their joint experience demonstrates that among official government sponsors and private companies there existed rather primitive ideas about film propaganda. Friend and foe alike employed film as a weapon, less in front-line terms than for psychological mastery over home and foreign populations. They used film alongside print to win sympathy for a national point of view. If some of the strident propaganda earned negative marks, both nations learned from the war what to avoid in the future.

From this precedent evolved Grierson's documentary film movement in Britain. As the visionary of the movement, he seized the opportunity to mould government sponsorship of film into a new credo for social democracy. He surrounded himself with loyal believers who, with his guidance and inspiration, carried the torch of the crusade. Together they shared a dream that film could provide the ordinary citizens and working men with a new collective consciousness that their humdrum daily life was something of consequence. Documentary's missionaries believed that film could weave the discordant and often contradictory elements of twentieth-century existence into a thematic whole portraying peace and international understanding.

Grierson saw himself as a political progressive, yet his first rule was to stay clear of partisan politics. He was a self-appointed missionary for an idea. What was remarkable was his ability to convince the governments of both Britain and Canada to give him a chance to develop that mission. In depression Britain, where the inspiration and movement were born and bred for ten years, Grierson propagandized as far as he dared, then began to cultivate commercial and international sponsorship when the inevitable backlash began to materialize. He did not wish to see the filmmakers he trained serve as apologists for the *status quo*. Recognizing the apparent contradiction of the movement's financial dependency upon government, he was exploring both industrial and international sponsorship when war clouds appeared on the horizon.

Grierson's idea of propaganda as education would have special application to Canada in the Second World War. The element of chance also played happily into Grierson's hands as the thirties drew to a close. He was planning to seek other sponsors on the international level when the Canadian government approached him to suggest a new cosmetic for the faded national image. He was brought to Canada to help clear up the impasse left by the moribund Canadian Government Motion Picture Bureau. He created a new agency, the National Film Board of Canada. The outbreak of the Second World War gave him an opportunity to use North America's commercial theatres as outlets for his inspirational propaganda campaign. Coincidentally, he could act as an agent to help the British in their hour of need: fire the enthusiasm of the Canadian population and then coax gently from isolationist America positive thoughts about the global conflict and Britain's will to survive it.

As well, Canadian wartime propaganda extended to non-theatrical film. The National Film Board widened a prewar system of non-theatrical distribution to reach every corner of working Canada. Films made for various government departments were often circulated through this network. Field officers took the pulse of the country by reporting on audience reaction to films and they could recommend to the central office in Ottawa what audiences thought the country needed. Grierson would try occasionally to channel this advice to the prime minister's office. As he described it later with more optimism than fact, 'the great development of the war was the decentralization of responsibility to the furthest corners of the state.'

From late 1939, he and his associates produced monthly issues for commercial theatres and information 'shorts' for non-theatrical audiences. As self-proclaimed propagandist and educator, Grierson continued his mission and encouraged a blend of non-partisan progressivism and idealism, promising a better world to come after the war. He orchestrated a system whereby the state was to act as a diffuser of information over all aspects of society. Through all these channels he intended to build national consensus and national will. It was a process he would call 'being totalitarian for the good.' The phrase itself smacks of extremism and might have contributed to the failure of Grierson's crusade. Perhaps, too, a certain political recklessness in combination with his fierce individual style of operating may have been a factor. Some could attribute failure to the crusade's simplistic underpinnings. There is some reason to believe also that the entire edifice may have been built upon sand. Zeal and enthusiasm characterize a crusade; the propagandists might have been taken in by their own idealism.

Mackenzie King's government was satisfied with the film propaganda and paid Grierson scant attention. Yet most political personalities, even while caught up with their own particular responsibilities, viewed the Scotsman as an outsider and a dreamer. The prime minister, perhaps the person most sensitive of all to political breezes, was never comfortable with the freewheeling Grierson. His attention lay elsewhere until Grierson drew political heat because of his dabbling with international themes, the prime minister's own jealously guarded area of expertise. King grew nervous because the films started to preach internationalism, understanding the Soviet Union, and a brave new postwar world no longer based on traditional concepts of balance-of-power politics. Until then, the lucky Scotsman survived the war years relatively unscathed, standing, as he put it, 'one inch to the left of the Party in power.' It was, in fact, one inch too far. Just as he was preparing to leave Canada for a fling at internationalizing his propaganda crusade, he slipped and the prime minister let him fall from public grace. Grierson watched in despair as the hungry Opposition pounced on the Film Board's 'political' and 'controversial' propaganda. The government dissociated itself from the internationalist propaganda line and messianic rhetoric of its film agency. Almost overnight Canada forgot Grierson and his crusade. A slimmed-down National Film Board remained for his successor, Ross McLean, to administrate. Wartime film propaganda had affirmed the importance of the individual in a democratic society and had appealed to collective action to ensure victory on behalf of society as a whole. Victory itself had become the Promised Land. Victory achieved, and the cold war developing, there was no place for propaganda about 'tomorrow.' Fascist aggression may have been crushed, but there would be no enjoyment of peace, no fulfilment of the years of promises, no swords beaten into ploughshares.

In so far as the government was concerned, the propagandists had been brought in to fill the vacuum created by the onrush of events. Once the crisis had passed, there was no need to preach about a better world to come. One is left wondering if, despite its measured success, the propaganda crusade had played itself out by the end of the war. To the surprise of few, fundamental political power relationships among international ruling elites remained unchanged as the media turned millions of minds toward the cold war. John Grierson and his propaganda missionaries stayed outsiders, who by definition were contenders not expected to win.

7 | Early Film Propaganda: A Canadian Flair and a British Movement

One of the best and oldest definitions of documentary film is that it dramatizes fact instead of fiction and attempts to render a creative interpretation of actuality from an immediate social situation. It might be fair to assert that documentary film has its roots in the very first moving pictures ever made, because the subjects were non-theatrical and real. Representation of the events themselves preceded the use of a dramatic framework. From the Lumière brothers' 1894 record of workmen filing out of their factory, early films promised to thrill audiences with the magic of movement while offering information and description. What they lacked and what documentary film would develop was the use of the record or reconstruction toward specific educational, political, and social ends. Primitively evocative early films had less appeal to the intellect than to the eye. But audiences preferred entertainment and fantasy to education or social purpose. Film meant that from twenty minutes to an hour they could escape humdrum reality with a ten-minute melodrama, a comedy, and perhaps a travelogue or interest film. Neophyte movie-goers enjoyed their new window on the world.

Most governments did not seem to be very impressed with the medium as a means of communicating with their citizenry in either an educational or political context. One exception was Canada, where in 1896 motion pictures appeared in the capital, Ottawa. Canada was one of the first countries to see the practical application of film for specific ends, namely to attract immigrants to settle its largely vacant Northwest. In 1900 Canada encouraged the Canadian Pacific Railway to advertise Canada's 'Last Best West' to potential homesteaders. Canada had the last open frontier in North America and the government supported an assortment of publicity efforts which portrayed the natural attractiveness of the land. Some keen minds at the CPR thought that film might promote British immigration and the CPR itself. Canada had become a British North American nation linked from sea to sea, ready to join the rest of the western world as a resource-based cog in its vast industrial machine as well as a supplier of staple foodstuffs. It all depended on immigrants coming to settle the West. Earlier governments had tried and failed to attract enough homesteaders to fill the prairies. Until the first decade of the century, excessive emigration had offset immigration, which itself was showing a disturbing tendency toward Americanizing the British North American identity.

The CPR films, known as 'scenics,' were called the *Living Canada* series, and after a January 1903 première were exhibited in England in corn exchanges, town halls, and numerous theatres, as well as in Ireland, Scotland, and Wales, accompanied by a qualified lecturer at each performance.[1] The CPR reported that the results from the emigration standpoint were most encouraging; government figures show that from 1900 to 1908, 440,419 British immigrants came to Canada, a figure which surpassed the 322,583 from the United States.[2] Early Canadian government promotional films also went to the United States, hoping to attract potential settlers and investors in Canadian agriculture. Other films demonstrated primary production in lumbering, fishing, and mining. The *Living Canada* series probably played some role in attracting British immigrants, though critical audiences most certainly would have seen that one of the earliest uses of propaganda was to suppress information as well as to inform: under order from the CPR, the filmmakers cut winter scenes because the sponsors wished to give no credence to the widely held British belief that Canada was a land of ice and snow.

In 1919–20, the CPR became interested in newsreel production and invested in a Canadian subsidiary of Associated Screen News of the United States, called Associated Screen News of Canada. The subsidiary would survive the demise of the parent company probably because the CPR controlled half interest in the Canadian company. With solid financial backing, it became the first successful film production company in Canada. Associated Screen News did not produce a newsreel series, but remained a news-gathering agency, sending material abroad. The first commercial productions occurred in the mid-twenties and were travel and promotional films for the continuing *Living Canada* series and later for industrial sponsors. Associated Screen News came to play an important role in the Second World War by supplying technical facilities to the National Film Board and producing a number of films for that institution.

The Canadian government had used film officially in peacetime before it developed the medium for wartime propaganda. In 1914, the Department of Commerce and Industry envisioned the future use of film as an adjunct to trade and promotion in other countries. From this the Exhibits and Publicity Bureau evolved, and by 1918 it was producing commercial film propaganda on a regular basis. The films concentrated on Canada's natural resources and industrial activities. Significantly, the Exhibits and Publicity Bureau was the first government film production unit in the western world. It sent its representatives abroad to stimulate interest in the country and its products. Theatrical distribution grew too as the *Seeing Canada* series met with increasing acclaim in Canada, Britain, the United States, Australia, New Zealand, South America, and Japan. These one-reel scenic films and high-quality travel pictures gave the world a new perspective on the north country and wilderness. They said nothing, however, about the people and politics of Canada. The Exhibits and Publicity Bureau's *raison d'être* was to increase trade and tourism. It succeeded by portraying Canada almost entirely in terms of picturesque landscapes. Travel films continued to be the Canadian government's major product and were as non-political as they were uncontroversial. The bureau became the Canadian Government Motion Picture Bureau in 1923 when it dropped its trade exhibit. By 1927, some seventy-seven government organizations, representing thirteen departments, had requested and received materials produced by the bureau, which had also expanded its theatrical and non-theatrical distribution on an international scale.

With characteristic Canadian duplication, each province also established a motion picture bureau, which generally speaking was an adjunct of, or in some way connected to, the board of censors of that province. In imitation of the federal organization, these film bureaus produced and distributed films for agricultural training, general education, and advertising provincial products.

One of the largest provincial sponsors of film was the Ontario Government Picture Bureau: in 1919 it began sponsoring tourism films which soon received theatrical distribution in large American cities near Ontario's border. By the mid-twenties, Ontario rivalled the output of the Canadian Government Motion Picture Bureau in Ottawa. Its films included a number of educational and community efforts and by 1926 non-theatrical distribution was in the thousands of reels per month from a film library of over two thousand film subjects. Saskatchewan also established regular production and distribution and was concerned mainly with agricultural subjects. Most of its films were produced under the auspices of the provincial Department of Agriculture, which sent regional representatives through the province to screen the films in churches and grange halls. Though production ended with the depression, the precedent of using this type of non-theatrical distribution was built upon by the National Film Board during the war years over a decade later. British Columbia also created a film service in 1919 and after a brief fling at the theatrical shorts market returned to producing educational and training films. The provincial film bureaus were phased out of existence as economy measures during the depression and none were left by 1939.[3]

Though the Canadian government had established the early precedent of communicating with its citizens through film, these films were notable for what they lacked. Neither political nor propaganda, they did not appeal to basic human emotions, nor did they try to define the national purpose or seek to elicit or provoke collective action. It would be during the national crisis of war that Canada, closely allied with Britain in the struggle, would discover the capacity for mass suggestion in film propaganda's verbal and visual message.

CANADA, BRITAIN, AND OFFICIAL WAR PROPAGANDA

If the First World War offered a seemingly limitless field for commercial news exploitation in the form of the newsreel, it also provided a suitable testing ground for print and film propaganda. All the belligerents produced general propaganda from the outset, mainly to encourage enlistment. Then as the stakes rose and the war became total, they turned to developing the propaganda film to obtain a positive and collective response to specific national goals. They found too that film provided a superficial cosmetic for political leaders. Canadian and British war propaganda films began to be made in response to the Austro-Hungarian and German enemies, who were using print and film as psychological weapons upon friend and foe alike. If war films were crude politically and almost totally lacking in ideological content, the war established the potential of film as a persuasive political tool. Neither the documentary film nor the documentary film movement would be born in the First World War, but the precedent of government sponsorship of film propaganda provided the seed-bed from which John Grierson's documentary movement would emerge a decade and a half later.

To publicize its position as an independent nation expressing imperial solidarity, Canada appointed Max Aitken (later Lord Beaverbrook) the Canadian Eye Witness, a liaison person with no specific duties or posts who acquired the rank of lieutenant-colonel in the Canadian militia and stationed himself in General Headquarters, France. Using the Canadian Armed Services, Aitken eventually became the voice of Canada in Britain. As the first war correspondent of semi-official standing, Aitken ran into stiff military censorship until April 1915, when the Canadian government intervened on his behalf. Thereafter, he could and did defy British censorship rules in propagandizing for Canada. Among his many activities as a publicist, Aitken started a daily newspaper for Canadian troops and participated in the Canadian war memorials fund, which commissioned artists to paint scenes of war. He developed a philosophy of propaganda which, oddly enough, would account for the future success of Canadian film propaganda in the Second World War. The British would miss the point in their own experience with film propaganda during both wars. In Aitken's words, 'No propaganda reaches the hearts and minds of the people unless it is so convincing that the public is ready and anxious to pay a price to see or read it.' Canadian theatre-owners would pay rental fees for government film propaganda in the next war; their British counterparts would receive theirs free, hence would often neglect to screen it. Aitken became absorbed with the visual impact of the war as well as with the printed word. In 1916, he was behind the appointment of an official

Canadian photographer at the front. Not only were the first photos of tanks Canadian; when the British press wanted to show a tank, they had to borrow the picture from Aitken's office. It was said by some that the impact on the United States of his Canadian war dispatches had been so great that Canada appeared to be fighting the war alone.[4]

Aitken also chaired Britain's War Office Cinematograph Committee, which worked in cooperation with the official cinema team, created in 1916. That same year the committee bought out the Topical Film Company and began producing its own regular newsreels. The committee took over control of film arrangements between Britain and Canada and, by the end of the war, showed a profit of nearly £72,000, of which £50,000 was distributed among war charities. D.W. Griffith's *Hearts of the World* was a spectacular success for the committee, earning for it some £13,000 in 1918.

Aitken's eye for publicity was captivated by the potential of film, though he must have known that newsreel companies were faking a good deal of their wartime footage. The mercurial Canadian did not stay with his task long enough to develop a philosophy of manipulating film to a specific end. He went only as far as taking film at its face value, as moving pictures which showed actual history in the making:

The new generation will see the Battle of the Somme as though we saw the Egyptian Wars of the Eighties, the Fall of Khartoum, the assault of the Canadians at Paardeburg, or the combattants at the Battle of Mukden; and Courcelette and La Mouquet will be as vivid to them in fact as any of the great events of history are to us in imagination.[5]

It would take other minds to develop the potential of film propaganda into a socially animating force aimed at progressive ends, but Aitken (Beaverbrook) earned himself a place in the history of film propaganda, not so much for developing the medium as for encouraging its development. Beaverbrook was soon off on other assignments, including Canadian record officer, Canadian military representative overseas, and finally the minister of information in Lloyd George's government. He was hardly to be envied, as one biographer put it, since most politicians distrusted propaganda as much as they distrusted Beaverbrook himself.

The absence of popular respect for propaganda was one reason why Beaverbrook's ministry came to have an almost exclusive concern with disseminating propaganda abroad. The ministry was supposed to have no concern with opinion at home, but rather to 'strike at and undermine enemy morale.' None the less, the ministry was to become involved in significant 'home front' propaganda and Beaverbrook would use personal contact to bring press correspondents around to the government's point of view. In the Second World War Canadian and British propaganda activities would be directed toward home audiences first and friends and neutrals second.

The ministry was most successful where Beaverbrook extended the work he had already been doing for Canada. Later on, he credited the newsreel with being the decisive factor in maintaining the morale of the population in the dark days of early summer 1918. But he failed to achieve establishment of a single government film agency.

Beaverbrook claimed credit some years later for having 'seized on the cinema,' the major medium of mass entertainment, for the dissemination of propaganda. His ministry expanded the application of the film tag, a two-minute film which incorporated a useful moral in story form, such as 'Save Coal' or 'Buy War Loans.' After the ministry concluded a standing arrangement with the three major newsreel distributors to add these film tags to their bi-weekly issues, about ten million people saw each tag. Government departments used the film tag for various appeals to the national duty in wartime. The ministry was about to exploit the possibilities of the story film when the war ended.[6]

The film tag was not exclusive to Britain. All the major adversaries used it regularly, including the Americans when they came into the war. Take, for example, a 1918 Famous Player/Lasky/Zukor 'Victory Loan' film tag, which was tailored especially for Canadian audiences. The film opened depicting a Canadian soldier recovering in hospital under the gentle care of a beautiful Canadian nurse (Lillian Gish). He dictated a letter to his mother which the nurse duly inscribed. Then a title card announced an air attack on the hospital, 'Under the bombs of the merciless Hun,' and all hell broke loose as the hospital was hit by a German biplane. The nurse refused to abandon her helpless patient and threw herself over him. The hospital collapsed in its entirety under the bombardment, killing everyone. A final message flashed across the screen, 'Buy Victory Bonds.' The stark contrast between the innocent soldier and nurse and the unseen German enemy who lacked a shred of humanity would have had a telling effect on the viewing audience.

The myth that was perpetuated would have it that in war the other side commits atrocities while one's own side is fair, human, just, and plays by the rules. Perpetuation of this hate campaign continued, typified in such British films as *The Leopard's Spots*.

As this film began, it showed two German soldiers striking down a French woman and baby. Then they appeared in postwar England, selling German wares in the countryside. A British woman, examining one man's goods, noted a 'made in Germany' trademark. She cast a scornful eye at the German and called a constable who dutifully threw them both out. A final notice flashed on the screen and warned the public that there could not possibly be any more trading with these people after the war. Under this statement appeared the words, 'Ministry of Information.' A member of Parliament, Leif Jones, criticized the ministry for this specific film (which he thought was entitled *Once a Hun Always a Hun*) and, in a not altogether unrelated connection, condemned sharply the ministry's leadership for being comprised primarily of men with business links, in his words 'a wholly formidable combination'; he alleged that the subject of the film could only benefit British businessmen. *The Leopard's Spots* (*Once a Hun Always a Hun*) was a dangerous example of how a government propaganda film had, without authority, tried to seize the initiative, to anticipate and set postwar policy, while the government had not yet discussed its plans publicly.[7] After the war, this sort of film propaganda was recognized as having a negative impact, and in the Second World War both Canada and Britain tried assiduously to avoid hate-mongering.

The Ministry of Information's limited successes under Beaverbrook did not disguise its major problem, its thorny relationship with other government ministries and agencies. In short, the word 'propaganda' kept its negative connotation. This may have been one reason for the ministry's constantly strained relations with the Foreign Office. Beaverbrook noted that he had to employ a full-time secretary simply and solely for the purpose of conducting diplomatic correspondence with the Foreign Office as with a neighbouring and none too friendly power. The War Office and Admiralty snubbed the ministry's requests for intelligence information after the Foreign Office snatched away the entire intelligence bureau that had been part of the Department of Information. Prolonged wrangling brought out the worst in Beaverbrook and wore him down physically. He threatened to resign. After further deterioration of his health, he submitted his resignation in October 1918. The ministry ended shortly thereafter with the conclusion of the war. Its passing was an ignominious one – virtually all of its records were burnt.[8]

THE IMPACT OF THE PROPAGANDA FILM

By the end of the war, some sort of revolution in communications had occurred in all countries engaged in the struggle. Though print remained the primary mode of conveying information and of improving public relations, a new era in electronic communication had dawned. To a limited extent, film had succeeded in directing the national purpose to specific activities such as recruitment and economy. Propaganda film had proven its value politically, too, both as a means of making politicians come alive to the populations they served and, in the wartime context, in its appeal to basic human emotions when addressing the multitudes. Propaganda was largely expressions of patriotic platitudes woven with sentiments of honour and duty.[9] Press and film had developed the power, wrote British press baron Lord Northcliffe, to telegraph a message to millions with damnable reiteration. In the world of information, power had come to be derived from mass suggestion, from a slogan or expression in the form of short phrases repeated again and again until it produced an instinctive reaction. Most would probably have agreed that the propaganda formula which applied to newspapers also applied to film: 'What you say about your product is just as important as the product itself. What other people can be made to say about it is even more so.'

In the long view, home-front propaganda was successful in establishing domestic goals such as recruitment, food economy, and national savings, and in this context film gained enormous prestige as an instrument of national purpose, albeit as a late arrival. Films in the First World War were all silent, yet there were those who saw their great attraction and potential. British writer Hall Caine took an idealist's point of view when he claimed that film backed by a human voice appealed to humanity as a whole. He thought that film should make all men kin. 'A story which is dramatic, interesting, picturesque and human, and makes so wide an appeal that it is freed from all national and local limitations, speaks to the world. But to make a universal appeal, it must be elemental; it must deal with obvious things – things that begin with the Garden of Eden and will go on till man's last hour.' Young John Grierson, who was at this time patrolling North Sea waters on a British minesweeper, would discover the same elements of simplicity and drama in the ordinary when he began to study film in the twenties.

While Grierson would reject Caine's vision of film as a talking book, Nazi propagandist Joseph Goebbels would in the Second World War return to the theme of the 'elemental' in a way which, ironically, seemed to support Caine; though Goebbels rejected the liberal and progressive insistence on the value of the individual that was crucial to the documentary film movement's ideology, he came uncomfortably close to the mainstream of that movement. His sentiment was that speaking, not writing, was the essence of effective propaganda, and cited his mother as a representative of the 'voice of the people'; from her he learned that the rank and file were usually much more primitive than governments imagined. Propaganda therefore had to be always simple and repetitious.[10] The documentary film movement would also reach out to represent the voice of the people on film. The critical difference was that the documentary movement gave people credit for being intelligent and discerning rather than for being primitive. The next war would test each side's philosophy and determine who was right.

The First World War had demonstrated how information as a whole played a valuable secondary role in what was now 'total' war. As an obscure clergyman had put it when he addressed the members of the film industry in Glasgow during the war, 'You are a profession whose duty it is to inculcate ideals in a pleasing way.' The double-edged meaning of his words no doubt could inspire both the believers in, and the haters of, democracy and liberal progressivism. Ideals, like truths, are neutral until they are put into a political context. During the national trauma of war, the task is easy. In the First World War, those directing propaganda had both to respond to the other side's propaganda and persuade their own participants and friends that Truth and God rested on their side. In both Britain and Canada, government sponsorship of film propaganda was limited to war-oriented themes for the duration of the crisis. Social problems and the idealistic attitudes and political inspirations which could have accompanied their interpretation were ignored. What is significant is that peacetime social issues would become the 'Oklahoma' or unoccupied territory which Grierson said years later was waiting to be filled by film. Here is where the documentary movement would take root.

Print and film propaganda had developed a new basis of communicating in the First World War. Both appealed to traditional prejudices of the nation and of each constituent group through language ties, social ties (like democratic customs and institutions), economic ties, interpenetration of the population, relative military confidence, and a thorough understanding of the tension level or tenor or the public psyche.[11] In Canada, the Canadian Government Motion Picture Bureau would continue to develop the new medium in the peacetime twenties and thirties, mainly to promote trade and tourism. Until 1939, Canadian film propaganda techniques were applied to advertising landscape and natural resources, while with few exceptions images of people and their daily life were excluded from the screen. The catalytic effect of John Grierson and his school of idealistic filmmakers would change all this and give substance to the argument that propaganda techniques used properly and in the national context might make a nation *more* democratic, especially if the viewers identified themselves, their values, and their national aspirations upon the screen. Canada would give him *carte blanche* to undertake a propaganda crusade along these lines during another cataclysm of world war. This would grow out of the successful documentary film movement in Britain. But first the 1920s thrust a reluctant civilization into an even more confusing era of contradiction, instability, and will to self-destruction. W.L. George, a contemporary sociologist and novelist, predicted for the decade that after so much pain, delight, love, and hatred, the survivors of the Great War might find life rather flat. By the end of that decade, John Grierson insisted that if the British government would sponsor him, he could through film bring to life a new and positive public attitude. Film could also stimulate empire trade. A few key people were prepared to listen to the crusading propagandist and the documentary movement was born.

EMPIRE FILM PROPAGANDA: THE EMPIRE MARKETING BOARD

By the 1920s, the British government had relinquished most of the special powers it had needed to wage the First World War. The period was characterized by a visible retrenchment from the powerful directing position government had enjoyed in wartime. If there was a genuine hope that 'business as usual' would characterize the readjustment process from war to peace, the word 'usual' had lost its meaning during the war years. And business, far from being usual, was erratic. The Stanley Baldwin government enacted preferential tariff cuts in 1923 and tried to encourage emigration of its unemployed to distant dominions like Canada and Australia. At the Imperial Conference of 1923, Prime Minister King was not enthusiastic; he thought British immigration would likely encourage Canadian emigration. Leo S. Amery, Britain's secretary of state for dominion affairs, failed to win King over and pushed for the establishment of an Empire Marketing Board whose main purpose would be to spend money on research and advertising to create a 'non-tariff preference' for empire goods in the British market. His belief that British emigration would stimulate increased empire trade met with King's lifelong suspicion of Britain's embrace. He would not listen to emigration schemes.[12] Trade, yes; more immigration, no.

Sentiments for empire assumed a new meaning at the Imperial Conference of 1926, as the British government explored cautiously the possibilities of sponsoring empire and film propaganda for peacetime commercial purposes. During the First World War British film interests had lost out to their American counterparts, and in the twenties the Americans succeeded in undermining whatever market strength remained to the British commercial film industry. For British film interests, the twenties were a decade of depression and insecurity. Sentimental imperialists and empire businessmen alike dreamed of an empire united both by common feelings and a single market. Related to this was the practical suggestion that more films screened in the British Empire should be produced by the empire and those films should project an ideal British image.

The conference's general economic subcommittee reported that there was a need for an increased production of films of high entertainment value and sound educational merit. In November, the conference issued a report which noted the importance of the cinema as an 'instrument of education in the widest sense of that term.' This pleased both the sentimentalists and the businessmen, since it was obvious that films not only promoted cultural values but also sold goods. Deliberations of the Imperial Conference led to a resolution that more of the films exhibited throughout the empire should be of empire production and that empire governments should take early and effective action to deal with the serious situation. As a whole, the Imperial Conference was an admirable, if somewhat unrealistic, attempt on the part of British imperialists to keep economic cohesion within the empire.

One of the major outcomes of the conference was to bring to life in May 1926 Leo Amery's 1923 idea for an Empire Marketing Board. The new agency was supposed to subsidize research on the preserving and transport of empire foodstuffs in the British market.[13] Its first secretary was the imaginative public relations expert Sir Stephen Tallents. Promised an annual budget of one million pounds sterling, Tallents used his extensive experience as a government publicist to develop the ideas of national presentation by the use of posters, newspapers, exhibitions, school classroom walls, and, to a limited extent, film. With his eye fixed toward promoting imperial products and sentiments throughout the empire, Tallents directed his energies to appeal to those people living above the subsistence level who could purchase highly finished goods. He sought to project to them a picture of British industrial quality. They were people, he believed, who were most susceptible to the new art of national presentation. Of a budget of £500,000 in 1926, only £150,000 was spent. The budget for 1927 was £600,000 with an additional £600,000 to be made available if necessary, though Winston Churchill used his power to keep the purse strings tight. With relative financial liberty, Tallents began to experiment with some new ideas to promote the empire. At this auspicious moment John Grierson would enter the scene and in a few years establish the documentary film movement. Grierson would begin his career as a public servant and film propagandist, chasing what he called, years later, 'the bluebird of Empire.' Thus, his hallmark and most successful film, *Drifters*, would be oriented toward empire commerce, though it was original in its progressive treatment of the common man at work.

ENTER JOHN GRIERSON

Grierson was born in 1898 in Deanstown, near Stirling, Scotland, the son of two teachers. His father was a Calvinist headmaster of the village school near his home and his mother served as an occasional substitute while managing a large family. His education at Glasgow

University was interrupted by the First World War, during which he served on a minesweeper on the North Sea between 1914 and 1917. After the war he returned to civilian life and earned a master's degree in philosophy from Glasgow, graduating with distinction in 1923. He lectured briefly at Durham University, then between 1924 and 1927 held a Rockefeller Foundation Fellowship in the United States. There he studied at the University of Chicago where professors like Charles E. Merriam, Harold Lasswell, Leo Rosten, and Walter Lippmann directed his interest in the dynamics of public information. He began by studying the patterns of assimilation adopted by immigrants to the United States. This led him to examine the psychology of propaganda. He studied the development of newspaper and film media and began to write on the modern problems of education and public information.

Grierson returned to England and, with a letter of introduction from the poet Robert Nichols, met Tallents. 'Brimming with ideas,' the young Scotsman was taken on at the Empire Marketing Board where he was given his head to explore the idea of national presentation through film. Tallents recognized in Grierson a man who had been steeped, but never dyed, in the colours of orthodox education: 'a man with a propagandist flair and a love of films, a twentieth-century radical, shrewd, forceful, no poet but a social prophet, an oxy-acetylene firebrand with the showmanship of Barnum and Bailey and the sincerity of Moody and Sankey.' The fiscally wise young man could also accept a totally inadequate budget to make an inadequate film which would produce a larger but still inadequate budget to make a more ambitious film. This was the stuff of which responsible public servants were made.[14]

The Empire Marketing Board was to promote trade, not politics. Tallents planned to create a school of national projection in the borderland which lay between government and private enterprise. Using all channels of communication, the new propaganda would inspire, not regulate. Few would have thought in 1929 that development of this sort of propaganda could become something more than an uninspiring task of making commercials to sell the sponsor's goods.

At the Empire Marketing Board, Grierson began his duties as films officer, a position he shared with Walter Creighton. Creighton had studied the impact of film in Canada and noted in 1928 that there was a fear of the far-reaching effects of showing American films exclusively. School children, in seeing only American achievements on the screen, were becoming convinced of their own inferiority. He recommended that all government cinema activities throughout the empire be organized so that they could keep in touch and show important events, developments, and customs. In short, he concluded, dignified and attractive artistic films could 'spread that intimate understanding of each other that alone can bind together such a diversity of lands and peoples as is contained in the Commonwealth of Nations.' He believed Canada would welcome a lead and encouragement from Britain.[15] This was the kind of philosophical approach that was already at the core of Grierson's thinking.

Before he could take his first step, Grierson drew flak and suffered embarrassment. Questions were asked in Parliament late in 1928 about the work of the Empire Marketing Board cinema officer who, it was admitted (to the amusement of the film trade) had no technical experience. L.S. Amery answered awkwardly that 'the cinema officer had not previously been engaged in technical cinema work, but he had had experience which was felt to qualify for the Board's particular requirements in this field.' Undaunted, Grierson wrote a series of memoranda on the position of film in different countries, stressing non-theatrical production. He wrote too about France, where educational cinema had been recognized and developed as early as 1896. Various departments and organizations had set up film libraries, but both distribution and production labours had been duplicated unnecessarily. Grierson hoped that Britain would not commit the same errors. To encourage more interest in British non-theatrical films, he arranged a series of foreign-made interest shorts at the Imperial Institute. The films emphasized national achievements, and Grierson convinced Tallents and other Marketing Board members to come view them monthly for their own instruction.

The Empire Marketing Board must have been encouraged. In a confidential report on 1 March 1928 the board's film committee, of which Grierson was a member, wrote that it was impressed by: 1 / the possibilities of cinema in fields of scientific research, agricultural instruction, and marketing propaganda; 2 / the need to attract commercial interests to this end; and 3 / the need to develop distribution facilities including a film library. The last point would bring him to Canada in 1930–1. Before long, Grierson began pressing Tallents about making his own film on national achievement.

The unpretentious subject of herrings was the tactical choice for the film that was to become *Drifters*, mainly because the financial secretary to the Treasury, Arthur Michael Samuel, had a mania for the subject and the Treasury was the biggest obstacle to overcome. Samuel had written a book, *The Herring: Its Effect on the History of Britain*, and it did not take much salesmanship to convince him to support a film on the herring industry. The Treasury allotted Grierson £2,500 to make his film. In explaining the subject years later, Grierson noted humorously, 'If the Civil Service or any other public service must have its illegitimate infants, it is best to see that they are small ones.'[16] *Drifters* was screened in 1929 with the first British showing of Serge Eisenstein's *Potemkin*, which had been banned by the British Board of Censors since its release in 1925. The impact which *Drifters* made was sensational. Grierson later remarked that the Russians, after a brilliant period in which the Revolution was starkly relived and all its triumphs registered, found it more difficult to come to grips with peace. They continued to praise triumphantly the spirit of revolution. Grierson felt that the technique of mass energies and significant symbols, suitable for the stress of revolution, only embarrassed the quieter issues of peacetime life. *Drifters*, as a counterpoint to the Russian emphasis, allowed the British to laud 'workaday Britain brought to the screen for the first time.'

A few months after completing *Drifters*, Grierson wrote an essay called 'The Worker as Hero,' describing the conception behind his film. It also gave definition to the film genre the world would recognize as documentary.

It is about the sea and about fishermen, and there is not a Piccadilly actor in the place. The men do their own acting, and the sea does its, – and if the result does not bear out the 107th Psalm, it is my fault. Men at labour are the salt of the earth: the sea is a bigger actor than Jannings or Mikitin or any of them: and if you can tell me a story more plainly dramatic than the gathering of the ships for the herring season, the going out, the shooting at evening, the long drift in the night, the hauling of nets by infinite agony of shoulder muscle in the teeth of a storm, the drive home against a head sea, and (for finale) the frenzy of a market in which said agonies are sold at ten shillings a thousand, and iced, salted and barrelled for an unwitting world, – if you can tell me a story with a better crescendo in energies, images, atmospherics and all that make up the sum and substance of cinema, I promise you I shall make my next film of it forthwith.

With camera and cameramen lashed to the wheelhouse, Grierson had found high adventure in the commonplace and ordinary life of North Sea fishermen. Some forty years later he would explain, with a glint in his eye, the success of *Drifters*: 'It made people seasick.' What he meant was that he had discovered that documentary film was, from the beginning, an adventure in public observation. He articulated this point in 1939:

It [documentary] might, in principle, have been a movement in documentary writing, or documentary radio, or documentary painting. The basic force behind it was social not aesthetic. It was a desire to make a drama from the ordinary to set against the prevailing drama of the extraordinary: a desire to bring the citizen's eye in from the ends of the earth to the story, his own story of what was happening under his nose. From this came our insistence on the drama of the doorstep. We were, I confess, sociologists, a little worried about the way the world was going. ... We were interested in *all* instruments which would crystallize sentiments in a muddled world and create a will toward civic participation.[17]

It is a little-known fact that Grierson experimented with the *compilation* film, at the end of 1929, just after he completed *Drifters*. The compilation film used archival and stock shot material which, with skilful editing, could persuade audiences politically or commercially. Esther Schub, a Russian filmmaker, had made a major contribution to the Russian political compilation film in 1926; predictably, the British used the compilation film primarily as a means of selling. In the film *Conquest*, made for school children, Grierson and Basil Wright employed Hollywood stock shots of locomotives, cowboys, and Indians and a materialist analysis to explain the importance of modern transportation in the taming of the American West. Advanced social organization and its technology brought about an end to pre-industrial nomadic Indian civilization. The technique of the compilation film was to become a most effective means of countering enemy film propaganda in the Second World War; but Grierson chose to develop the British documentary film along the lines of *Drifters* rather than those of *Conquest*, probably because the technique of *Drifters* let the producer and director determine tempo and action. This allowed greater artistic control than did manipulating dated newsreel or stock footage. The difference between the two types was significant: though both kinds of films were consciously persuasive, the compilation film was limited by what someone else had recorded previously about the subject, while in documentary film the director and producer had much wider creative scope. The latter enjoyed the luxury of time; the former was dictated by the urgency of war and lack of time. Grierson's close associate Stuart Legg perfected compilation film technique using a 'voice of authority' narration to illustrate the images in Canada's two wartime theatrical series.

FROM THE EMPIRE MARKETING BOARD
TO THE GENERAL POST OFFICE

The dramatic success of *Drifters* established Grierson's reputation, and before long the Empire Marketing Board was sponsoring the first Film Unit, a school of documentary filmmakers which Grierson trained between 1930 and 1932. By July 1933 the Film Unit had grown into a documentary school of over thirty members who were committed to the principle of collective filmmaking. From this school would emerge some of the outstanding figures in British documentary film: Basil Wright, Arthur Elton, Stuart Legg, Paul Rotha, John Taylor, Harry Watt, Donald Taylor, Edgar Anstey, Evelyn Spice, Marion Grierson, Alexander Shaw, and J.D. Davidson, to name only a few.

In 1930, the Imperial Conference was held in London, in part to search for a collective approach to the depression. There emerged a recommendation that contact in film production be established throughout the empire. This gave Grierson reason to visit Canada at the beginning of 1931 to see films and establish contact with film people at the Canadian Government Motion Picture Bureau and the Ontario government's film bureau. Captain Frank Badgley, head of the former agency, made available enough material for Grierson to return to England in 1931 to set up a library which was to become a major source of non-theatrical films for schools and others. In its first year, the library had an audience of one million; it tripled the next year.[18]

While the early successes established firmly the credibility of the documentary film movement, the overriding factor which influenced thought and politics in this period was the Great Depression. In 1931, the

Labour government under Ramsay MacDonald contemplated bringing in deflationary measures to cope with its fiscal woes, short of touching unemployment benefits. In August, the cabinet met in an atmosphere of urgency to discuss the worsening financial situation and decided to apply universal economic cutbacks in all government spheres. The Empire Marketing Board appropriation was to be reduced £250,000. Its *raison d'être* was snuffed out at the Ottawa Conference of 1932, where Canada, South Africa, and the Irish Free State blocked formation of a general customs union. To weather the depression they pursued a policy of individual national self-interest, thereby ignoring traditionalist calls for imperial unity. The Empire Marketing Board ended officially on 30 September 1933, leaving behind it a Film Unit which had produced nearly a hundred films under Grierson's guidance. Fortunately, the documentary film movement still had its guardian angel in Sir Stephen Tallents. He was invited to join the General Post Office staff and accepted his appointment provided he could bring the Empire Marketing Board Film Unit and Film Library with him. Thus the transition to the GPO from the EMB was very smooth and hardly disturbed the young filmmakers.

The Empire Marketing Board was gone, but Grierson had achieved his aim of establishing a permanent documentary film school. He was grateful for what Tallents had done to help make it possible. 'Tallents marked out the habitation and the place for our new teaching of citizenship and gave it a chance to expand. In relating it to the art so variously called "cultural relations," "public relations" and "propaganda," he joined it to one of the actual driving forces of the time and guaranteed it patronage.' The Film Unit had been just one laboratory among others for discovering the terms of the relationship of the artist to the art or idea he was communicating. Tallents' need and Grierson's purpose created an alliance between public relations and documentary film which grew so close that had there been any desire to commercialize the documentary film movement it would not have been possible. What emerged was an especially strong alliance for the British government.[19]

IDEAS WHICH FUELLED GRIERSON'S CRUSADE

One wonders in light of the Tallents-Grierson relationship what constituted Grierson's intellectual roots as the seminal figure in the documentary film movement. While studying at the University of Chicago from

1924 to 1927, he became intrigued with Walter Lippmann's analysis of twentieth-century democracy, in which Lippmann stated that the ordinary voter could never make informed judgments because of his lack of relevant information and time for consideration. Grierson understood Lippmann's pessimism but would not integrate it into his own beliefs. He interpreted Lippmann's articulation of the problem as a challenge. Henceforth Grierson would focus all his energies on trying to reveal to the ordinary voter the pattern of the twentieth century so that those who were part of it could feel that they had a stake in the future their leaders were planning. Grierson chose the medium of film on the offhand suggestion by Lippman that the effects and influence of film might be more easy to study than those of the press, since the basic data, box-office results, were easier to obtain. He began by studying the impact of film on the 'melting pot' idea of the Americanization of immigrants and ended up with a theory of film as a tool of education. His experience at Chicago produced the amalgam which became the core of the documentary film movement.

Lippmann's pessimism stemmed from the logical dead end of the nineteenth-century liberal individualist and rational theory that individuals were expected to know and to understand all the issues of public life. Not only was this a dead end in educational theory; if applied to twentieth-century politics, it meant that the only course for mankind to follow was to let the few do the thinking for the many. Here Grierson resisted stubbornly. There must be a way, he thought, of presenting the modern scene dramatically to its millions of inhabitants. The educational system was not equipping the individual mind with a reference point in a fast-moving world. Education, then, became the central point of Grierson's philosophy. Years later he wrote about his father's misapprehension of where education was supposed to lead, and what he had learned from his father's error. He wrote that his father's operative philosophy in education had been liberal in the nineteenth-century sense of eternal truths and the natural rights of man. There was an individualist ideal at the root of the liberal dream which implied that education for free men in a free society would create a civilization unique in the history of the world. Grierson thought that the logical extension of his father's philosophy would be a dream of creating a system in which every workman was a gentleman in a library in deep pursuit of truth and beauty. What actually happened was quite the opposite. Men started to think and became less satisfied with their miserable pay. They organized. There were strikes and lockouts. The nine-teenth-century liberal dream shattered. Grierson the elder and his son learned two important lessons: first, education could not be detached from the economic processes and what was happening in the world; second, the individualist dream in education was impossible in a world which operated in terms of large integrated forces. Grierson the elder could do little but realize the error of his ways. His son matured with a realization that mankind was into the new world of facts before it was out of the old world of attitudes.

To young Grierson, education became the tool to reorient the world and to serve as an active instrument of the democratic idea. There was no difference between education and propaganda because both func-tioned 'in the quiet light of ordinary humanism.' To Grierson, the task was to be undertaken by speaking intimately and quietly about real things and real people, which in the end would prove more spectacular than the spectacle itself. Grierson's use of propaganda went straight to the Catholic origins of the word – *Congregatio de Propaganda Fide*, the College of Propaganda instituted by Pope Urban VIII in the seventeenth century to educate priests for missions. In the modern progressive sense, Grierson wanted to organize a movement to preach, spread, and maintain the doctrine of democracy and to maintain the democratic faith by inspiring the citizenry. Thus, until the end of his career, Grier-son would pursue the inspirational message rather than the narrow political message or a critical analysis of existing institutions. Grierson explained his position years later:

We can, by propaganda, widen the horizons of the schoolroom and give to every individual, each in his place and work, a living conception of the com-munity which he has the privilege to serve. We can take his imagination beyond the boundaries of his community to discover the destiny of his country. We can light up his life with a sense of active citizenship. We can give him a sense of greater reality in the present and a vision of the future. And, so doing, we can make the life of the citizen more ardent and satisfactory to himself.[20]

It might be worth while to pursue some of the intellectual compo-nents of Grierson's thought, though instead of a clear-cut and easily identifiable individual what emerges is a composite man of overlapping attitudes and roots, some contradictory, others vague and some even impossible to label. Here was an individual whose lack of identifying political signature might leave both the ideologue and the polemicist dissatisfied in their compulsion to define. Complexity often escapes categorization. Depending on the angle of observation, intellectually speaking, John Grierson was a materialist, a Marxist, a Hegelian, and a non-religious Calvinist. Overriding all of this, he showed an instinct for political survival. Survival meant abstaining from partisan politics and associating the documentary with a non-religious crusade based on widely held concepts of morality. But in the long run these elements were the very obstacles which prevented the movement from becoming an agent of social change.

In his study of documentary film, Alan Lovell has stated that the starting point of Grierson's intellectual position was a technological / collectivist view of modern society in a neo-Hegelian context. Grierson was most conscious of the fact that technological developments in communications had made people throughout the world aware of, and more dependent on, each other. Technology, or the material factor, was in a very direct way in the vanguard of social change and had forced collective organization to become the logic of the twentieth century.[21]

This was historical process at work. Humanity had only to understand it. Yet Grierson wished to deal neither with the existing hierarchical order of society nor with questions of class conflict. From a practical point of view, had he dealt with these issues, he would have earned the label of Marxist. Traditionally, most governments in liberal democracies conduct the least amount of official intercourse possible with Marxists, whose universal aim is to eradicate capitalism. Thus, Grierson's identification with the Marxist cause would have caused the doors of government sponsorship and financial backing to be slammed shut against him. As a pragmatist, Grierson thought it better to deal with the commonality of all men; this, he thought, would break down the barriers which keep men alienated from each other and objectified as members of classes. Still, his failure to deal with this basic Marxist precept of class ensured that the documentary movement would remain an articulation of working-class Britain by the university-educated intelligentsia. Speaking then from a strictly orthodox point of view, Grierson was a very poor Marxist.

But he was looking for more than a passage from capitalism to socialism. He believed that socialism, as defined in the late nineteenth and early twentieth centuries, would never come. He explained why in the early forties:

That surely was plain when the Workers' Soviets with all their Socialist dreams of workers' control in a classless society were driven out of industrial management in Russia and Republican Spain, and by their own leaders. They were driven out not because Socialism did not represent a high ideal, but because given the conditions of modern technocracy, workers' self-management represents an unpractical and inefficient one. My view, if any, would be that we are entering upon a new and interim society which is neither capitalist, nor socialist, but in which we can achieve central planning without loss of individual initiative, by mere process of absorbing initiative in the function of planning. I think we are entering upon a society in which public unity and discipline can be achieved without forgetting the humanitarian virtues. ...

He warned that men had to grasp the historical process and not bother about recriminations or moral strictures. Men were all the fools of history, he concluded, even the greatest and the best of them. One could argue that this might include himself ultimately, because he failed to see the shift of world economics toward monopoly capitalism. If Grierson missed this change in the forties, he was not alone – most public men either could not or would not acknowledge this evolving aspect of capitalism for the next thirty years.[22]

Late in life, Grierson would be more open about the influence of revolutionary Russia upon him, not only in terms of the Russian film directors (Grierson had helped title the version of *Potemkin* first screened in Britain and North America), but also in terms of revolutionary attitudes toward art which emerged from the Revolution. He credited Trotsky with being the source of the phrase 'art should be used as a hammer not a mirror,' and there is some evidence that this idea was a powerful influence in the direction his own thinking took in the thirties. Grierson also acknowledged and imitated the tempo of Eisenstein and Pudovkin. In fact, he followed the course of Russian films so closely and intimately that on one occasion in the thirties the documentary movement got ahead of Russian technique. He agreed with the Russian writers who emphasized that the key to the future lay with people in the community finding and believing that they had the means to be creative and useful. In documentary film this became an effort to make aesthetic shapes from men's lives in their environment.

Let us look, for example, at the ideological impact on Grierson of a short Russian primer by Ilia I. Marshak (M. Ilin), called *New Russia's Primer*. The book was designed for children from twelve to fourteen and aimed to explain the Five-Year Plan begun in October 1928. Grierson claimed many decades later that this book served as an important motivating force to him and to his film school. The book presented in graphic form Russia's preoccupation with science, technology, and machinery, while revealing the temper of the revolutionary movement and the large human goals toward which that movement tended. The social vision rather than the political vision was what attracted Grierson. This vision was expressed through the book's concern with the relation of education to social planning. The conclusion summarized the social vision, which closely paralleled the social vision of the documentary film movement: 'Do we do these things merely in order to change Nature? No, we change Nature in order that people may live better.'

Grierson never revealed the specific reference to the phrase 'art should be used as a hammer not a mirror' and he felt free to borrow some of Lenin's ideas on art as well. Lenin was alleged to have said that it was not of much consequence what art means to a few hundred or even thousand out of a population counted by the millions. To quote Lenin more extensively:

Art belongs to the people. Its roots should be deeply implanted in the very thick of the labouring masses. It should be understood and loved by these masses. It must unite and elevate their feelings, thoughts and will. It must stir to activity and develop the art instincts within them. Should we serve exquisite sweet cake to a small minority while the worker and peasant masses are in need of black bread? It goes without saying that the following is to be understood not only literally but also figuratively: we must always have before our eyes the workers and the peasants. It is for their sake that we must learn to manage, to reckon. This applies also to the sphere of art and culture.[23]

Grierson could not have agreed with Lenin more. After the Second World War, he would state, 'My own view ... is to say with Lenin that if you pretend to any leadership of the people – and art is certainly a form of leadership – you must forever go where the people are.' However, there were other intellectual threads running through Grierson's thought which were difficult to reconcile with Lenin's Marxism. The neo-Hegelian aspect of Grierson's philosophy was an interesting counterpoint. He took a very idealistic view of the state as 'the machinery by which the best interests of the people are secured.' He said the same thing again in 1947. Lovell mentioned that the revival of interest in Hegel in late-nineteenth-century Britain was a concern with freeing the political role of the state from any notion that the state existed to serve partisan interests. He might also have made the connection between neo-Hegelianism and the rise of British Liberalism from about mid-century, because Grierson was influenced to no small degree by the Liberal idea. That idea was to free men, politics, and the state from the antiquated practices of patronage and to pay homage verbally and in practice to moral improvement, moral effort, and rationality. The Liberal hope, expressed rationally, was that society as a whole might be improved. Moral improvement began with each individual. As one historian of the Liberal era has written,

For the nineteenth century man, the mark or note of being fully human was that he should provide for his own family, have his own religion and politics and call no man master. ... The great moral idea of Liberalism was manliness. ... Thus, *being* a Liberal (rather than just promiscuously recording a Liberal vote) was something that could not come about without great changes in the circumstances and horizons of classes hitherto outside the political nation – changes creative of moral pressure which overflowed into a traditional parliamentary culture, full of banality, and very little ready to be moralized. That is the paradox of Liberalism.

And Liberalism was not just individualism; there was a specific role for the state. It was in this context that the state in the late nineteenth century had a new duty thrust upon it, a duty which became a crusade. Moral improvement, which was understood to be the aim of persons, politics, and the state, took on an economic and Christian dimension. This dimension was expressed in class terms by the newly emergent bourgeoisie, which invariably referred to God's wishes at all points of their political and domestic life.[24]

Thus, Grierson's idealistic view of the state as 'the machinery by which the best interests of the people are secured' was in a direct line with the Liberal tradition, which itself was partially reflective of neo-Hegelian philosophy popular in certain British and Scottish intellectual circles from 1870 to 1920. It is not surprising to learn that Grierson's studies at Glasgow were in philosophy and neo-Hegelian philosophy was especially influential in Scotland at that time. Once his philosophy crystallized, Grierson emerged with a vision of the state, exclusive of politics and politicians, which more or less embodied the Hegelian dictum, 'The truth is the whole.' To Grierson, the state not only embodied the truth/whole, but also was the vehicle which revealed the truth to the populace. Divorced from politics, the state became the ideal and one of the pillars of Grierson's philosophy of documentary film. The truth which was to be revealed was a democratic faith and that faith was revealed through propaganda or education. Where Grierson would face an irreconcilable contradiction years later was in another classical dictum, 'The whole is the sum total of all its parts.' In terms of the state, as each of its parts came under closer scrutiny, the whole seemed to become more and more fuzzy and incomprehensible. The world of politics, the reality of government sanction, the class structure of society, and the very magnitude of the technocratic world he was trying to give meaning to would overwhelm him and relegate him to the realm of dreamer. The stone wall of reality would prove to be something quite different from the idea.

Linked to these characteristics was the driving force which gave Grierson the strength to maintain his convictions for a lifetime. This last component was faith, which stemmed from a strong Calvinist tradition, and which gave Grierson confidence and authority in the midst of twentieth-century discord and incongruity. Very late in life, Grierson would define his odd brand of Calvinism: 'there are three forms of the elect. One is having their duty to their community, and another of duty to God. And the other is of the elect having no duty. Being elect anyway. That is a falsity.' In an abstract sense, Grierson considered himself one of the elect whose duty was to the community, or in his words, 'conditioning the imagination of mankind,' like every rabbi, prophet, and priest before him. Like them, he believed he derived his authority from Moses. 'Masterminding is a valid activity of the human spirit and medicine men are worthy of their hire. They all represent controls – all represent imaginative discipline, seeking of the power which will enable them to operate.' This sort of Calvinism was distinctly outside conventional religious tenets. As he put it, 'I've been brought up as a Calvinist. The more I've lived, the more I think that the Christian religion was a savage attack on the human race by the Jews. When I think of religion, I believe in Spinoza's God. ...' Quoting an obscure French duchess writing about religion, he concluded, 'C'est comme le sexe. Je le fais souvent, mais je n'en parle jamais.'[25]

But Grierson was embarked on a religious crusade without the trappings of dogma. He felt he was 'serving the greatest mobilization of the public imagination since the Churches lost their grip.' And public imagination was to be mobilized into some sort of public faith in civilization. As he put it succinctly, 'I do not mind confessing that I would sooner have an educational system based on the Church and on the Christian virtues than a national educational system that is so busy with mere knowledge that it has no faith to give.'

If one senses contradiction in the man, it is because the twentieth century had not yet worked out its own contradictions. And as a child of the twentieth century, Grierson had a sense of being a very unusual kind of totalitarian man. This did not mean he was authoritarian or dictatorial for evil purposes; rather his authority was a power he exercised for good. As he explained,

Some of us came out of a highly disciplined religion and see no reason to fear discipline and self-denial. Some of us learned in a school of philosophy which taught that all was for the common good and nothing for oneself and have never, in any case, regarded the pursuit of happiness as anything other than an aberration of the human spirit. We were taught, for example, that he who would gain his life must lose it. Even Rousseau talked of transporting le moi dans l'unité commune, and Calvin of establishing the holy communion of the citizens. So, the kind of 'totalitarianism' I am thinking of, while it may apply to the new conditions of society, has as deep a root as any in human tradition. I would call the philosophy of individualism Romantic and say we have been on a spectacular romantic spree for four hundred years. I would maintain that this other, 'totalitarian' viewpoint is classical.[26]

In developing his idea of communication he was careful to avoid having the few preach to the many. Information was a two-way process between state and people, people and state. He would encourage the two-way process of communication in the years of the Second World War, in the non-theatrical film circuits of Canada and in the regular use of polls to report the tenor of public opinion to the government. His belief was that the group of filmmakers which came to be called documentary were specialists for and on behalf of people and not specialists from without.

These contradictions may have put Grierson in an awkward intellectual position, subject to challenge from many quarters. But the ideas were at least clear, and even if they lacked an academic's depth they did have a visionary's perspective. Grierson's philosophy also allowed him to avoid being labelled. What was important was activity toward inspiration, inspiration of the public. Unfortunately for him, this reliance upon inspiration would suit his political masters only for the duration of the national emergency. Theirs was a game of pragmatic and dogmatic politics. Grierson's ostensible policy was to skirt basic political issues and, as a public servant, to maintain a neutral political posture. This enabled him to move adroitly through the corridors of politics and power.

DOCUMENTARY: RADICAL IDEOLOGY
OR APOLOGY FOR THE STATUS QUO?

Using hindsight, it is easy to criticize documentary films for being advertisements for the establishment, and therefore for the *status quo* of that miserable decade, the thirties. Years later, Grierson's defence was that national propaganda policy followed the 'consensus of the House,' or stayed in line with government purposes. Besides having 'about half the Cabinet popping into our private theatre to see what we were about,' he explained, 'the prevailing sense of participation by ministers in a common inquiry and adventure gave much spirit to the whole development. One missed it in later years. The carrying out of departmental orders by detached and sometimes servile technicians is not the same thing.' The underlying guidelines were political but beyond party. At the Empire Marketing Board, the guideline was in response to the Statute of Westminster (1931); Grierson and the Film Unit attempted to instruct the British people about the new relationships within the commonwealth. At the GPO they exploited the whole story of communications, national and international, with sound film, giving the documentary school a new characteristic theme and *raison d'être*.

Given the period, politics were as inescapable as they were dangerous. These were years of choosing between extremes: extreme fascism at home and abroad and the emergence of extreme leftism at the opposite end of the political spectrum. Grierson's policy was to wend his way around and through politics rather than to become mired in them. The social vision had to remain foremost in his mind as he attempted to enunciate and articulate for the first time mass man's place in the world. On the one hand, he could paraphrase Bertrand Russell and claim that he was trying to 'make peace as exciting as war.' On the other hand, he could explain that what he was doing was not taking place in a vacuum but in the real world of people and material interests. He best explained his position in a 1933 article:

In documentary there is this difference. The producer does not always serve purely commercial interests, unless, that is to say, you take the Marxian point of view, on which all service of the status quo is purely commercial. He can, however, give himself the liberal satisfaction of serving such interests as education or national propaganda: which, in any sensible definition is itself a species of education. Or the producer may act on behalf of a business concern, large enough in its operations and its outlook, to turn publicity into education and propaganda into a work of development.

Documentary suggested broad answers, not specific or radical solutions to social problems. The right wing of the political spectrum found little to carp about and Grierson escaped partisan political debate. Was he a glib apologist for failing to criticize the faults of the system, as a contemporary critic, Arthur Calder Marshall, charged? 'Mr. Grierson may like to talk about social education, surpliced in self-importance and social benignity. Other people may like hearing him. But even if it sounds like a sermon, a sales talk is a sales talk.'[27] His task, Grierson felt, was to lead the sponsors of propaganda and education to a knowledge of what was involved. 'In that respect,' he added humorously, 'It is well that the producer should know how to talk soothingly to children and idiots.' Film critics who had despaired at the 'meagre mental standard' of contemporary films found new hope in what Grierson was trying to achieve. Perhaps they sensed along with Grierson that 'documentary then was not just the runaway from the synthetic world of contemporary cinema but also was a reaction from the art world of the early and middle twenties, including Bloomsbury, Left Bank, T.S. Eliot, Clive Bell. ... It was a return to reality not unconnected with the Clydeside movement, I.L.P.'s and the Great Depression.'[28]

In 1936 Grierson was able to capitalize upon luck and his own gift of salesmanship in enlisting the talents of Benjamin Britten and W.H. Auden to make the now classic documentary *Night Mail*. Both artists had already cooperated with the GPO Film Unit in making Cavalcanti's 1935 documentary, *Coal Face*, which was intended to provoke a social protest about the miserable life of coal miners; but then the attempts to synthesize Auden's verse and Britten's music only partly succeeded, and the film was not a great success. In the preparation of *Night Mail*, Grierson approached both men individually and told each that the other had accepted an offer to work on the film; characteristically Grierson, this action was taken before either man had committed himself.[29] The appeal to their egos succeeded and their collective contribution synchronized to the film's use of direct sound made it one of documentary film's great tributes to the working man. It happened that Ross McLean, secretary to the Canadian High Commission in London, was doing a report on the documentary movement in Britain and sat in on the sound recording of this epic film. He was convinced Grierson should be invited to Canada and, from then on, the wheels began to turn in that direction.

The documentary movement rejected the lyrical-artistic approach to film, associated with the style of Robert Flaherty, whose insistence on the beauty of the 'natural' in films was at the expense of a socio-political foundation. *Nanook of the North* was the archetypal naturalist documentary, setting man against the merciless elements in the Canadian North, and even when Grierson found himself in Canada, he shunned Flaherty's romantic approach to film. (Grierson had coined the 'documentary' as a genre in a review of Flaherty's *Moana* for the *New York Sun*, 8 February 1926.) Flaherty found very brief employment with the first documentary school in England, but Grierson had to let him go because of his extravagant shooting methods. The two men remained lifelong friends despite this unhappy episode and embarked on what Grierson called a 'dialectical pub-crawl across half the world.'

Grierson's school began to branch out and deal with social themes of a more controversial nature. It was the logical direction which documentary had to follow, although it was too much to expect the Conservative government to embrace, despite the fact that the films were related to Conservative measures to fight the depression. For example, *Housing Problems*, made privately by Arthur Elton, Ruby Grierson, and John Taylor, whose sister Margaret was married to Grierson, was an antecedent to the *cinema vérité* school founded after the Second World War. The film took viewers into the slums of London and let them see and hear the poor tell their story. The filmmakers lived in a poor area of London for a month, then set up their equipment to record the people's stories about living conditions there, with the element of humour, not despair, pervading the film. It is hard to forget a housewife's matter-of-fact irony in describing the killing of a rat.

If Grierson approved of this kind of treatment, it was because the Conservatives were behind the crusade for housing and health. He believed he was studying the degree of sanction at every point and had a constant active concern with the rising of the degree of sanction. But he drew the line at being 'party to false witness.' Yet it was the unofficial informal censorships from unnamed but powerful sources, representing their own peculiar concept of the *status quo*, which harassed the documentary movement most. They sought to embarrass the honest picture of Britain tearing down slums, building anew, and facing up to unemployment problems. Grierson detested these people who wanted to show only the superficial and pretentious elements in the British scene, which he called 'synthetic nonsense.' But *Housing Problems* was among the several films which the British Council's film committee censored unofficially for viewing at the New York World's Fair because they were too honest. To no avail, Grierson fulminated in print against those who were 'anxious to substitute for the heartfelt interpretation of responsible artists the synthetic lie of partisan interests.' The films were not included as part of the official British exhibit but were included in the American science and education pavilion.[30]

There were numerous individuals and groups who were suspicious of Grierson's progressive instincts. Some even alleged that the documentary school and Grierson were communists and that control and supervision should come from Treasury. One official looked into the Conservative Research Council accusation that Grierson and his friends were communists. This could be found in their work, went the charge. After examining the issue further the official wrote, 'For communism read realism and a certain healthy liberalism and there might be something in it. But I am convinced we can't have Treasury butting in.' The charge of communism seemed to follow Grierson at the most inopportune moments in his public career. Harry Watt, an early innovator in documentary method, remembered how, in trying to present an image of the working man that differed from the Edwardian, Victorian, capitalist version, Grierson's embryo filmmakers were suspect:

We were always financed by the Establishment and the Establishment basically regretted that they'd started this thing. To start with we were left-wing to a man. Not many of us were communists, but we were all socialists and I'm sure we had dossiers because we demonstrated and worked for the Spanish war. Grierson overtly never did. Now what he did behind the scenes – I knew nothing about his political beliefs. But we were on a razor's edge. ... It would have been utterly impossible, we'd have committed suicide, to have come out and made completely left-wing statements. As you know, in the EMB days, a detective was put in as a trainee editor, a man from the Special Branch. And we all knew who he was and we made his life such hell by going behind the cutting room door and saying, 'All right for tonight, Joe? Got the bomb? The job's on.' He twigged of course immediately that he'd been spotted. ... But there were always people until the late thirties who were wanting to shut us down and cut us off. We weren't permanent civil servants or anything like that. Our life was really precarious. ...[31]

Watt's testimony at least provides some feeling of the atmosphere in which the young film movement had to grow up and makes it somewhat easier to understand how and why Grierson was cautious in choosing themes and directions to explore. Had the documentary filmmakers gone any further left in their films, they would have lost their source of financial support. Clearly, however, they were not acting solely as apologists for the *status quo*. Like most left-wing bourgeois intellectuals in the thirties, they were ashamed of 'poverty in the midst of plenty' and were trying to do something about raising public consciousness wherever they could. Also, they would have been the first to admit the absence of revolutionary or even radical sentiments in their films.

The limitations of government sponsorship were evident to Grierson quite early in the evolution of the documentary film movement. In the late thirties he remarked caustically that the censor, J. Brook Wilkinson, stood by a slogan of 'no controversy' which meant 'no reality.' Grierson was being hamstrung in bringing cinema to its destiny as social commentary, inspiration, and art. He wanted film to 'bite into the time and from its independent vantage, contribute to the articulation of the time.' The only alternative was to cultivate other sources of sponsorship, like the public utilities, which were much less sensitive to politically controversial themes than was the government. He hoped that the example of non-government sponsorship would spread abroad and possibly in the United States where this sort of approach could prove useful publicly. It was logical that private enterprise 'should prove that its private opportunity was a public responsibility and that its enterprise was such as to relate to the people's needs and, therefore, to their imagination.' He continued to believe that much of the underwriting of the nation's art and education could derive from private enterprise.[32] This was indeed a far cry from the reactionaries' allegations of communism. Grierson was optimistic for a while because a number of prestigious films were made in the corporate realm for British Petroleum, British Commercial Gas Association, and Imperial Airways. They were, in the long run, exceptions to the rule in corporate and industrial advertising.

Though Grierson had given up the post of producer of the GPO Film Unit in July 1936, he stayed on until June 1937. Then he decided to resign to start something independent of the government and of industry, to provide continuing stimulation and encouragement for the documentary idea, particularly on the international level. The resulting effort became the Film Centre. There, with Stuart Legg, Arthur Elton, and administrator J.P.R. Golightly (who was Grierson's complete right-hand man and shadow), he established a headquarters for research, consultation, planning, and contact. Film Centre set the precedent for public relations films when they devised a programme for the production of seven films for a screen survey of Scotland for the coming Empire Exhibition in Glasgow. Financing was shared by industry, government, and interested groups.

Grierson next embarked on a 'brief, bright excursion to Geneva,' at the invitation of the International Labour Office. With Basil Wright he presented a scheme for the ILO's enlightened use of the film medium.

Their idea was to establish an international exchange system of industrial education films, to propagate high standards in every field of industrial and social welfare. The scheme collapsed as the rush of events toward war sealed Europe's fate and redefined the documentary movement's *raison d'être*. Grierson's dream to lift documentary film out of the national into the international context was delayed by the coming war, though, from here on, the international element would lie at or just beneath the surface of films he produced.

Thus, by 1937, the documentary film movement had become a useful, if limited, part of the British scene. Looking back at the first eight years of sponsorship and production, Grierson could be satisfied with what had been accomplished, some sixty trained technicians in four distinct film units. (He had produced forty-three films and directed one, *Drifters*.) There were many in 1937 and 1938 who did not share Prime Minister Neville Chamberlain's optimism about prospects for peace. Grierson was one of these people, and following the ILO rebuff, he re-established a loose relationship with the British government when he became film adviser to the Imperial Relations Trust. They commissioned him to travel to Canada, New Zealand, and Australia to prepare a preliminary report on the film production which might be undertaken with a view toward strengthening the link between Britain and the dominions if war came. The Imperial Relations Trust wanted to see him set up a film centre in each of those three countries.[33] And Canada, wrestling with its own publicity problems, thought he could do something for the ailing Government Motion Picture Bureau. He set sail at the end of May 1938.

War would change everyone's plans. Britain's Ministry of Information became an indifferent step-parent to the first documentary school and bore a large part of the responsibility for undermining the morale and sense of élan which Grierson had nurtured so carefully for so long. The British documentary movement floundered about during the conflict. Its wartime documentaries suffered from a lack of thematic coherence because the Churchill government chose not to enunciate war aims. Brought to its knees, Britain tried to weather the onslaught which threatened its national existence. Churchill treated information as a whole with relative indifference.

As for distant Canada, the late thirties found some men in government looking toward the British documentary experiment as an example to emulate in their search for a fresh approach to national imagery.

It was a happy coincidence that Grierson was exploring the possibilities of transplanting the documentary idea to an international level or elsewhere in the empire. Luckily for him, the coincidence of the Imperial Relations Trust assignment and Canada's invitation provided him with a perfect growth medium to continue his propaganda crusade. War made Grierson Canada's propaganda maestro and he seized his opportunity with characteristic vigour. While serving Britain and Canada, he would perpetuate the documentary idea. A missionary crusade began: its purpose was to reveal, inspire, and focus on Canada's place in a world of upheaval.

2 | Political Cockfights and the Wartime National Film Board

CANADA INVITES GRIERSON

The Canadian Government Motion Picture Bureau's official film propaganda in the twenties and thirties had been aimed mostly at promoting tourism from the United States. Its early audience of twenty-five million had fallen to three million by 1934. The bureau's films had consisted largely of travelogues extolling Canada's scenic wonders. Repeated austerity budgets in the depression years had led to a general hardening of the arteries at the bureau. Most films reflected a predictable mediocre content and style and remained unchanged even after sound arrived in the late thirties. By then Canadian government films deserved the poor reputation they held abroad.[1]

In fact, as early as November 1935, Ross McLean and Vincent Massey were discussing the possibilities of developing something along the lines of Grierson's documentary idea. Both men had just emerged as significant contributors to Mackenzie King's return to the post of prime minister in a landslide victory over R.B. Bennett in the election of October 1935. They had been involved in the publicity effort for the election for some six months. Following King's victory they left in November for prestigious new posts in London, Massey as high commissioner and McLean as staff secretary. As mentioned earlier, McLean began making contacts with Grierson and the documentary school and soon became greatly influenced by the GPO unit's activities. Having sat in on the final sound recording of *Night Mail*, he later said that session was the catalyst in his decision to recommend Grierson to come to Canada.[2] This recommendation first appeared in a February 1936 report to Massey, but it was not until two years later that it would reach the prime minister. In the spring of 1938, McLean approached Lester Pearson, then first secretary of the High Commission in Britain, and said that as Grierson was so far ahead of the Government Motion Picture Bureau, he should go to Canada to show Canadians what he was doing. Subsequently Massey wrote to Prime Minister King and recommended Grierson.

At about the same time, McLean sent a memorandum to the minister of trade and commerce, W.D. Euler. McLean described his disenchantment with the use of Canadian films in Britain because of their failure to meet audience demands or to provide representative information about the Canadian people and the Canadian scene. This, he believed, directly hampered development both of mutual goodwill and understanding between the countries and of mutual trade interests. McLean stated his case directly in terms which Euler could understand:

There is no sounder basis for the expansion of trade than a deeper and wider knowledge of differences in tastes and modes of life. These can be conveyed most effectively by interpreting in a wider sense the functions of the Motion Picture Bureau, by improving the quality and enlarging the quantity of Canadian films by adapting them more consciously to the demands of the British public.

McLean recommended that the government invite Grierson to come to Canada to advise it as to ways and means of extending its film work and of planning its production with a view to meeting the demands of British audiences.[3] The arguments were convincing and Grierson set out for Canada in May.

When Grierson had made an earlier trip to Canada on behalf of the Empire Marketing Board, he had established a cordial relationship with Motion Picture Bureau chief Frank Badgley. Now, he was to review the position of the bureau, to 'put it back into business as leader of the pack,' he would say. It soon became clear that Badgley was retarding government film efforts.

Grierson completed and submitted a report in June and sketched a large picture of film potential, carefully avoiding naming names. He viewed government film propaganda as serving four objectives: general information, trade publicity, departmental information, and national prestige, that is, theatrical appeal. All these types of film worked together and had to be considered in building an overall information programme. Both Canada and Britain needed to establish a strong coordinating policy and an enduring film unit. Here would lie the genesis of a new government film policy. Grierson avoided neatly any hint of politics or threats to already established government film enterprises like the Motion Picture Bureau. The key to success, he argued, was a central agency to coordinate government film work. To effect this, he suggested the appointment of a government film officer to advise the government on production and distribution of films, an increase in the creative talent in the Government Motion Picture Bureau, and a widening of the scope of the film production programme. He hoped that the Motion Picture Bureau would loosen its ties to Trade and Commerce and become the central film agency for all government departments. Those films intended for broad distribution would come under the aegis of the central agency. To avoid duplication of services, distribution was to be centrally coordinated. The National Film Society would be able to help secure cooperation of outside bodies in the area of non-theatrical distribution. His report completed, Grierson returned to England in July and waited. He was called back to Canada in November to 'develop a plan for the coordination of the film production and distribution activities of ... the Dominion Government in accordance with the proposals set out [in his June report] ... and otherwise to assist in the interdepartmental discussions for making the plan effective.' Here was the opportunity to transform eventually the overall Canadian film programme and film policy. He would preach to citizens about their democratic responsibility toward and involvement in society; he would also preach internationalism to an international congregation. All this was within the framework of his assignment for the Imperial Relations Trust, to set up a North American propaganda base to urge Canada and (more important) the United States into an active partnership with Britain at war, if war should come. He remained on the payroll of Imperial Relations Trust until mid-1941.[4]

King's advisers knew Grierson was working for the British, though it is unlikely they knew the details of his assignment. Their interest in him grew as they perceived Canada's deficiencies of image and the potential of government-sponsored film as a remedy. It was remotely possible too that some may have been thinking of preparations for the coming war, part of which would have to be a war of ideologies, with film serving as a significant weapon. In January 1939, O.D. Skelton, under-secretary of state for external affairs, referred to Massey's recommendation and suggested to Prime Minister King that Grierson would be 'a good man to get for a year or so.' Skelton too had become aware of the importance of publicity and was looking 'for an effective use of motion picture publicity centered at Ottawa – both for external and internal effect.' Skelton had recently been told by Norman A. Robertson, one of his young lieutenants, that there was presumptive evidence that Badgley, a good technical man, was not the person to be given administrative responsibility for a new publicity effort. As an outsider, Grierson would be 'much better equipped to smooth out the interdepartmental jealousies' which were partially responsible for the inadequate work of the Motion Picture Bureau.[5]

W.D. Euler, as minister, was responsible for presenting the legislative bill in the spring of 1939 which gave life to the National Film Board. The bill was the political brain-child of Grierson, though J.F. McNeil, of the Department of Justice, framed the actual wording. Euler's attitude, at least in public, seemed to be somewhat different from Grierson's and Skelton's. He addressed Parliament in March and stated that the National Film Board was to control the film activities of various government departments, though each department would have the power to initiate its own films, subject to approval by the central board. The Motion Picture Bureau was to continue to make films for the government as far as possible; the primary rationale behind the board was to provide for improvement and efficiency in the preparation and distribution of government films. The board directorate was to be comprised of only eight persons, who would be responsible to the Privy Council; two were to be members of cabinet, including the chairman who was the minister in the Department of Trade and Commerce, three were to be from the civil service (or later, defence services), and three were to be from the citizens of Canada. All, except ministers, were to be three-year appointments. The film commissioner was not to be a member of the board, but was to be the only paid man in the organization. Euler believed the new agency would be an adjunct of the Department of Trade and Commerce; he had no visions of creating a new branch of government complete with personnel, only a publicity organ to drum up business. He finished his presentation by saying, 'I may add, in conclusion, that this board is not being established with the intention of providing jobs for anybody. There is really to be only one paid man in the organization.' He stressed a final point that the National Film Board would not enter into competition with private business.[6] The bill faced little opposition in debate, save for the weak protests of some economy-minded individuals loyal to Badgley. The bill passed its third reading without debate on 16 March 1939 and received royal assent on 2 May. The Department of Trade and Commerce continued to think of the Film Board as its special responsibility because the ministers, first Euler, then James A. MacKinnon, remained as chairmen of the board's directorate until the minister of national war services, J.T. Thorson, assumed that role in 1941.

By the fall of 1939, the members of the National Film Board had been selected, with the exception of film commissioner. The board directorate thought that the position should be held by a Canadian but there was no one with sufficient film experience available. Grierson found himself in Hollywood in September and was preparing to go to Australia and New Zealand to fulfil his assignment for Imperial Relations Trust. He postponed his departure when war in Europe was declared and spent the next few weeks commuting between Washington and New York, planning a film distribution centre to circulate 'democratic' films. The Ministry of Information in London rejected the plan because it feared commercial distributors would be disturbed. They were further annoyed that Grierson was not using code in his telegrams to London from the embassy. He was off on the wrong foot.[7] In October, the Canadian government called upon Grierson to become film commissioner for six months – until a Canadian could be found. He agreed and postponed his trip again, this time for several months. Now the fledgling National Film Board was constituted with a staff of five: Grierson, Ross McLean (assistant film commissioner), Stuart Legg (production supervisor), and two secretaries.

Once he agreed to become film commissioner, Grierson would be plagued by the very problem of interdepartmental jealousies he had been hired to iron out. He wanted to avoid the bureaucratically top-heavy example set by Britain's Ministry of Information, and to prevent the Film Board from becoming another extension of the civil service. He had ensured that this be stipulated by the act: that the film commissioner would not be subject to the provisions of the Civil Service Act or of the Civil Service Superannuation Act; that the National Film Board would assume all authority and coordination of government film activities; that all departments of the government must clear projects with the commissioner who would 'arrange for the technical carrying out of the work'; and that distribution must also be cleared through the commissioner. The significance of all this was that Badgley, under an exaggerated impression that he had been responsible for Grierson's being invited to Canada, would find himself with diminishing influence and power. When Grierson was named film commissioner, Badgley considered him an interloper and became dead set against Grierson's kind of film.

Within six years, this innocuous organization which 'had no intention of providing jobs for anybody' would become a well-oiled film propaganda machine of nearly eight hundred which would rival qualitatively the film propaganda efforts of the most sophisticated nations. The Film Board would succeed in both formulating a national image in the minds of Canadians and translating the national programme of communication into an international programme. Grierson's unique interpretation of progressive internationalism would come to constitute a major thrust of Canadian documentary film in the last two years of war. This was not to be accomplished in a vacuum. In 1943 he would take the helm of Canada's faltering wartime propaganda agency, the Wartime Information Board. This meant playing politics near the top, where an ever-dissatisfied prime minister wanted better coordination of public information. Grierson's public image as the founder and animator of the documentary film movement often overshadows the lesser-known political creature who, like other King servants, played a loyal and unquestioning role.

INFORMATION: MORE THAN WORDS

The war that Prime Minister Mackenzie King thought appeasement could avoid stirred his already sharpened powers of concentration and clarity. If he thought he was an instrument of Providence in this his supreme test, he knew too that he had to be on top of all issues all the time. To achieve this, he made information an immediate priority. Control and dissemination of information meant power. King thought about forming an information bureau as early as 9 September 1939. He wanted information to be more than just 'words on war events' and thought that the bureau should 'help speakers in what was being said on the radio, etc.' This was an oblique reference to his own perceived need for help in projecting himself publicly and was rather a narrow view of what could be done.

The prime minister was in a kind of personal despair in the early months of the war, particularly when he was listening to Winston Churchill's broadcasts. According to his secretary, J.W. Pickersgill, King wanted to project his own image in much the same way that Churchill at the Admiralty was making his mark on the British public. It is probable that King's awkwardness as a public speaker and public personality led him to search for the cosmetic an information bureau could provide. Radio too was a disaster. Commenting on a radio speech in October, King confided to his diary, 'Once or twice found it difficult to realize that I was really talking to anyone.' Leonard W. Brockington, former head of the Canadian Broadcasting Corporation, would try unsuccessfully to help King. But the prime minister felt ungainly reading Brockington's words. According to Pickersgill, King needed plenty of time to assimilate what had been prepared for him and 'insisted on painstaking revision which, all too often, stripped what he had to say not only of rhetoric, but also of life.' No arrangement ever fully satisfied the prime minister, he claimed.[8]

Perhaps too King put great importance on the bureau because he was annoyed with press opinion of itself as being able to make and unmake public men and public opinion. A government information bureau would be an effective counterweight to the press where there was 'far too much power in the hands of a few men.' Evidently he respected that power enough to pass over his own preference for Brockington as information bureau chief because of the latter's previous battle with the press. He did not want to 'fight Associated Press,' so by December he chose Walter S. Thompson, director of public relations for Canadian National Railways. Brockington had to settle for the post of counsellor to the prime minister.

Thompson opposed the bureau idea, favouring instead talking with the press, learning what they wanted, and telling them how to get it. The prime minister did not want a director of censorship (radio speeches could be 'censored from a war point of view' from the studio) but rather someone to keep an eye on different censors. Mindful of the link between information and power, King wanted all matters of general policy to be under the prime minister and the Cabinet War Committee.

The prime minister was cautious about 'propaganda.' The government's attitude, King wrote in his diary, was not to have propaganda as that term was understood, but rather an interpretation of information using different media for the purpose. He did not wish to see public information having two sides. His position was clear and philosophically liberal: his government was not seeking to mislead anyone, least of all to advertise itself. Canada's war effort had to be made better known.

And so, somewhat inauspiciously, the Bureau of Public Information came into existence in December by an Order in Council. A month later ill health forced Thompson to retire and G.H. Lash became director. The bureau's mandate was straightforward enough. It was to collect, coordinate, and disseminate to the public information concerning all phases of the Canadian war effort. It was also to coordinate the existing public information services (radio and films) and to originate and employ other means of disseminating information. Besides weekly press conferences between ministers and press and consultations with the association of broadcasters, the bureau would arrange for and advance production of documentary film through the National Film Board. In this last point John Grierson's hand was visible. He knew that if the National Film Board was to become more than a mere coordinating agency, it would have to undertake production. Though the prime minister had vetoed Grierson's idea of a film unit to accompany the Expeditionary Force to Europe ('much too expensive,' wrote the penurious King), Grierson would obtain the cooperation of the Bureau of Public Information to finance the *Canada Carries On* theatrical series, the bureau's single largest item in that year's budget. *Canada Carries On* would make the National Film Board a familiar name across Canada.[9]

GRIERSON'S PLAN FOR FILM PROPAGANDA

In November 1939, Grierson outlined his plan of film propaganda in a letter to A.D.P. Heeney, principal secretary to Prime Minister King. Film was to have two aims: to develop national unity and to describe war activities and related themes. Grierson planned to use the wartime situation for the 'emphasis of themes of long term importance to Canadian life.' Thus would he 'prepare the peace.' In the same letter, Grierson described his discussions with N.L. Nathanson, manager of the largest theatre group in Canada, Famous Players Canadian Corporation, owned by Paramount Pictures of Hollywood. Nathanson's mind was set more directly on doing a job for Britain and on using Canada as a base for propaganda efforts in the United States. Grierson noted that there had been violent reactions to Allied propaganda in the United States since the last war and American opinion was supersensitive to any crude exploitation which might create ill will which could surface after the war was over. He continued:

... while the voice of Canada must inevitably develop great importance in the United States at the present time, it may be wise to determine with great care and foresight the nature of that voice. I have advised the Embassy at Washington to concentrate for the time being on an intensive development of cultural relations between England and the United States by film and other media. The same policy might be adopted by Canada with a judicious introduction of information concerning Canada's war activities, its views on the war, and, particularly, its national interpretation of the democratic issue at stake.

Coincidentally, this was the very policy which Prime Minister King wished to establish.

It would appear from this portion of the letter that Grierson had taken on the task of initially coordinating the British wartime information effort in North America. His aim was to instruct the North American public of the issues without instigating a campaign of vilification of the enemy. There was also a need to avoid Canada's exploitation as a North American base for the cruder forms of propaganda which some people would have liked to see developed in hopes of bringing the United States into the war. This is not to detract from the underlying purpose for which Grierson wanted to develop the documentary film; but the urgencies of war would have to assume priority over his long-range planning, and it was in this vital capacity, he admitted years later, that he thought he was serving the British government. Ross McLean has, to an extent, corroborated this theory.[10]

In closing his letter to Heeney, Grierson sketched plans to develop a monthly reel along the lines of the renowned *March of Time* newsreel.

(This idea would develop and expand eventually into the two success-ful series *Canada Carries On* and the *World in Action*.) He mentioned that Famous Players' Nathanson was so enthusiastic about helping that he had pledged the automatic inclusion of some eight hundred Famous Players theatres across Canada in the distribution network to be estab-lished.[11] A significant percentage of a regular Canadian movie-going audience had been presented virtually gratis to the government by pri-vate (American) capital, an extraordinary event in Canadian economic history. In Britain, commercial distribution took two years to become organized satisfactorily. In later years Grierson was fond of claiming that the film industry in North America was one hundred percent Jew-ish; hence, from his point of view, the Second World War was a Jew-ish war. This fact doubtless had some connection with the willingness of commercial theatres to allow the distribution of government film propaganda. On the other hand, Grierson would claim glibly that Can-ada's commercial theatres were cooperative because he threatened legislation that would force them to show twenty minutes of govern-ment-sponsored film at each performance. This threat was supposed to have convinced them to show National Film Board films voluntarily. But there appears to be no proof of this claim, and David Coplan, at that time sales manager for Columbia Pictures of Canada, denied its credi-bility. None the less, one cannot rule out the possibility of this calcu-lated Griersonian political gesture. He was never afraid to use bluff to achieve desired ends. As Ross McLean explained, a 'carelessly' dropped phrase at a cocktail party to his associate and henchman Arthur Gott-lieb might be inflated tenfold before reaching the ears of the intended recipients. The upshot of it all was that there was virtually no problem in distribution from the commercial theatrical sector for the balance of the war. As for non-theatrical distribution, Donald W. Buchanan, erst-while founder of the National Film Society, used his contacts to organize a substantial non-theatrical network which by 1942 reached a Canadian audience of more than a quarter million a month.

Grierson's letter to Heeney had sketched a pattern for government film propaganda that he would adhere to faithfully. On the same day as the Heeney letter, Grierson addressed a letter to Walter Turnbull, soon to become Mackenzie King's chief personal secretary. The greatest amount of Grierson's correspondence to the government during the war years would pass through Turnbull's hands. Unaware of King's own intentions, Grierson unveiled his plan to establish a Canadian counterpart to Britain's Ministry of Information. Canada could avoid the formation of a civil service organization fraught with heavyweight officialdom if there was formed a Bureau of Information which in effect would be 'a small group of liaison officers or Secretaries of Information – one for each medium which the Government wishes to use – with a principal Secretary of Information who would report directly to the Prime Minister and convey policy decisively to the others. The idea of 'Secretaries' is important as conveying the idea of liaison with high authority.'

The group forming the information service would be something in the nature of a flying squad, 'proceeding from specific job to specific job and cooperating with people only in respect of specific jobs.' This was to be no civil service organization; it was to be free of restrictions which normally might hold the entire body in check. Grierson wanted *carte blanche* as coordinator, 'but ... with the authority of the P.M. [sic] in the background'; he thought the organization should follow a considered and single policy with respect to the problems of 'national unity, presentation of Canadian views to the United States, advising the British Information service on Canadian realities, etc., etc.' He warned, however, that it would be necessary 'to keep the lunatics in leash' and this could best be achieved by several rather than by several score watchmen. Supervision would be coordinated by 'a single person, maintaining personal contact at key points and with the distant authority of the Prime Minister.' Here, Turnbull marked the margin in red pencil, 'Turnbull,' evidently viewing himself as the possible liaison between Grierson and Mackenzie King in the proposed information set-up.

There would be no cumbrous Ministry of Information in Canada, Grierson concluded. 'The very intangibility of the Information set-up I suggest, would probably be its principal asset ... it all comes down to a choice of imaginative and active personnel; and four, five or six chosen absolutely because of their qualifications for the job – and with no other considerations whatsoever allowed to enter – would do the trick.'[12]

But Grierson made little headway in reaching King, who was already thinking about Thompson. If the Bureau of Information was quite remote in conception and practice from Britain's Ministry of Information, so too was the National Film Board from its British counterpart, the Films Division of the Ministry of Information. The National Film

Board suffered a disadvantage in its early days by being an adjunct to the Department of Trade and Commerce, but Grierson had his mind set on single-handedly organizing the operation with the assistant to the commissioner and later deputy commissioner, Ross McLean. Some officials at External Affairs disapproved of the choice of McLean and eyed with some suspicion Grierson's powerful and often manipulative approach to people and politics in his host country. The atmosphere of distrust which Grierson the outsider engendered, especially in senior civil servants, would be a factor in the rejection of Grierson's choice of successor in 1945.[13] On the positive side, however, what seemed to be most characteristic about organization of film propaganda in Canada was the absence of the confusion and lack of direction that marked developments in Britain. Perhaps this was because the Nazi menace was thousands of miles away. Canada's transition from peace to war was a slow process, but there was a clear government mandate for documentary film production, and Grierson did attract imaginative and active personnel. He did not miss the opportunity in December 1939 to affirm film propaganda's *raison d'être* in the war in such a way that the King government could only agree with him: 'We shall use the film, I hope, to give visual significance to the words of Mr. King when he said that the spirit of mutual tolerance and the respect for fundamental human rights are the foundation of the national unity of Canada.' It may have been politically shrewd or it may have been genuine loyalty – or both. Grierson would always try to publicize King favourably, much to the chagrin of the parliamentary opposition. The reasons for Grierson's strange sense of loyalty to King go further than the mere fact that King was, by some distant blood tie, a fellow Scotsman. Grierson would say in later years that, whoever might be the prime minister, 'he is the only Prime Minister you've got.' This was not only a politically astute and safe position to take: he really believed it. It was an example of his deep-seated respect for existing institutions, despite an inner drive to challenge the *status quo*. Paradoxically, though Grierson's progressive ideology may have seemed out of the mainstream and even left-wing to some, it was, in fact, quite close to house policy. In this context he could operate freely within the Canadian political system. At the same time, Grierson's position lessened the likelihood that his film propaganda would encourage or countenance radical change.

Propaganda was education stirring a people's loyalties and even promising a better world to come – but the changes would all be encompassed in Liberal programmes.

Putting this into perspective, by March 1940 the National Film Board could claim only ten persons on its staff and the Government Motion Picture Bureau was little better off, with a staff of twenty-nine, located in a former lumber plant on John Street in Ottawa. There was no lack of demand for films in the early days of the war. National Defence required them to help in recruiting and training. Munitions and Supply wanted to convince Canadians of the urgency and importance of the industrial front. Months later, the Wartime Prices and Trade Board would wish to explain controls and rationing to the public. Also, the War Finance Committee would enlist films to help sell bonds and war savings certificates. The first National Film Board production was a War Loan film. This greatly impressed J.J. Fitzgibbons, who had become president of Famous Players Canadian Corporation. He congratulated Grierson: 'It is positively one of the finest films of its kind we have ever seen and will be a welcome subject on every program in every theatre everywhere.' More specifically Fitzgibbons had renewed Nathanson's pledge to screen government film propaganda in almost eight hundred Canadian theatres.[14]

But this was only the beginning of the task. Grierson knew that if his contribution was to be significant, he had to extend the power and scope of the National Film Board without squandering the public purse. There was much to overcome before he could expand staff and production within the narrow mandate given by the government. In applying his progressive philosophy, Grierson never abused personal power, and this gave him a stronger position in the political battles he would face in the war years: in those frays he would disregard paralysing civil service procedure, abandoning those who lacked initiative or a progressive approach to their work.

Grierson brought in four men who, between them, set the guidelines and established the working methods of the wartime National Film Board. Stuart Legg, who arrived in early summer 1939, became the political scientist; Stanley Hawes, who arrived in October 1940, a former director at Strand Films, became the poet; J.D. Davidson, who, besides having taught Grierson camera skills in *Drifters*, had done jobs

NFB field representatives reported that audience discussions were usually intelligent and positive. 'Very constructive consideration of social issues came to the fore.' (NFB)

Rural children trudge three miles to see a non-theatrical NFB film. (PAC 129914)

Stuart Legg described his task in the global upheaval as trying to take hold of the growing points around a given subject and organizing it. He constructed a visual story to which afterwards he fitted words 'like a vine.' (NFB)

Lorne Greene's fatherly, reassuring voice of democracy, associated with *Canada Carries On* and *The World in Action*, provided audiences with consistency, hope, assuredness, and sense of purpose. (NFB)

Grierson, flanked by two military officers, censors a screen battleship in 1940. (NFB)

Prime Minister King botched this 1940 sequence a half dozen times before overcoming his wooden screen presence. Of this performance before Arnold Heeney (left) and Walter Turnbull he wrote, 'I loathe my own appearance on the screen. The thought of having it reproduced destroys every natural feeling of joy in preparing anything.' (NFB)

Lucio Agostini, who composed much of the music for the NFB theatrical series, employed musical crescendos to punctuate Legg's phrases of narration. (NFB)

for him in almost every conceivable mechanical discipline of the film business for a decade, became the craftsman; and Raymond Spottiswoode, a graduate of the GPO Film Unit, came from Hollywood in 1941 to become the teacher. Legg created the theatrical series, Hawes set the basic patterns for non-theatrical films, Spottiswood organized technical aspects and drafted the plans for the instrument that the National Film Board eventually became, and Davidson imparted the relevant and essential skills and crafts. Together they trained and prepared young Canadian recruits to take over from them, though the international composition of the staff still grew steadily over the years. Guiding the entire enterprise stood the paternalistic Grierson, who provided the direction, coordination, and inspiration.

His policy of hiring the creative staff was diametrically opposed to that of the British counterpart, the Ministry of Information. Creative staff was hired on a temporary basis, neither subject to civil service regulations nor secured in their positions by such regulations. He did this 'to specify responsibility and to encourage initiative.' Employees' practical politics were irrelevant so long as they remained personal.

The following account of Grierson in action in these early days is worth quoting at length. The late Graham McInnes remembered his first encounter with Grierson when he was hired to write a script for a film of Canada at war:

'Sit down, sit down!' he barked. 'So you got here all right? Good! Now I want you just to try to understand what we're endeavouring to do. You have to see the perspectives, the growing points behind what's going on up here on the Hill. A nation at war; but still bemused. Still half asleep. You have to search, to analyze, to articulate the potential of Canada and make it so compelling that people will want to plunge their hands into their own pockets. Their *own* pockets. You understand?'

I wasn't quite sure I did. The barked torrent of words flowed on over me: a cataract of verbiage with unknown phrases sticking up like sharp rocks to confound the frail barque of my self confidence and perhaps overwhelm it. He had a habit of jabbing a hole in the air as he spoke; of running his finger round quickly inside his collar; of jerking his head impatiently; of scratching his scalp; above all of hoisting his feet up onto the desk – not in a lazy man's way, but with knees bent, poised like a coiled spring either you thought, to push his own chair back and send it skidding the length of the room, or else to leap right on top of the desk to harangue some imaginary mob. He was wound up tighter than a watch and gave a tremendous sense of controlled strength, of bounding energy and bursting vitality barely held in check by the diminutive body.

He appeared to be driven by a tremendous force, yet when he stood up to say farewell, after bruising me verbally for half an hour, I was astonished to see that I was a good head taller than him. Sitting behind a desk he gave the impression of being very large, or at any rate of being larger than life; of sizzling vigour. An alert acrobatic allusive converse bombarded you like a hail of birdshot and at the same time questioned enough of your accepted myths, prejudices or teachings to make you want to protest at every fifth word. Protesting but also fascinated. Numbed by the coruscating flow of ideas, but filled also with a heady sense of freedom and devil-may-care abandon. Because if he – perhaps your prospective employer and certainly at forty-two, which he then was, a man half a generation older than yourself – if he was so iconoclastic, could not you be so too? Could not you too sway along behind his chariot, thumbing your nose at the mighty, even perhaps letting off a loud idealistic belch or an intellectual whistle in their direction? As he rose, I rose.

'Sit down, sit down,' he growled again, for he hated – or pretended to hate – big men to overtop him, even in the mere physical matter of height which of course none of us can help. He started to pace the room with a swift jerky lope; a cross between Groucho Marx and what, in my imagination, I had always imagined as the walk of Edward Hyde. He shot words, phrases, sentences over his shoulder like a stream of smoke and sparks from a turn-of-the-century locomotive breasting the Rockies.

'You can script in something about closer living, up here. Across the Line it's all still pie-and-ice cream and mazuma. They haven't really grasped the fact that it's their war, for all that Roosevelt's a greater man than most. And here they're searching for leadership, scratching around in the dark looking for matches. You want to take images that will straighten their shoulders, brighten their eyes, put spine into them. It's there, but they don't know it. Things seem unreal to them. Pull out the images that they know – street corner hockey rinks, sap flowing in the sugar bush, the hard clear line of the Laurentians, men and clattery combines on the Prairies. You know the kind of thing! You may not know much about visuals yet, but do us an outline. Write a script to time for nine minutes, and put in your visuals on the right margin, a guide to the director. All right, you got that?'[15]

Thus would Grierson hammer, cajole, and inspire the creative talent he attracted to the National Film Board. Sometimes his view was both too expansive and too expensive. Early in December 1939 the ever-frugal prime minister vetoed Grierson's plan to spend $125,215 on creation of an overseas film unit to accompany the Expeditionary Forces.[16] Another year and a half would pass before an RCAF unit would begin to be trained – by the Americans and for free, underscoring the notion that the prime minister conducted the war as one of limited liability for Canada.

Amidst the hectic pace of organizing, training, and producing, suddenly in January 1940 Grierson left on his twice-delayed assignment to Australia and New Zealand. He wanted to fulfil his prewar commitments to the Imperial Relations Trust, commitments which now took on a special meaning in the wartime context. In the period between January and April, Grierson helped set up information machinery in both countries, and, it would appear, attempted to coordinate their government film distribution in such a way that by November 1940 he would claim, 'The circulation of certain films has been as intensive in New Zealand and Australia as in Canada itself.' The work in Australia and New Zealand was connected with Grierson's attempt to set up a worldwide network for documentary films, first in their wartime capacity, then, he hoped, in a postwar context. This all seems to be plausible in the light of what Grierson would write in a 1945 report (marked 'secret') on the results of his wartime labours:

The documentary approach today effectively controls the policy of the British Ministry of Information Film Section, also the National Film Board of Canada. In a lesser degree the film information activities of Australia and New Zealand. Failed to do so in the U.S.A. where, of course, the scale of Hollywood's industry made documentary development less relatively important for propaganda and morale purposes.[17]

As far as the government was concerned, in January 1940 Grierson was going abroad for a short while, fulfilling a commitment he had undertaken before he became film commissioner and for which he was still being paid. In wishing Grierson farewell for the prime minister, A.D.P. Heeney said, 'We shall all look forward to your return, however, before too long.'

But Grierson had spread himself too thin. He had undertaken a juggling act which nearly cost him everything he had built up to the time he left, including the government's good will. While he was gone, the National Film Board was rocked by a crisis from which the repercussions went directly to the prime minister's office and at one point led an exasperated Walter Turnbull to ask, 'Where's Grierson?' – only to be reminded that the man responsible for the operation of the National Film Board was thousands of miles away in the Pacific. The crisis erupted when, during the federal elections, a brief segment of film propaganda on behalf of Mackenzie King in a Grierson-inspired film raised the hackles of a jealous Ontario Premier Hepburn.

A MIRE OF POLITICAL EMBARRASSMENT

The story begins in October 1939, when Grierson approached Louis de Rochemont, producer of The March of Time, the highly popular American screen journal series, to undertake a joint production with the National Film Board. The March of Time, controlled by Time-Life Incorporated, enjoyed vast North American exposure and was at the height of its popularity, playing to a weekly audience of nearly twenty million in over nine thousand theatres. Raymond Fielding, who wrote a history of The March of Time, has claimed that the series was not a newsreel, 'but a kind of documentary film whose structure represented a compromise between the traditional newsreel and the socially conscious discursive forms of the British and American documentary traditions.'[18]

Grierson's publicity instincts were attracted by the popularity and vast audiences of the series and he devised an idea how best to initiate the Canadian war propaganda effort. Late in October, he requested and received from the prime minister's office authorization for undertaking a joint production with de Rochemont, to be called Canada at War. Grierson explained to de Rochemont that he wanted 'to show just what happens to a country's national organizations when it goes to war,' not only describing the military aspects of mobilization, 'but what happens in the reorganization for war of economic, financial and other related aspects of the national life.' De Rochemont offered his crews to do the photographic work and to 'make available to you all cuts not used in our release.' Grierson agreed and told him that the government would keep control of the film so that nothing would go out of the country without permission. Grierson obtained the right to supervise the picture both in Canada and in New York and arranged to waive customs and immigration restrictions for the Americans. He told de Rochemont that war conditions made the film subject to the terms of national censorship and that he, Grierson, would supervise such arrangements on behalf of the government. In setting a precedent, Grierson assumed personally the final responsibility for censorship of Film Board films. In August 1940 the Privy Council gave him authority to dispose of films seized in censorship for examination.[19] He acquired the title 'custodian of enemy films' and told filmmakers they could recut enemy propaganda to suit Canadian needs. Of course military censorship operated too, especially when secret or defence items, such as radar or explosives experiments, were being filmed for non-public screening. The film commissioner remained the last person to vet propaganda within the board. Above him the process could continue ministerially right up to the prime minister who would on at least one future occasion exert his authority to withdraw an item. The Department of External Affairs was consulted rarely, and had a tendency to see films after they were finished. It would occasionally complain that its input should have been solicited earlier.

Before de Rochemont began shooting in Canada, Grierson was off to the Pacific. He left supervision of the production to Ross McLean. It is far from clear how Grierson was able to give the impression of being in firm control of film production while he was thousands of miles away. In Britain, Documentary News Letter reported in May 1940 that Grierson 'made a brief but electrifying appearance in the act of censoring a screen battleship in a March of Time production for a February, 1940 release.'

Before leaving, Grierson recommended that Colonel John Cooper, head of the Canadian Motion Picture Distributors' Association, be invited to act as temporary film commissioner during his absence. This was Grierson's first major political blunder and perhaps underscored his disadvantage as an outsider not attuned to Canadian politics. Ross McLean has said that the Cooper affair threw a shadow over Grierson's activities ultimately and led King's lieutenants to doubt the film commissioner's style of politicking and scheming. Grierson chose Cooper in the unrealistic hope that he was tying the hands of Famous Players Canada Corporation during his absence. What he did not take into account was that the ardent Tory Cooper could and would play politics, hoping to cost King a setback in Ontario in the federal elections of March 1940. Whether or not his fears were justified, Grierson was counting on Cooper's influence to prevent Famous Players from wrecking the young, fragile National Film Board and to keep commercial distribution of government films from being altered. But he missed the wider political ramifications of his choice. Cooper would use his power and friendship with Ontario Premier Mitchell Hepburn (King's fellow Liberal and presently jealous foe) to try to undermine the prime minister.

The crisis began over the joint production with the *March of Time* of *Canada at War*. McLean, with Walter Turnbull behind him, naturally enough wanted to help steer the film in such a way as to depict Mackenzie King in a positive and favourable light. This was not easy to do, since in one segment King botched his line repeatedly. The room had to be cleared of all but the camera and sound persons and the 'on screen' audience of Heeney and Turnbull. A half dozen takes of the shot later, King almost looked natural as he spoke with firm resolve of Canada's significant role in the war. To himself, he was fulminating against Liberal Premier Hepburn. Later that day he confided to his diary that he was fatigued and overwrought with the Ontario leader for his legislative resolution which condemned the King government's war effort. This was an unforgivable sin, for he noted bitterly that Hepburn united Ontario Liberals with George Drew's 'Tory gang.' He was dismayed that a fellow Liberal had betrayed Liberalism and Liberal principles. 'It is all part of a threat that he would destroy me whether in so doing he would destroy the party in provincial and federal field alike,' he wrote. This *March of Time* film was becoming a nightmare to him.

King's immediate preoccupation was Hepburn but in truth he could never feel comfortable before a microphone or camera. His strength was neither personal charisma nor publicity. 'I loathe my own appearance on the screen. The thought of having it reproduced destroys every natural feeling of joy in preparing anything. I become filled with a sort of fatal dismay.' King detested publicity in the context of the war. It was, he thought, self-advertising, something he always despised.[20] For a twentieth-century politician this seems a critical flaw. King's ability to remain Canada's longest-serving prime minister is explained most by his supreme ability to monitor every detailed movement of his party, machine and politicians alike. That knowledge meant certain power.

He predated by several decades the politician who was part and parcel a media package, an image, a saleable consumer item. Not being charismatic, he was by nature the man always in the middle of extremes, the publicly restrained individual, the conciliator, the mediator. He was the quintessential Canadian.

King's small flirtation with film propaganda exacted a psychological price, as evidenced by his diary, but for ex-Liberal publicist Ross McLean the film was a piece of publicity which could do no harm. King called for a federal election at the end of January.

Anxious to contribute to the prime minister's re-election as he had in 1935, and aware of the film's value, McLean rushed the negatives to New York City to print the final copies, since printing in Canada took too much time. He returned to Canada by plane with nineteen prints and gave them to RKL Pictures of Montreal, the distributors. They fixed a release date early in March to coincide with the election campaign. Colonel Cooper, however, was sympathetic to Ontario Premier Hepburn, who by now was publicly nearly at war with Mackenzie King. After seeing the film and realizing its political value, Cooper pressed heavily on Fitzgibbon, president of Famous Players, to hold back on releasing the film in Ontario until after the election. Fitzgibbon agreed. McLean was furious, called Cooper and asked for an explanation. Cooper, technically his superior, told him coolly, 'Why don't you call the Prime Minister?'

Turnbull then summoned Cooper and told him angrily. 'You are playing politics and playing Hepburn's game. He is using you as a front.' Turnbull demonstrated aptly to Cooper how politics was a two-way game: he threatened to keep Famous Players' American parent, Paramount Pictures, from passing its films through Canadian customs. Cooper was sufficiently frightened and told Hepburn that the film would be released. But the war of nerves was not over. Cooper had caved in to the pressure, but Premier Hepburn was not going to be intimidated. Hepburn prevailed upon the Ontario Board of Censors to ban the film in Ontario. Turnbull was soon on the phone to de Rochemont in New York. De Rochemont was upset that a *March of Time* film was becoming a political football. He issued a press release stating that *The March of Time* did not play partisan politics and that this was the second time a *March of Time* film had been banned, the first time having been by Hitler. The association of Nazi tactics with Mitchell Hepburn could not have been more blunt.[21]

Hepburn's antagonism to King stemmed from a slight he suffered in 1935 when the prime minister had refused his nominations for the federal cabinet. Also, he both resented Ottawa's unwillingness to assist Ontario in exporting hydro-electric power to the United States and opposed Ottawa's intrusions into provincial areas. By the summer of 1939, it appeared that Hepburn would do all he could to thwart the King government in a federal election.[22] Through the fall of 1939, he thought that King's war effort was inefficient and in January, he condemned the King government publicly.

King seethed with anger. Worse yet, Cooper, wanting revenge on McLean, came up from Toronto and told him flatly he was fired and could not return to his office. King then exploded and wanted to fire Cooper. Turnbull sensed the danger of making Cooper a *cause célèbre* and prevailed upon King to resist the impulse. Making the best of an embarrassing situation, Turnbull was behind the advertisements which soon appeared in Ottawa, announcing the showing of the film across the river in Hull, Quebec: 'See the Film Banned in Ontario.' Among other factors germane to the campaign, public opinion in Ontario seemed to indicate a sense of outrage against Hepburn's flagrant confrontation with Ottawa. The federal elections followed. King, expecting to lose between 30 and 40 seats, saw the Liberals capture a majority of 117 over the combined opposition, the largest ever majority until then and 51.5 per cent of the popular vote. His party held 57 of Ontario's 82 seats.[23] It was a gratifying triumph for the prime minister.

In preparing his victory speech, King intended to refer to Hepburn's as a Nazi mentality making its evil pressure felt. Two of his advisers, J.W. Pickersgill and Leonard W. Brockington, urged him to modify his language, but King boasted in his diary that he insisted in bringing out that this was one of the factors which had contributed in no uncertain way to the result.[24] Years later there would be some public reconciliation between the two, though in his heart King never forgave Hepburn for betraying Liberal solidarity.

Following the successful outcome of the elections, Dana Wilgress (no doubt with the approval of the prime minister) asked McLean personally to return and resume his position as assistant film commissioner, though it would mean still working under the now sullen Colonel Cooper. McLean agreed and returned to work. He did not have to wait long before Turnbull called upon the prime minister to slay the dragon. 'Not once or twice, but at least six times I have been told that Colonel Cooper is doing everything he can to embarrass and annoy the men who are trying to produce pictures for the Government,' Turnbull complained to King. Both Herbert Lash, director of public information, and Stuart Legg, supervisor of film production, said it was impossible to carry on with Cooper. Turnbull was not worried about a successor. 'In any event, the question of a successor is not as important as getting rid of Colonel Cooper before he does any further damage.' The discouraged and politically outflanked Cooper left quietly for Toronto shortly thereafter and returned to his position as head of the Canadian Motion Picture Distributors' Association, much the worse for his political wounds. Some weeks later, Grierson was back in Canada and resumed his post as film commissioner. The damage had been done and repaired; Grierson's improvident choice of Cooper may have convinced at least one King adviser to be wary of the freewheeling newcomer. Turnbull was more willing to forget the whole episode, though he had developed some scepticism about Grierson, who he thought 'was trying to cover too many bases.'

GRIERSON STEALS THE THUNDER
FROM THE MOTION PICTURE BUREAU

The Colonel Cooper affair was a prelude to the major confrontation which was to occur between Grierson and Frank Badgley of the Canadian Government Motion Picture Bureau. The struggle stemmed from the fact that, as film commissioner, Grierson was not the chief agent for production or distribution; he was, however, to be consulted before work on film for the government was begun. The chief agent was still Badgley, who with his group of loyal followers seemed to be constant thorns in Grierson's side. Relations with the Motion Picture Bureau were deteriorating into near-open hostilities by May.

The crisis started when Audio Pictures, owned by Grierson's close associate, Arthur 'Killer' Gottlieb, produced a two-reel film for the Department of Fisheries called Teeming Treasures. Gottlieb suggested that the film be edited to one reel before being released for distribution.

J.E. Michaud, minister of the Department of Fisheries, agreed to have the film cut, but sent the matter to Badgley's Motion Picture Bureau 'for their final opinion.' Michaud asked Walter Turnbull to oversee the problem and told Grierson to make arrangements with secretary Turnbull. Turnbull was sympathetic to Grierson, yet was afraid to undermine actively Badgley's privileged position. Grierson appealed to Turnbull: 'Let us get hold of that film right away and gear it to distribution realities. I shall take account of Mr. Michaud's political problem in regard to it. This means that the film should be handed over to me fairly soon to get ahead with.'[25]

The film's fate is unknown. The months that followed were clouded by Grierson's and Badgley's mutual antagonism. If Grierson signed a memo releasing some of his people to work for Badgley, Badgley would refuse to send them back to the Film Board even if he had nothing for them to do. Exasperated, Grierson decided to force the issue by making himself the expendable pawn. He sent in his resignation to National Film Board chairman James A. MacKinnon on 27 November 1940, despite the Film Board's request that he remain. He hoped to force the Motion Picture Bureau to be brought under the administration of the National Film Board and to establish direct contact between the Film Board and the Treasury.

In the letter of resignation, Grierson expressed fears that the Film Board would be associated too closely with the administration of the Department of Trade and Commerce (the Motion Picture Bureau's parent body). He stated bluntly, 'This presumably is to ensure that the National Film Board, like other departments will jump through every hoop of Civil Service regulation. It is, I am sure, a mistake. The creative media cannot always be "packed into that narrow act."' Grierson criticized the tug-of-war between the civil service and his creative people. The former's procedure weakened the latter's vitality and paralysed initiative. This was a theme that he was to enunciate throughout his entire public career. 'One notices that wherever the weight of influence has lain with the Civil Servants, the spark has gone out and the use of the creative media has not been remarkable.' His recommendation was that the government bring the Motion Picture Bureau within the administration of the National Film Board and let the film commissioner, with his executive, relate government procedure to creative practice. In short, radio, information, and film should be brought into a close constructive relationship. As Grierson put it, 'I believe that the strength of the country's Information Service may represent the vitamin D of both Canada's war effort and of its rehabilitation after the war.'[26] It was a blueprint he would follow until 1945. He wrote to his old associate Basil Wright in England explaining the essence of this 'old fight on my hands. ... The issue is the same – youth and activism against the bureaucrats and the mediocrity and complacency and death of the spirit they represent.'[27]

His letter of resignation was not without effect. Leonard W. Brockington still had seven months of good will left before the prime minister would lose confidence in him. He tried to use his influence when informing King of the situation. He surmised that at the root of it all was a political disagreement between the Treasury Board, some members of the civil service, and the National Film Board. There was no doubt in his mind that Grierson had engineered some of the 'finest creative work that has been done on a national basis.' He concluded the memorandum in the strongest possible terms. 'While, no doubt, Mr. Grierson has some temperamental weaknesses, as all creative people have, he is recognized as a world authority, and I believe his resignation to be a national calamity.'[28] Eight days later King spoke of the resignation to the Cabinet War Committee and said it was desirable to retain Grierson's services. He would take the matter up with the minister.[29] A month passed and nothing changed.

Grierson waited until late January 1941 to communicate directly with Mackenzie King. Characteristically, he did not make a personal bid for power but asked that a young Canadian be appointed film commissioner. He offered to stay only for a period to help his successor with the 'various possibilities and practices of this work.' He asked that two simple but effective administrative changes be effected: that the Motion Picture Bureau be brought under the administration of the National Film Board, and that the board be enabled through its own treasury officer and by direct contact to relate its creative needs to Treasury practice. As for the Film Board's request that he stay, he concluded that any decision to stay 'must depend on the creation of a state of confidence regarding fundamental points of policy.' Here he was implying that if MacKinnon's view as chairman of the National Film Board and (now) minister of trade and commerce remained radically different from his own, he had no choice but to resign and permit MacKinnon a 'clear field for the policy he espouses.'

Turnbull was sympathetic. He wrote to the prime minister on the same day as had Grierson and confirmed that the Department of Trade and Commerce had a tendency 'to departmentalize the Film Board' and to prevent it from serving as the agency of all departments. Turnbull thought the answer was to limit the number of representatives from Trade and Commerce who sat on the board to one, the minister, who would be chairman. The secretary should be chosen from another department and the Film Board should have its own Treasury representative.[30] This scheme would be adopted some months later, after more political struggle.

Was Grierson's resignation sincere? It did appear that he was serious, since he could not continue to function while being hamstrung by Badgley and MacKinnon. He had appealed to King for personal support while affirming his intentions to step down. From the prime minister there was characteristic silence and delay. Some two weeks later, Grierson reiterated his position to MacKinnon. First, it was time to hand things over to Canadians. From a personal viewpoint there was less need for him now and he was anxious to be in a position of more direct service to British Information. But these considerations aside, Grierson's major reason for resigning was his opposition to codification of the Film Board's activities and its more definite integration with the departmental workings of Trade and Commerce. He would remain as an associate only if the commissionership were handed over immediately to a young Canadian. The Motion Picture Bureau could be left, for management purposes, within the Department of Trade and Commerce. But, he emphasized, 'the Board's powers to determine the style and manner of purpose of production and distribution are necessary, if the Bureau is to be the leading instrument of the Board's plans.' There was little room for doubt as to the change of status envisioned for the Motion Picture Bureau. Grierson suggested that MacKinnon appoint a separate commissioner to govern exhibitions and stills (an obvious reference to Badgley) while the Motion Picture Section should come under the aegis of the Film Board. Further, besides having its own direct relationship to Treasury, the board should have only one representative from Trade and Commerce so that other departments could be represented. Finally, Grierson asked for regular monthly meetings to consult with MacKinnon. The letter closed with the explanation that these were not conditions, but proposals for consideration by the Board and 'for possibly still higher consideration.'

In fact, these were conditions for Grierson's continued presence as film commissioner. MacKinnon had already intimated to the press that the film commissioner was staying and told Grierson personally that he would do his utmost to give effect to his suggestions. But Grierson, in a personal letter to Walter Turnbull that same day, expressed reservations about MacKinnon's tendency to let things ride indefinitely: 'I sometimes suspect that Mr. MacKinnon regards time as an all healing principle. It derives from a great sensitiveness about changing anything or disturbing anybody, but of course that is of no use to us on this occasion. Certain alterations have to be made, even if they produce a temporary ruffle in particular quarters.' The temperamental Grierson was not to have immediate satisfaction. MacKinnon was to become deeply involved in wartime wheat policy. Though Grierson withdrew his resignation, little seemed to be happening. In April it was noted that his salary was fixed at $6,600 a year from 1941 to 1943 while Badgley's was $2,000 less. The board also gave Grierson the right to spend up to $5,000 on the telephone without going through normal Treasury channels, something he called, years later, 'a wonderful lubricant with which to get things done.' He complained to Turnbull on 30 April: 'I'm afraid nothing concrete has been done in respect of undertakings given when I withdrew my resignation and the conditions which led to the previous issue still prevail.' He asked Turnbull to tell the prime minister of the existing situation.

The next day Turnbull wrote to Mackenzie King: 'Mr. Grierson is now recommending that, under the Transfer of Duties Act, the direction of that part of the Motion Picture Bureau having to do with films be vested in the National Film Board. This device had not occurred to me but it appears to be legally sound, and should, if agreed to, clear up the problem which is still causing the strained situation.' On the same letter, a note dated 12 May was scribbled in pencil at the bottom in the prime minister's hand, stating that MacKinnon had been seen for the second time on this subject and later Wilgress and then Mr Grierson.[31]

To his diary, the prime minister confided how he had sorted out the problem. He consulted with the key members of the board directorate, MacKinnon, Wilgress, and Crerar, and made up his mind that 'the work of the media of information in Canada's war effort would have to be more effectively coordinated, and the whole effort dealt with by someone with imagination, the whole work assigned to a separate ministry.'

King then had Brockington and Grierson to dinner and agreed not to let Trade and Commerce do this work. He was incisive in his evaluation of the probably over-eager Grierson: 'I was much impressed with Grierson's knowledge of the whole work of propaganda, publicity, etc. but not particularly taken with his personality.' But Grierson was the best man available to carry out a really effective programme for films of the war effort, and so, King concluded '[I] have asserted my authority in seeking to get action in this matter.'[32] He was probably put off by Grierson's and Brockington's wheeling and dealing. On second thought, four days later, he realized that both men were trying to control the information programme, the department, and the minister and thought that Brockington had 'overplayed his hand.'[33] It was the beginning of the end of his counsellor's usefulness. King expected his underlings to see the world through his eyes and to pay him respect as the wise and prudent power broker. He said nothing more about Grierson, though one suspects there was now a seed of doubt planted in King's mind, perhaps by the Scotsman's politicking, his independence, or his métier as propagandist. Mackenzie King used his authority and the log jam was broken. Next day the Cabinet War Committee met and learned of King's decision to review the various public agencies involved with public information. They discussed how to improve public information services along the lines he indicated.[34]

Grierson believed he had engineered total and complete reorganizational success. Seven and a half months had passed since he had first tendered his resignation to force the issue. On 11 June 1941 the powers defined by the National Films Act to the minister of trade and commerce were transferred from that department to the new minister of national war services, J.T. Thorson. Grierson, though not governed by the Civil Service Act, took over the Motion Picture Bureau staff which had been appointed under that act. Thus the National Film Board was to include civil servants from the bureau and its own non-civil-service personnel who had been hired on a three-month or per job basis. One of the most sensitive issues, annual salary increases, was handled by Grierson with characteristic aplomb. He broke with the civil service practice of annual salary increases, instead reorienting salaries to the quality and amount of work a person produced. This system encouraged those with talent and ambition and discouraged those who were only seeking tenure and security through years of service. He was able finally to achieve peace between both staffs by hiring some relatives of the Motion Picture Bureau personnel on at the Film Board. He thought this would appease those who had felt a strong allegiance to Badgley. The move was practical as well as *politique*.

By August, the Motion Picture Bureau's Stills Division was transferred from the Department of Trade and Commerce to the National Film Board. It became the Photo Services section of the National Film Board under the broader Graphics Division. Subsequently Graphics would control the Poster and Publication Design Section. Grierson now left temporarily for Britain to set up the Military Film Unit for the Department of National Defence and returned to Canada at the end of October.

As for Captain Frank Badgley, that hapless official found himself stripped of power and the loser in the political game. His already poor health was further aggravated by personal problems and within a year he was dying. Grierson, never one to hold a personal grudge, went to visit Badgley in hospital shortly before he died.[35]

The net effect of Grierson's success in reorganizing the National Film Board was that he found the chance to apply his philosophy of education through film propaganda in a practical manner. The victory over Badgley was neither personal nor political in the shallow sense. To Grierson's mind, before he could develop his plans and policies fully he had to rid himself of the bureaucratic entanglements associated with the Motion Picture Bureau. There was now an opportunity to develop out of the war's logical needs an integrated education in practical citizenship. If he had 'won his place' in the King government on the political battlefield, he had no intention of spending a comfortable tenure enjoying the privilege of position or the fruits of political victory. Now there was work to be done, especially to find means of disseminating propaganda to wider audiences. With characteristic energy and fanatic resolve, Grierson continued his self-appointed mission of uniting propaganda and education with inspiration. Meanwhile, the rest of the government's propaganda apparatus seemed to drift on aimlessly.

3 | Image of Wartime Canada: Publicity, Information, or Propaganda?

In 1941, Prime Minister King reached a conclusion that if his country-men believed they were now engaged in 'total war,' there remained serious problems to overcome in terms of delivering information relevant to that war. He was unhappy because there was no effective coordination by the media of Canada's war effort. The agency he had envisioned as a kind of helping hand to speakers like himself had become the undistinguished Bureau of Public Information. By 1941 it was the 'sick man' of the publicity world. The bureau had faced strident criticism in and out of Parliament during its first years because of the unfocused nature of public information policy. Member of Parliament and rising Liberal star Brooke Claxton wrote to the prime minister early in May about the weak information services which he described as 'unimaginative, uninspiring and late. What was needed was to create in people a general feeling of confidence which makes them identify themselves with national action.'[1] But King himself had been responsible for keeping the agency little more than a 'facts and figures' organization. He so much as admitted it in mid-May when he complained in his diary, 'Our Information Office has fallen down completely, simply on facts and statistics, which is what they were formed for.' He concluded that what was needed was 'someone to see that all available agencies of different departments were used as media to get out information that was needed.' His disappointment with the bureau was that in trying to publicize, it was 'continually avoiding getting information in a form that different media of publicity could use.'[2]

Most complaints centred around the ineffectiveness of the bureau's material. It would send out to newspapers background material and general information which few of them ever used. But the prime minister was also partly to blame. Though overburdened with the myriad details of running a country at war, he still found time to meddle in publicity, reflecting his omnipresence if not omnipotence as Liberal leader. For example, he could protest in council against the style of poster he had seen and then veto the use of radio for political discussion. 'Our Ministers are far too limited on these matters,' he confided to his diary. More likely, he was jealous of any other ambitious politicians seeking public limelight. It was his practice if he recognized bald political ambition in his underlings to withhold reward and even punish with banishment. For example, in November 1941, when Leonard W. Brockington suggested he be sent to England to speak on Canada's war effort and broadcast to Canada, an incensed King wrote privately, 'As far as I am concerned, this incident ends Brockington's relations with my office.' Brockington's failure to clear this plan with King convinced the prime minister of his underling's selfishness and inability to render any real service to others.[3]

King decided that the information apparatus needed someone with imagination, perhaps even a separate ministry. He talked the situation over with James A. MacKinnon, now minister without portfolio, T.A. Crerar, minister of mines and resources, and Dana Wilgress, who also sat on the directorate of the National Film Board.[4] Whatever their input, it would take over a year to identify specific reforms which needed to be undertaken and to begin the reorganization.

The Bureau of Public Information had been failing all along on the external side as well. In Washington, DC, it was not the fault of King's heavy hand that there was no Canada Information Office. Two months before Pearl Harbor, President Roosevelt, displeased with British and Australian publicity efforts and probably mindful of strong isolationists in America, told the Canadian minister in Washington pointedly that he was opposed to such an office. The next month he requested Canada to send a representative to work with Colonel Donovan, the coordinator of information, in his new organization. The president hoped that Canadian information officers would be associated closely with the Canadian legation there. King's predictably cautious response was to defer the question until a later meeting of the Cabinet War Committee.[5]

The information effort went from bad to worse. One cynical member of Parliament even suggested that Canada forget information and bring in Americans to generate tourist propaganda. J.T. Thorson, minister of national war services since June 1941, was responsible for the bureau and tried to defend it in November that year by claiming that it did not edit or censor material from other departments, but only acted as a distribution body. He could disguise neither the inefficiency of the government's information service nor the shortcomings of its leadership. As chairman of the National Film Board, Thorson might point to the bureau's only notable success, its sponsorship of the popular theatrical film series *Canada Carries On*. He could not, however, deflect the barbs aimed repeatedly at the directorship of the bureau. One member of Parliament attacked Director Herbert Lash and claimed he was 'neurasthenic and a fascist.'

A month later the Japanese bombed Pearl Harbor. President Roosevelt did not wish to overplay his hand or have foreign-inspired propaganda steal his thunder. In the hours following the attack he allegedly communicated to Mackenzie King that there was a strong feeling in Washington against any attempt on the part of Canada to influence the people of the United States in a way which might be held to be political; namely, Canadian propaganda should not try to bring the United States into the war. The prime minister claimed later that he had been asked by the highest authority in the United States to avoid any move by which it could be said that Canada was trying to influence public opinion in the United States to come into the war.[6] Canada resisted meddling with American public opinion, though it could have appeared to the public that the Bureau of Public Information was once again falling down on the job.

There had also been a noticeable lack of central direction with respect to censorship. From September 1939 a Censorship Coordinating Committee had existed, but there seemed to be confusion of responsibility between the provincial and federal governments and no means of establishing an effective policy. By May 1942 the minister of national war services assumed final authority in this area – the postal, telephone, telegraph, press, radio, and broadcast censors now reported to him and he also remained responsible for the National Film Board. The streamlining helped, but the information services' propaganda and counter-propaganda efforts needed boosting.[7]

On the national level, there were two problem areas. First, the government was suffering from an image of Canada as a producer and
banker rather than as a fighter. There was also a noticeable lack of
ideology and too strong an emphasis on winning the war first in all its
propaganda. Second, there was the severe morale problem to be dealt
with in the aftermath of the conscription vote plebiscite of 27 April
1942. The country had released King from his 'no conscription' pledge
of 1940 at the cost of alienating Quebec. Brooke Claxton appealed to the
prime minister for a national publicity campaign. He wanted to see a
scheme to promote unity and deal with Quebec 'to lift Canada out of a
state which in some quarters approaches despair.' He wanted Quebec
to feel it was included in Canada as part of the national enterprise and
thought a national campaign of emotional appeal could create a militant Canadianism. 'Only a militant Canadianism can overcome two
militant racisms,' he wrote. 'The people are ready for a new policy that
will give them a new start as well as a way out. The beginning point of
this is pride in Canada and her achievements.'[8]

Thus on both the national and international levels, the Bureau of
Public Information was ineffective. Perhaps M.J. Coldwell, leader of the
Cooperative Commonwealth Federation (the socialist parliamentary
party), best illuminated the bureau's failure when he asked in June
1942 why the ordinary common masses of the people in Canada could
not talk to their counterparts overseas.[9] This simple feature was, after
all, what public information was all about. King's private secretary,
Walter Turnbull, asked Lash finally why he was dragging his heels.
Lash replied that he was 'waiting for a green light from the Prime Minister.' An irritated Turnbull reminded Lash bluntly that, when driving
down a highway, one did not stop at every intersection.[10] Left alone to
muddle through, Lash had to accept responsibility for the crippled public information effort. Beneath him were personnel unsuited for the job.
There was a heavy concentration of corporate public relations execu-
tives, advertisers, and promotion men, most of whom reflected right-
wing class interests. There were no newspaper publishers, editors, or
top-rank writers.

Publicity relations with the United States continued to suffer, mostly
from neglect. On the one hand the Canadian position was essentially
negative. United States citizens heard almost nothing about Canada. On
average, the typical newspaper there mentioned Canada in connection

with the war only once in forty-five days. The impression was that Canadians were doing very little of anything. In the Cologne air raid early in 1942 one thousand of the six thousand pilots were Canadian, yet in the Associated Press story there was only an indirect reference to Canadian participation. On the other hand Americans would read of Ontario Premier Hepburn's insulting remark about the US Navy in February 1942 and think that this was the way all Canadians thought of the United States.[11] Also, rumours that Canadians were obstructing Alaska Highway construction needed to be squelched. The fault lay with Canada's poor handling of the news. There was a need for local facilities in Washington and New York to answer questions.

All these points came to light in a report on publicity presented to the King government by Charles Vining, president of the Newsprint Association of Canada, in July 1942. The Vining Report became the basis of total reorganization of Canada's propaganda effort. Vining's recommendations promised to be the Vitamin D that information and publicity needed. He thought that information should not become a ministry, since that route promised to create interdepartmental jealousies. Find new personnel, he said, and make the daily news the dominant focus of the agency, replacing the present stress on books, pamphlets, and mimeos. The Americans needed to be reached through news and newsreels. (The National Film Board was already enjoying success along these lines with its new theatrical series in US markets, *The World in Action*.) What was essential in this reorganization was to convince the members of the government to change their attitudes and to value information. He put it in a simple summary: 'This is a war of mind and spirit as well as a war of manpower and weapons.' If the reorganization were to work, the government had to find the right man, someone who could conceptualize and develop the right attitude, someone to plan centrally for decentralized education. He should remain in close connection with the Cabinet War Committee, the 'chief source of big news in Canada.' The penchant for pretentious titles (like 'director' of news and information) should be dropped for simple descriptive words, as the Americans had done with their Office of War Information. The new agency should have members from the major ministries – External Affairs, National Defence, Munitions and Supply, Finance, National War Services, Labour, and Agriculture – all representing their respective ministers. There should also be a domestic and external division.

The Vining Report looked fine on paper. Prime Minister King echoed almost verbatim Vining's words about the war being one of mind and spirit. The Bureau of Public Information was to be replaced by the Wartime Information Board in September 1942. The Cabinet War Committee told the new board to cooperate with the War Expenditure Committee to expose false rumours regarding the Victory Loan and war profiteering.[12] But the question of finding the right man was still the key. Newspaper heir Victor Sifton's name circulated for a while, then the job fell to Vining himself. True to his plan, he concentrated most efforts on external publicity, concentrating heavily on the United States. He established offices in Washington, New York, London, and Canberra as well as in Latin America. In its first months of operation, the Wartime Information Board acted primarily as a facilitating agency rather than itself engaging in media activities. The Vining regime embarked on a limited and cautious policy, giving departmental information services a sense of security from the pressure of 'government propaganda' or the government's masterminding of information efforts. This was in direct contrast with Goebbels' Ministry of Propaganda in Nazi Germany from which all information emanated and different still from Britain's Ministry of Information which suffered from top-heavy officialdom and lack of direction.

The major weakness of Vining's coordinating body was that it was not equipped to deal with the information needs of other government departments. Vining's own personality quirks did not help either. The unhappy chairman, Norman A. Mackenzie, summed up perhaps too directly the general feeling that Vining was 'a backside kisser to everybody above him and a sadistic tyrant to all below.'[13] Vining was aware of the inadequacies of the information set-up, but failing health made it difficult for him to reorganize the structure. Too ill, he resigned in January 1943. Before leaving, he recommended that external and domestic informational activities should be combined under a single unified administration. He suggested that National Film Board film commissioner John Grierson become general manager of the Wartime Information Board and assume executive duties under chairman Mackenzie and vice-chairman Philippe Brais. The minister responsible, J.T. Thorson, had claimed the previous June that it was never possible or desirable for publicity, public relations, or public information agencies to come together exclusively in one department or administration, but he had been overruled. The prime minister, anxious to clear up the 'war information business,' had concluded in August that 'nothing was so important as the war information,' since the government and country were suffering from not having proper publicity. It might be said too that King was probably hoping the new board could help him with his still unconvincing public image. He wrote in his diary the same day that it was the frightful obligation of facing further speaking engagements or broadcasts or press interviews in Britain that weighed on his mind more than all else.[14]

For Grierson, this was an opportunity too good to pass up. He was willing to don two hats for the two tasks. The position of manager of the Wartime Information Board carried no pay, only a provision for out-of-pocket travelling expenses. It would provide Grierson with the power to unite information policy, direct it toward a single end, and put into practice almost verbatim the terms of his November 1939 letter to A.D.P. Heeney. His only provision was that the post of general manager be temporary until July 1943. He hoped to extend the Wartime Information Board's function to 'increasingly act as the administrative agent of inter-departmental committees dealing with special informational needs and supported by the Cabinet in the programs they outlined.' This policy, he agreed, 'admittedly went in a direction different from that envisioned by Lash and Vining.' Though he was independent, he was responsible to a board of governors and told them, 'For two hours, once a month, it is your privilege to rake me over the coals.' This independence allowed him more than a chance to interpret the Canadian idea; there was an opportunity to create an active sense of social progress. Grierson wrote to Walter Turnbull in the fall of 1942, 'I don't think I am putting it too high if I suggest that out of these war needs can be created the appreciation and progressive achievement of a social platform of the first order.' The platform would be non-political, having developed from the war effort's own intrinsic nature, 'yet, at the same time, it might take rank as a radical political achievement equal to anything that might be urged from partisan and *a priori* political sources.'[15] The practical implications of such a policy meant the establishment of a central coordinating agency which would articulate the new world the war had created. Information would be 'total' in the sense that total war had created a need to direct both aims and goals externally and internally toward a larger prospect than victory for its own sake.

To achieve the desired ends of his 'radical' programme of information, Grierson began employing academics, especially from the social sciences. Their idealistic vision fit more comfortably with his radicalism than did the views of the advertising men and right-wingers who preceded him at the Bureau of Public Information. Those of the early agency who remained at the Wartime Information Board would find themselves rendered largely impotent.

In his unpublished history of the Wartime Information Board, William Robert Young referred to the board as 'the home of a group of parched idealists who were anxious to throw themselves into a cause.'[16] Grierson, himself a somewhat less parched idealist, would harness their energy to hammer out the propaganda line that this was a people's war and that concrete measures for postwar reconstruction would diminish poverty and assure broadly based prosperity and social equality. This vision coincided precisely with the prime minister's 1939 war aims of social security and human welfare.

In the first months Grierson divided the board into two operations. The first continued the external news and reports services of the Vining regime, but under the general manager's much tighter control. The reports branch, for example, under Davidson Dunton, began surveying labour, American, foreign language, and daily press reports. The second operation was less specific in orientation. This was primarily a 'think tank,' which tried to propose social action projects and media coordination efforts. Among other endeavours, Grierson had them undertake studies of voluntary war workers, art and information exhibitions, newspapers' views of information work and their use of government publicity material, industrial morale, youth morale, and consumers' information.[17]

At both the Wartime Information Board and the National Film Board, Grierson tried to use the relatively direct access he had to the eyes and ears of the powerful in order to translate the needs of the Canadian public into government policy. Vining had tilled the field which Grierson was to sow and he had left the Wartime Information Board with the hope that the board policy would be based on the 'inward flow' of information. To achieve this, Grierson decided to consult regularly the Canadian Institute of Public Opinion and the Gallup Poll. The Cabinet

War Committee demurred and ordered him in January 1943 to desist. Grierson disagreed and argued that, although publication of results tended to crystallize opinion at the point of questioning (the Cabinet War Committee's position), the poll allowed the ordinary man's views to be heard in Ottawa. Polls also revealed gaps and confusion in popular information and truly reflected public opinion. Such polls, he continued, were used by the Wartime Prices and Trade Board and the War Finance Committee as a test of their public approaches and were used officially by the United Kingdom and the United States. Finally, polls were essentially democratic. Grierson's argument convinced the prime minister to throw his weight behind a proposed confidential monthly survey which Grierson thought would be of real value to the Cabinet War Committee and others with whom the surveys were concerned, but King warned that considerable care would have to be taken in the matter of its distribution. All printed surveys would have to be numbered. By March it was agreed that the board could use the poll method;[18] Grierson would use them regularly throughout the war to test public opinion. Though the value of such polls is often questioned today, in many wartime reports to the prime minister and his cabinet Grierson used poll results to argue for a point or policy. In a few cases he was successful in influencing a government decision.

The Cabinet War Committee's reluctance to see poll results circulated might also have reflected a fear of having the information fall into the opposition's hands, where it could have been turned against the government. It might be argued less convincingly that polls violated *laisser faire*, long a Liberal principle; probing the public might actually cause the beast to stir. Unafraid, Grierson took the nation's pulse and reported the findings to his superiors.

From January to May 1943 there were nine issues of Wartime Information Board surveys. A chronological breakdown of themes reveals that most of the surveys were probing questions of morale: 'good' news was having a positive effect. The surveys measured expectations about postwar Canada and attitudes to the war effort and further taxation. They also ranged over issues like wartime information and trust in government. There was a probe into rumours and a poll seeking to know about 'participation' in general and reactions to the war budget. Another survey tested the sense of Canadian nationhood and national morale. A specific issue in April was Canada and Soviet Russia and how to create an atmosphere of mutually friendly postwar relations. A query about the state of public opinion preceded current information needs and the last issue in May dealt with manpower allocation, rationing, and living costs.[19]

Even though the poll results were kept secret, this five-month sample demonstrated the democratic element in Grierson's application of the information process. Information went traditionally from the leaders to the led. The surveys added another dimension, making the movement two-way, from the people to Ottawa, from the led to the leaders in specialized fields of industrial and consumer interest. They were also useful politically to the government. Grierson established communication with a hundred and forty communities across Canada.

If the intricacies and practical complications of this two-way approach caused some people to question its usefulness, Grierson was unwavering in his resolve and confidence. Shortly after his accession to the Wartime Information Board he wrote one of the most revealing letters of his public career in answering Sir Stephen Tallents' letter of congratulation to him upon his new appointment. Tallents had opened the doors for Grierson to found the first documentary film school in Britain. Grierson knew he was an outsider, though he could not help but be caught up in Canada's national awakening. He wrote:

February 16, 1943

Dear Tallents:

It was kind of you to write me on this new W.I.B. job. I thought you would perhaps be pleased that at least one slab of territory had come into our keeping, but, of course, the whole thing is surprising, and not least to me. Canada, as I have told you, has a deep sense of her growing nationalism: mostly subconscious, but all the more effective in primary decisions. It works out this way, that your alien – and particularly the alien who has served England – may be treated with all respect, but is not often taken seriously. I did not, therefore expect this translation and I am still surprised at it. ...

Then he turned to his new post as director of the Wartime Information Board and offered some remarkable insight into the Canadian national character:

Information in Canada has a bad history and three predecessors have gone down on it. The curious thing is that the service on the whole has been very good. It's just that the Canadians have not thought so. Again, it is part of the national incapacity for conscious self-measurement. They don't realize it, but they have a fantastic sense of want. It is articulated in a thousand different directions, few of which have any relation to the actual nature of the want. Partly it's young-nation stuff; partly a growing sense of destiny vis-à-vis the United States to the south and Russia over the right shoulder; partly it's a sense that the pluralist political shape they are dedicated to, is too difficult, and a craving for what seems a greater and more dramatic simplicity in others; partly it's a sense of the common economic illness. The last appears especially ridiculous in a country that has far more production power, agricultural and industrial, for its twelve millions than any country on the earth; yet, paradoxically, it is closer than most to the primitive dreams of personal fortune that go with a pioneer state.

You may well understand, therefore, why Directors of Information fall hereabouts. They have taken complaints at their face-value and trimmed their sails to every wind current and often very competently and with every desire to do a good job, and still they have fallen. The second last regime tried to meet every demand and was blamed for doing too much unnecessarily. The last regime, wary of doing too much, lost all face by seeming to do nothing. And that is where I start. All I am certain of is that we are going to reverse the unconsciously Fascist process and concentrate far more on information from the people to the Government, than from the Government to the people. That will take care of itself if the Government does what is intelligent to do on things like labour-management, selective service, prices, social reconstruction and the rest. We shall operate, in other words, far closer to the political scene than Informationists are expected to do. It is dangerous, of course, but personally I don't care a damn. We are certainly not going to try to dope people into a false estimate of things that are badly, or unimaginatively, or unprogressively done. We are not going to, because we couldn't get by. On the outgoing part of Information, we are going to put the media very much under their own steam and concentrate on easing the sources of information then, when it lays the department open to public criticism.

If he seemed a little flippant, the essence of his thinking had not changed. He admitted that the war itself was less important than the planned use of propaganda as education. He wanted to create a kind of Ministry of Education. Information, education, and propaganda were interchangeable words inspiring activism, that is, a new sense of citizenship in the modern cooperative state. At one point he described his philosophy of information as being 'totalitarian for the good.' He put it candidly,

I hope it isn't spotted too early, or wrongly, but I confess I can't every get very excited about the war effort per se, and feel that any information regarding it must somehow try to get behind the shot and the shell. The surface values – the guns and the campaigns and the braveries and the assembly lines and the sacrifices – are, I think, taken by themselves, the greatest bore on earth. The Americans are managing by superb showmanship to make a great spectacle out of it and some Canadians, of course, imagine we ought to solve the information problem in similar fashion. But even if we had the great store of national images and the ability – which we haven't – I am sure we'd still be wrong. We shall, instead, concentrate first on a clear-cut system of information or education, touching people as producers, and another, touching people as consumers. I expect we shall concentrate on a new activism in education and a sense of education in action and by action; close, I hope, to where the new citizenship of the cooperative state is even now, in spite of all the confusion, asking to be articulated. The general lines of the first [producer's] scheme I'll enclose to demonstrate the argument, but, of course, the next stage is the vital one: to put down the actual projects in radio, film, etc. by which the word is realized. Films are already on their way with well-considered schemes touching Conservation and Nutrition, and it is largely a matter of finding similar growing-points in the other media. If, as I hope, we get all the relevant departments behind these concrete schemes, so that all our information is tied to some extent to common ends, we shall have in relatively short order more of a Ministry of Education than anything else. I figure that if the planning is extensive enough, a few reactionary let-downs, which are inevitable, won't affect the bearing of the whole. ...[20]

Almost a month later he wrote to his brother-in-law, Duncan Mc-Laren. He reiterated the goals he had established for information, and painted a candid picture of wartime Canada's strengths and weaknesses. One still gets the sense of a complex, idealistic mind at work on behalf of democracy. He concluded:

Inevitably the lack of unity (which I find healthy and interesting) and the lack of ready cooperation (which is in the nature of things economic, geographic, national, racial and what-not), are blamed on the weakness of the Information service. For the moment I'm the ho presto man and the one they'll be blaming and bumping off, they think, anytime within the next six months. But we'll see about that, because this time the animal is going to be very malevolent and will defend itself, you may take it. They're not bumping me off, just because of their bloody geography. Apart from all that, it's an interesting business, and I have the illusion that I know more about it than anybody alive, outside Goebbels, and I like it. By the time I'm through it's pretty certain I'll have done something about education that will stick, and that's the main thing. There's a big chance, too, to do something on the social and reconstruction side, out of the information services associated with industrial morale, consumer education and agricultural production. I have gone down all three holes like a triple of terriers, and the dirt will be coming up in a flurry any time now. ...[21]

Both letters reveal how Grierson planned to put into practice his aim of channelling information from the people to the government. 'Being totalitarian for the good,' Grierson the idealist and crusader thought he enjoyed the luxury of being controlled by little more than his own sense of what was right and what was necessary to achieve. In practical terms his 'democratic' approach was not to be taken literally. In fact, he intended outside people, that is, primarily from press and media, to build upon the themes and aspirations which emanated from a hub or centre presided over by himself. He would in practice develop a personal relationship with as many newspaper editors as possible throughout the cities of Canada. If they were, by virtue of their class status, close to the ruling elite, they were a credible and relatively independent source (among other sources) from which he could take the nation's pulse and report it to the government.

The centre stood close to, took its cue from, but was not in fact the government. As a kind of national moral conscience, it would provide some sort of 'continuing purpose.' Besides press and media, the outside people could include those with no direct lines or responsibilities to the government. It was a good plan, given his predecessors' failure, because the sources of information would allegedly be made accessible to the critics who then might be less likely to put pressure on the director of information for doing too much or too little.

This was one way in which Grierson thought he would avoid partisan politics while pursuing his ideals. His methods were not perfect but it was his crusading idealism on behalf of the people which sustained him. This idealism separated him from the opportunist, who also displays great personal drive, but believes in nothing more than himself. As to the practicality of the idealism, the Aristotelian philosopher in him (perhaps in opposition to the Hegelian side) confirmed that the effort to reach the ideal is as important as achieving the ideal itself. This posture seems unlikely, especially for a twentieth-century public servant, and indeed Grierson was unique. One could not easily unite a crusader and a servant in the same person. He admitted that he had been paraded at various times as an uncomfortable character for a public servant to be. His defence reflected his unusual philosophy: 'I have always fought my battles as though I intended to win them. This was always a difficult situation, for ... it is only if the State is fighting for democracy that it has a dog's chance of coming through.'[22]

About the same time as the March letter, Grierson presided over a meeting at the Wartime Information Board of the industrial morale section. His articulation of the question of morale demonstrated how information was to have an impact at every level of wartime society. He said that industrial morale was one of the most vital areas of information and was necessarily concerned with a wide range of factors including health, transportation, safety, nutrition, and taxation. He emphasized that industrial morale had much to do with a worker's sense of status and with how workers participated in the national war effort. To realize this, he was working on bringing to the workers a monthly programme of war information under the auspices of labour and management. (This was in reference partly to the system of industrial film circuits then being organized by the National Film Board.) To illustrate, the Coal Labour Supply Committee had asked for a morale-building programme in the coal-mining industry. Grierson demonstrated how 'total' government information efforts should be employed. Not only should there be a major film on the subject, but also there should be twenty items to build morale. (See the Appendix for complete articulation of this morale-building programme.)[23] Within nine months the complete programme was in place. Films and film circuits were to be complimented by at least three radio broadcasts on coal and an extensive graphics programme including news photos, features, wall poster displays, photo panel displays, and booklets. To defuse the historically difficult labour situation in the industry, he recommended formation of labour-management committees and a change in the taxation system for miners. Finally a series of newspaper stories and articles on coal mining were to be circulated and were to appear in Canadian newspapers and magazines.[24] The net effect of this saturation campaign cannot be calculated or traced directly; following an illegal miners' strike in Alberta and British Columbia in 1943, relative peace was soon restored in the industry. A government move to reform the worst abuses of labour early in the new year surely was a significant factor. But one would not wish to ignore the morale-building effects of the board's propaganda effort. Grierson intended to strengthen the social side of morale and to analyse social and working conditions, instead of following the well-worn path of either chauvinistic flag-waving or of dampening popular discontent.

One wonders if Grierson's superiors approved of or even understood his intentions to play down the war effort per se; it seems doubtful, given the nation's total commitment to the war, that they would have agreed to such a policy. They did, however, have a Liberal vision of propaganda in wartime which coincided with Grierson's vision of propaganda both in peace and war. They understood the value of devoting energies to issues like educating the public and encouraging producers and consumers to practise conservation and nutrition. Also, labour-management committees were preferable by far to militant unions. The propaganda chief's articulation of these issues would in return help gain public support for the government and more sacrifice for the war effort. The government was using this idealist for its own purposes, though in June 1943 a practical and cautious Lester Pearson warned Norman Robertson, under-secretary of state for external affairs, to 'watch out for St. John and his disciples.' Grierson was trying to use his position to wage an idealist campaign. There was never a doubt about who benefited most from the relationship, since Grierson's idea for a Ministry of Education never materialized. It was too aggressive for traditional slow-moving Canadian Liberalism. There would follow a programme of information aimed at industrial morale, consumer education, and agricultural production. Inevitably, the war would continue to be the focal point of virtually all information, and, with the return of peace, information would cease to be a national priority.

After six months at the Wartime Information Board, satisfied that the machinery was now established, Grierson considered returning to full-time duties at the National Film Board. Heeney, as Mackenzie King's close adviser and clerk of the Privy Council, also won the prime minister's support for most of the Information Board's decisions. He felt Grierson should stay on at the Wartime Information Board and thought it 'would be serious if at this stage in the development of the W.I.B. Grierson were to sever his connection with it as General Manager, particularly in view of the chops and changes of the last year.' Heeney asked the prime minister to arrange with Major-General L.R. LaFleche, who now as minister of national war services was also chairman of the National Film Board, to allow Grierson to remain as general manager of the Wartime Information Board. Mackenzie King wrote in the margin of the memorandum, 'This had been settled,'[25] and Grierson continued to remain in the dual capacity until January 1944.

There was another side to the propaganda maestro which was either too radical or too messianic for the ministers and government he served. Grierson sent a copy of a speech he planned to make at the American Informational Association meeting in Montreal early in June 1943 to Brooke Claxton to vet. A month earlier, Claxton had become parliamentary assistant to the president of the Privy Council (the prime minister) and was fast becoming a trusted insider in the Mackenzie King government. His Liberal vision of 'information' differed from Grierson's on one critical point. He insisted that Grierson had erred when he asserted that the job of an information service included persuading people to accept government policy. Not so, argued Claxton. The information service should be used only to persuade people to adopt a line of policy when that policy was something more than government policy. Persuasion should only be used when government policy coincided with the general will of the nation. Claxton articulated the Liberal notion of government information, a service that should endeavour to put all the facts before the people fairly so that they could understand the matter and make up their own minds. His admonition to Grierson was loud and clear: 'The Government cannot and does not want the information service to be an instrument for securing the implementation of government policy except in so far as this is generally accepted by other considerable groups.'[26]

Grierson had to pull in his reins or at least rephrase his idea of propaganda so he did not appear to be practising methods of totalitarian regimes on the Right or Left. His speech avoided mention of persuading people to accept government policy. He hoped that information, now regarded as a passing nuisance, would become an 'accepted public service.' His mind was clear on this: *laisser faire* was no longer a tenable government attitude – the power of initiative now rested upon governments. Information needed to be seen in the larger context of 'securing the necessary element of cooperation on a basis of understanding.' It was a matter of constitutionally agreed national necessity – as long as initiative was allowed to or demanded of the government, public information was a continuing force, not a temporary expedient. The secret was 'to carry information about ourselves along every channel through which men crystallize their sentiments and form their loyalties.' To Grierson, it was all a matter of morality. He believed that democracy had enough moral stature to command the loyalty of all men. Information had to contribute to the creation of harmony and the elimination of discord.[27] Grierson's high-blown rhetoric stopped short of his initial (and, to Claxton, unacceptable) position, but like many idealist positions, especially in wartime, it seemed pure, wholesome, and unassailable.

Claxton was a politician who had sensed danger in Grierson's over-enthusiastic application of modern information mechanisms. Yet five days before his admonition to Grierson he himself was dealing with the most sensitive and potentially divisive social issue of the war in the crudest practical political terms. He was discussing steps that might be taken to prepare Quebec for the introduction of conscription. (It would not become necessary for nearly another year and a half.) His was a plan to indoctrinate the Quebec population and he wanted the Wartime Information Board to help. The board should pay junior newspaper reporters to write replies to questions and forward suggestions. Personal visits and the use of the Gallup Poll every three months could verify their reports. He wanted to mail regularly to the key half dozen men in each parish something appealing. He hoped the Quebec Information Bureau could become a front for Ottawa and suggested that those speeches by the Catholic clergy that were sympathetic to Ottawa be circulated regularly. He favoured newsreel shots of what he saw happening – French-Canadian soldiers walking arm in arm with their girls on the terraces of Quebec. There were altogether a dozen major manipulative tactics he thought could be used: praise, exploitation of Quebec heroes, Canadianism, the prime minister's speeches, even a French edition of the *Reader's Digest* would all contribute to gearing

Quebec to accept conscription. Claxton wanted six Wartime Information Board members to study the problem and make suggestions.[28]

Grierson must have had a hard time reading these contradictory sig-
nals. In all probability Claxton would not have perceived it this way.
With respect to conscription, English Canada was virtually united in
support of it, while in Quebec something had to be done since time was
not on the government's side. Claxton had envisioned the Wartime
Information Board's activities there as more covert than overt. As for
Grierson's crusade, idealism was fine so long as government manipulation was not heavy-handed. Claxton was cautious of political pitfalls in
Quebec and wanted to use the tools for the dissemination of information subtly. Grierson's pontification about persuading people to accept
government policy was not subtle. The missionary approach was not
the Liberal way.

How far then was the general manager to go? Some weeks later
Grierson wrote to Heeney, at the Privy Council, about how he intended
to bring departmental representatives together so that a pattern of
approach could be worked out for the particular field of information
concerned. Grierson threw himself into this task with his usual fervour.
Aware of the board's new responsibility to edit *Canadian Affairs*, a
magazine for overseas troops, Claxton encouraged articles on reconstruction and Grierson started organizing postwar rehabilitation material for overseas troops.[29] What began to emerge was a plan for postwar
reconstruction, which Grierson had been anxious to launch since January. The premise was that the society of the future would grow out of
present patterns. The new democracy would have to base itself on
incentives other than traditional pecuniary gain. New motives were
already in operation – selflessness for the war effort was occurring in
the workplace. Those incentives already in operation needed to be perpetuated.[30]

Under the spell of his own propaganda, Grierson believed that all of
this was leading toward a new kind of democracy. There was a current
belief that the government's involvement in national consciousness
and its imposition of a pattern of life tended toward fascism. He could
not disagree more and wrote, 'If national planning is conceived as a
process of cooperation for self-improvement, bureaucracy need not
result. As a matter of fact, the great development of the war is the
decentralization of responsibility to the furthest corners of the state.'
He never believed that the few would do the thinking for the many;

hearkening back to documentary film's message of the thirties, he wrote, 'If you cannot teach the citizenry to know everything about everything all the time, you can give them a comprehension of the dramatic patterns within a living society.' His own crusade demonstrated this principle: 'The essence of the educational process has been taken over by governments and industry in the name of propaganda.' Now there was great power in the hands of the private educational systems maintained by the big corporations. 'One might say that we had removed the Church influence from education only to hand it to the bureaucrats of public and private enterprise. ...' He concluded that so long as government and industry retained the power of initiative they must maintain and share this power with professional educators and constitutional authorities.[31]

One practical application of this was to encourage the Wartime Information Board's adult education group to organize radio-listening groups to discuss various reconstruction issues posed during the weekly half-hour radio series, 'Of Things to Come.' The ever-vigilant prime minister was not amused by his underling's initiative, which by late July had put the board ahead of the government. He took strong exception to the idea of launching a plan before his government had decided on one. Heeney wrote to Grierson that King opposed any project dealing with reconstruction and ordered action suspended.[32] By November King made it known to the chairman of the Wartime Information Board, Norman Mackenzie, that he wanted Grierson and the board to keep Claxton 'fully informed of its work.' Besides his numerous other activities, the prime minister, as president of the Privy Council, was also responsible for the board. Claxton remained his conduit, contact person, and occasional travelling speech-reader.[33]

From this time Grierson no longer dared openly to encourage the adult education group's freewheeling discussions. W.R. Young believes this incident increased the Liberal government's suspicion of progressive civil servants and caused Grierson's resignation from the Wartime Information Board in January 1944.[34]

PRACTICAL POLITICS INTRUDE

It would appear that Grierson was becoming involved in practical politics in spite of his claim to be a non-partisan propagandist for ideas and education. At least that is how it appeared when it came to poll-taking or offering unsolicited advice regarding labour and wartime wage controls. First, the background. An Order in Council issued in December 1940 had provided that the 1926–9 wage level be the norm for a fair and reasonable wage. Wages below this level could be increased, but only by 5 per cent and under for any one year, plus a cost of living bonus of $1.25 per week. By 1941, 32.9 per cent of the wage-earners were earning less than $450 per year and only 6.8 per cent were earning over $1,949 per year.[35] Between 1939 and 1941 an inflation of 20 per cent had eroded hard-won gains and strikes affected many areas of the war economy. Employers continued to resist recognizing unions. From November 1941 a National War Labour Board came into existence with powers of investigation and recommendation on wages and conditions. Two major strikes in 1943 were based on money issues, a ten-day illegal walkout of 9,000 Alberta and British Columbia coal miners and a ten-day 'summer holiday' of 21,000 Montreal aircraft workers. In Ottawa, the government asked the National War Labour Board to inquire into 'Labour Relations and Wage Conditions in Canada.' Hearings began in April 1943 and within two months it became abundantly clear that wage control must be lifted from lower-paid workers and 55 cents an hour should be the national basic wage. A national labour code based on the United States' Wagner Act was essential for unions to achieve recognition by employers. A novel recommendation for a system of family allowances also emerged.

King decided to keep these findings secret.[36] Grierson's optimistic interpretation of Wartime Information Board surveys might have influenced him. The board had spent the summer taking polls on numerous public opinion themes: the effectiveness of the war effort, American attitudes toward Canada, national pride and reactions to the Sicily campaign, attention to war news, civilian morale, public perceptions of sacrifice, regional grievances, and anti-inflation controls. On the last point Grierson sent a confidential ('Dear Jack') letter to J.W. Pickersgill, another of the prime minister's personal secretaries, in mid-September. He stated that, in a survey undertaken by the reports section, there was 'no considerable public demand for the abolition of the price and wage controls.' Attached was a summary of a public opinion poll which Pickersgill subsequently underlined in key areas. The public approved of the government's policy to prevent inflation, despite imperfections in functioning and inequalities toward different groups, especially labour, which was concerned about lower-paid industrial workers. Finally, the public was willing to sacrifice more for the war effort. Pickersgill marked the top of this report, 'The PM to see.'[37] Grierson's interpretation was that the poll seemed to confirm the *status quo* and it indicated no urgency. Despite his disclaimers, he was getting close to political questions, especially since the Wartime Information Board surveys tended to confirm rather than to challenge or provoke. Perhaps that is a function of government surveys or polls that sample all classes of society. (See the Appendix, p. 292, for an abbreviated list of Wartime Information Board survey questions from January 1943 to July 1945.) The fact was that Canada was experiencing its worst year of strikes since 1919. King delayed. In February 1944 the cabinet passed an Order in Council, PC 1003, which provided the machinery for unions to follow formal certification procedures in virtually all sectors of the economy.

Another side of the coin was Grierson's involvement as an active agent. Here he found himself ignored in his attempt to get a better deal overall for labour. Eleven days before the 'Dear Jack' letter, he had written personally to King about the increasing morale problem in the 'labour situation.' He recommended that the prime minister take over the labour portfolio, 'in order to work out a new deal for Labour.' Such a move on the part of Mackenzie King 'would galvanize national attention toward the essentially progressive nature of your policy if, as it were, the Old Maestro were to step in when the going was tough.' This, he argued, would provide an opportunity for reattaching Mackenzie King's political philosophy and political record to the progressive cause in general. But King was never to read Grierson's appeal. One of the prime minister's secretaries pencilled the word 'file' at the top of the letter, and the lack of any other markings on the letter means that in all likelihood King never saw it.[38] King initialled and dated most correspondence which he read and his secretaries noted when he saw a letter. Turnbull explained years later that such a proposition would have been regarded as impractical, as it was generally considered to be poor politics to fire a minister unless it was absolutely necessary. Hence, he would not have forwarded Grierson's suggestion to the busy prime minister.

This incident does, however, shed some light on what some call the 'power behind the throne.' Even someone with direct access to the prime minister's office was still at the mercy of the prime minister's aides and secretaries who 'screened' material and, in a case of something as controversial as this, prevented the prime minister from receiving the advice. The obvious danger of such a practice, then and today, was that a leader could lose touch with the citizenry and be deprived of hearing the single voice commenting upon the emperor's proverbial new clothes. Grierson's well-intentioned but unsolicited advice to King the former labour relations expert never found its intended recipient. The Ministry of Labour, under Humphrey Mitchell since 1942, was in a frightful state, but it was unlikely that King would have been reckless enough to take on yet another portfolio. (On Mitchell's arrival he had written in his diary that he thought the minister would be a real strength to him.) As an enduring politician with some progressive instincts, King preferred to muddle through from crisis to crisis and let the labour imbroglio settle itself gradually. Grierson, the enduring progressive and man of decisive action, had limited experience in the slow, cumbrous ways of Canadian politics. He abandoned his lobbying efforts on behalf of labour, realizing that as an outsider he could not penetrate the screen around the prime minister on this subject.

There were, on occasion, stumbling blocks which arose from Grierson's own tactical blundering. For example, in September 1943 he probed into a dangerous area when he sounded out the prime minister on a plan which would lead effectively to monitoring cabinet ministers' public statements from King's office. Grierson asked King to request ministers to 'send in to your office drafts of such statements as might have repercussions in other countries. An opportunity would thus be provided for reviewing the manner of presentation, in order to obviate any possible misunderstanding.' A subsequent note in the margin by Heeney said that the prime minister felt the suggestion could not be acted upon.[39] The politically sensitive prime minister would never have risked the isolation of his entire cabinet by such unilateral and authoritarian tactics. King was more subtle, hence more effective, in the personal way he kept touch with his ministers' every move.

To balance the preceding picture, if the prime minister was not always available to Grierson's ideas, King could not have been displeased with the work Grierson was doing to bolster national morale and publicize Canada. In April 1943 the Wartime Information Board came under attack nationally as 'Canada's Publicity Jamboree,' consuming a half-million-dollar annual budget. The prime minister found himself defending Grierson personally in the Commons that month after one member complained that a statement by Grierson to the press in March was a policy statement which it more properly belonged to a minister of the government to make. Though no specific press reference was given in the debate, the criticism may have been directed at Grierson's statement of the aim of the Wartime Information Board, which was read into the parliamentary record early in April. Its aim, he had said, was to develop an overall contact with the public, without which Ottawa could not expect to keep adequately in touch with the people and their activities in over four thousand miles of territory. The Wartime Information Board was not immediately concerned with the information services of individual government departments, but had the duty of seeing to it that, in consultation with the departmental officers concerned, wastage of effort was kept within limits, campaigns were related, and contradiction was avoided. King's response to the criticism of Grierson was that he believed that Grierson was 'merely giving the position of the board in this matter.'[40] Conveniently forgetting his stop order on Grierson's rehabilitation programme, a few months later the prime minister asserted baldly that he had not interfered with the Wartime Information Board or its work and he preferred to maintain that attitude.[41] Grierson must have swallowed hard, but he said nothing.

There was political value in his work for the prime minister, and Grierson did not miss the opportunity late in 1943 to try to exploit this fact. From August he attempted to expand the Wartime Information Board into domestic information policy. The Food Requirements Committee wanted a half million dollars for a food conservation programme, and the Cabinet War Committee approved of the board's participation.[42] King deliberated and delayed. Grierson wrote him in October. If the prime minister would approve of such expansion, he said, 'We can, in fact, kill two birds with one stone: giving the administration the "break" that has been denied it in the past twelve months and relating the war record of the administration to the larger matter of the repute of Ottawa and parliamentary institutions.' He concluded that the prime minister 'has always been very kind to my work and to the ideas of national information which I try to articulate. I think that very much would be gained if you could, at this juncture, see your way to approve the scheme in principle. ... When you have rested and have time, we could together go into the detail of the particular fields of activities I have noted for action, and make said alterations as you see fit.' Grierson attached a brief asking for an additional $425,000 for the remainder of the fiscal year. King marked the brief 'approved' on 20 October,[43] and the Privy Council approved of the Food Conservation Programme a week later. That same month the general manager could report that Canadian information to the United States was showing marked improvement and, despite tightness for space in American periodicals, Canada was improving its position.

Grierson's inexhaustible energy must have left observers fairly breathless. He set a rigorous pace of a sixteen-hour work day, working at the Wartime Information Board until six in the evening, then on National Film Board affairs until midnight. On one level at least, some results were useful politically. By January 1944, weekly confidential memoranda to the members of the cabinet reflected the tenor of the country and public opinion in general. He began each memorandum: 'The following observations on Canadian public opinion have been reported to the WIB during the past week. While open to possible later correction, they come from sources which we have found reliable in the past.' The memoranda ranged from generalizing about the public mood ('tense expectancy' in early January in relation to the impending Allied invasion of Europe) to reflecting industrial labour's uneasiness at the possibilities of immediate and postwar layoffs. Additional items that month dealt with the problems of rehabilitation of ex-servicemen, the other provinces' jealousies of Quebec's apparently favoured position in regard to rationing, and a Gallup Poll survey which showed that just over half the public would favour the continuance of general economic control, that is, government anti-inflation policies, in peacetime.[44] No doubt this information was valuable to the King government, which could use it to gauge the speed at which it could or should act on particular problems. Grierson felt satisfied that he was channelling the public's will directly to the government and thereby strengthening the democratic and progressive roots in which he so firmly believed. The weakest link, however, was in King's government, which would never respond as quickly or dramatically as the times seemed to warrant. Grierson's radicalism must at last have touched raw nerves. He tendered his resignation as general manager in January. It was accepted promptly.

What had gone wrong? His work to promote social morale was going nowhere. The food conservation information programme was held up in cabinet by minister of agriculture J.G. Gardiner, who feared a slur on the achievements of Canadian farmers. Further, Grierson's plans for an economic stabilization information programme to support wage and price controls failed first because of opposition by Donald Gordon, chairman of the Wartime Prices and Trade Board, and then because J.L. Ilsley, minister of finance, was opposed to arguing a contentious issue with public money. Also, earlier opposition from the Department of National War Services had forestalled Grierson's plan to establish an ethnic information service and a youth information programme. Similarly, the industrial information programme had run into trouble with the Departments of Munitions and Supply and of Labour.

It was an ironic tribute to his efforts that his own chosen successor, Davidson Dunton, unstuck many of the board's blocked programmes. Dunton was more of a 'team' Liberal man who did not crusade or make waves. He continued to apply social science methods using public polling techniques and scientifically channelled field reports from representatives in communities distant from Ottawa. The Liberals used these reports also for their political value in making decisions about the continuation of postwar controls and in discerning public attitudes toward both postwar immigration and Germans and Japanese.[45]

When Grierson had taken over the Wartime Information Board the year before, the government was content to let him do a job which it believed was on its behalf. The object was simple: to use every possible medium of information to unite all Canadians in total effort to make a maximum contribution to the war. To achieve this, Grierson would fine-tune some nine different print information sources at the board's publications branch: these included the board's fortnightly surveys, information briefs and bulletins, reference papers, facts and figures weekly, press surveys at home and abroad, enemy broadcasts, and the monthly *Canada at War*. To him these sources were valuable beyond nationalist or chauvinist sentiment; his focus was to try to develop the idea of Canadian nationhood looking toward a postwar and international context. This theme became especially evident in the work of the National Film Board. Propaganda was supposed to show how the war had become a people's war and midwife to a new social order. Though the Wartime Information Board did not take any initiative in French-language or ethnic information work, it did undertake information programmes about consumer matters, economic stabilization, labour, armed forces rehabilitation, and reconstruction. To this end, the three large expenses of the Wartime Information Board in 1944–5 went to three committees: economic stabilization information, food conservation, and rehabilitation information. Perhaps Grierson's critical error in 1943 was getting ahead of government policy in his planned reconstruction programme. More likely, he remained an outsider to his superiors, though he was occasionally useful to them. The Liberal government supported its agency's nationalist information programmes because it could convince Canadians that the Liberals, not the socialist-leaning CCF, were inaugurating wartime and postwar measures to assure material satisfaction and social equality. And knowingly or not, Grierson undermined opposition to the Liberal government's political power grip by hiring many officers who supported the CCF. If these officers voiced support for housing, social security, and family allowance programmes, it was the Liberal government that would take the credit. This at least is what King's minister Brooke Claxton tried to do: he stage-managed the nationalist information programmes to serve Liberal purposes.[46] Grierson, a believer in a brave new world, predicted that government would continue to regulate Canadian daily life, inspiring the citizenry after the crisis of war had passed. The practical-minded Liberals wanted only to ensure perpetuation of their regime.

While the propaganda chief had been putting Canada's information agency into a solid position, he continued his duties as film commissioner at the National Film Board. The evolution of that organization had fitted neatly into the scheme of propaganda which Grierson had inaugurated and orchestrated at the Wartime Information Board. In the whole organization of information, it was found that films had a critical role to play in his crusade. A confidential survey in June 1943 of the values of various media in public appeals had revealed several startling facts. Information was not penetrating all classes of the population evenly. People in low-income groups, the poorly educated, young people, and women were badly informed in comparison with high income groups, the well-educated, older people, and men. Surveys demonstrated that radio and newspapers took the highest position for the country as a whole, while posters and printed booklets as means of telling what Canada was doing received the lowest support. Statistically, only 23 per cent of the population considered films in movie theatres as the most effective channel of communication. But most significantly, film (and posters) appealed to the less literate and young.[47] It was clear to Grierson that the National Film Board had more to do to win the minds of the less literate and young. The watchword was *more*. Film propaganda needed to be more inspirational and more ideological.

Grierson and Legg:
An Ideological Approach
to Film Propaganda and
a *Carte Blanche*

Grierson's victory in the Badgley affair did not seem to impress the Treasury Board, which in the fall of 1941 refused to raise salaries and hire more people at the Film Board. Production continued none the less as some twenty-nine non-theatrical and twenty-six theatrical films were either completed or in production. There was an excessive demand on equipment, time, and personnel. Home was 22,000 square feet of an old lumber mill in Ottawa, so the board's staff worked virtually around the clock. The day shift would use cutting rooms and laboratories for their own projects while at night a different group would come in to work on other productions. At the same time, young Canadian recruits with imagination and talent needed to be trained in film skills. Stanley Hawes trained James Beveridge and Donald Fraser, while Stuart Legg instructed Tom Daly. Gordon Weisenborn, an American, was also Legg's apprentice. The nucleus of a francophone group would be formed by Philéas Coté and Vincent Paquette. Once the penurious Treasury eased up monetary restrictions, the international composition of the staff grew steadily too, with the major requisite being talent rather than citizenship. The lack of facilities was redressed in part by assigning production to already established firms like Associated Screen News of Montreal, Cinecraft Studios of Montreal, General Films Ltd of Regina, Audio Pictures Ltd of Toronto, Vancouver Motion Pictures of Vancouver, and Crawley Films of Ottawa.

Following his return from Australia and New Zealand in the spring of 1940, Grierson had again become a teacher of documentary technique and a propaganda missionary. With the Nazi onslaught into France, Grierson began calling groups of filmmakers into his office to boost morale and to inspire joint effort. Filmscript writer Graham McInnes, who made non-theatrical films for departments with special wartime functions, described one such meeting and conveyed vividly Grierson's infectious drive:

We watched Grierson pacing back and forth and rubbing his sparse, sandy hair, the very picture of sulphurously creative disruption, and we heard and we wondered ... Grierson stormed up and down. ... And he hardly once stopped talking. ...

'There's no use pretending we're not in a terrible mess. The Gairmans [sic] have knifed right through our collective individualisms, precisely because they were individual. And there'll be rough times ahead for the Brits. We must oppose discipline to discipline. Ours to theirs. But you discipline a democracy by creating the collective will from within; not by imposing it from without. This is what we have to do. All of us. And in the next few months. For the British it'll be weeks, because they've only the Channel. We have the Atlantic. Don't let's cherish the vain illusion we can squat behind it. Otherwise all it'll turn out to be is a bigger and wetter Maginot Line.

Now let's see you all get going, with a conscience and a head of steam; analyse, project, get at the truth. And don't forget it's a many headed monster and you may have at times to make people believe what they ought to believe rather than what they want to believe. Especially now. All right. Off you go.'

Pretty heady stuff for young men in an uncertain world with as yet uncertain guidance ... with Grierson's magic touch even the clichés sounded dynamic and exciting. It was something in staid safe Canada three thousand miles from any fighting, to feel that you were wanted; that your own particular skill was valid and needed; that you could make a contribution.

... the talks inspired us at our desks, behind our cameras, in our cutting rooms; to work fast and tirelessly, to probe deep and to think big and wide. How had Grierson done it?[1]

The answer was Grierson's supreme ability to inspire a feeling that the films were made as a joint venture, involving maximum effort from every person involved. Margaret Ann Adamson (now Lady Elton) joined Legg's *World in Action* unit as a research assistant, idea woman, and expert at locating stock shots. Legg called her brilliant at finding material which could interpret his themes and believed that without her the series would have been impossible. She has said, 'The sense of being overworked, suppressed and underpaid was important to the whole staff. They *liked* being driven. ... They felt that they were engaged in doing the job of the century.' Equally important, she noted, was the fact that Grierson put a 'ring of steel' around the artist and kept the critics at bay. Beth Bertram, who was in charge of the negative room, remembered Grierson's admonition, 'Senior people never leave till 7:30 p.m.' This meant that the National Film Board staff was expected to stay later than their colleagues at the Canadian Government Motion Picture Bureau who, as civil servants, left at 5:00 p.m. Needless to say, there was no such thing as overtime pay. Evelyn Spice Cherry, whose films provided practical education and enrichment especially to agricultural Canada, has remarked that Grierson's effect was to make the filmmakers feel that 'something had stirred in the country – it was some sort of impact upon the people.' Grierson's advice to her was characteristic of the whole propaganda exercise: make the propaganda educational and honest while informing the people what was going on in regard to the war.[2]

Grierson's guiding hand seemed to be present everywhere, but Canadian wartime propaganda film could not have developed without the broad analytical mind and skilful editing craftsmanship of Stuart Legg. Legg became Grierson's closest associate in Canada after having spent years with the original documentary film school in Britain. He had come to Canada in the winter of 1939 to make two films for the Motion Picture Bureau and the Dominion Youth Training Programme, *The Case of Charlie Gordon* and *Youth is Tomorrow*. As trial balloons, these films heralded for Canada the wedding of the documentary idea to the national setting. Charlie Gordon was an unemployed youth found in the slums of the coal town of Glace Bay, Nova Scotia, who, as portrayed by the 'human story' method reminiscent of the British documentary approach in *Housing Problems*, found work ultimately with the help of a Youth Training officer. Some Canadian critics had displayed hostile reactions to the showing of these darker sides of Canadian life. This had led Grierson to come to Legg's defence, arguing that while it was perfectly natural that Canadians should think well of their country and desire others to do likewise, it was disrespectful to other countries to believe that they would think well of an account which was distorted to the point of portraying the pattern of the national achievement out of its human context. Grierson was unafraid of ruffling Canadian sensibilities; he believed that where the commonness of man was forgotten the common man himself was disenfranchised. It was the task of documentary film, he concluded, with all its powers of juxtaposition, to take the scraps of reality, the rough with the smooth, and bring them to order and significance and therefore to beauty.[3] This was an essential documentary principle in war or peace. Where unpeopled landscape had characterized the Motion Picture Bureau's films, Legg's portrayal of wartime Canada was quite different. Industrial Canada and its workers would soon fill theatrical screens. Legg had gone in 1939 to New York, where Louis de Rochemont of the *March of Time* had put him on the payroll. There he learned the methods and techniques of the renowned series. In exchange, Legg probably offered his hosts insights into his experience with the GPO in Britain. He returned to Canada in the spring of 1940 and the theatrical series *Canada Carries On* was born. Its logo was a turning globe, symbol of Canada's new world role. The plan was to produce a film a month, divided annually from 1942 between the National Six and the International Six, for home and foreign audiences respectively. Besides Legg, the *Canada Carries On* team proper consisted of Tom Daly, Gordon Weisenborn, and Margaret Ann Adamson (Lady Elton).

From its first issue in April 1940 until its last wartime release in 1945, *Canada Carries On* put into practice Grierson's functional principle of modern propaganda as education and inspiration, against a backdrop of total war. Legg and Grierson wanted the series to serve democracy by revealing the national pattern. *Canada Carries On* would articulate six major themes: it would urge Canadians to focus their collective energies, find purpose in their activities, understand the strategy of war in the Canadian context, respect women for their new wartime roles, unite in collective purpose to crush the tyranny of fascism, and prepare to usher in a new postwar world. If the series' propaganda was directed mainly at home audiences, the films also provided Canadians with a unique window on the world revealing an international perspective they had never before seen. The propaganda made it clear that there was no room any longer for the luxury of insularity and isolationism. *Canada Carries On* helped nudge Canada, the reluctant and gangling giant, into the maelstrom of world events. The films spoke with author-

Grierson kept secret the extent to which enemy films had been seized or used; he did not think it was in the public interest to know. (NFB)

Lifting this shot from *Triumph of the Will*, Legg turned it neatly against the Nazis with the comment, 'The little painter from Austria was gazing down upon the gigantic spectacle of a nation moulded to his own brooding image.' (PAC 130023)

A 'Men of Valor' series poster took the best propaganda line it could following the disastrous Dieppe raid of August 1942. (PAC 87124)

ity and convinced millions that something enormously vital was being decided for the present and future. As the fatherly reassuring voice of democracy, narrator Lorne Greene would be associated with practically all the wartime releases. Less austere than the *March of Time*'s 'voice of the tomb,' Westbrooke van Voorhis, Greene's narration cut through the stirring music and provided the consistency, hope, assurance, and sense of purpose that film-goers needed in the seemingly endless years of war.

Often the films focused upon how Canadians were mobilizing the individual and collective energies of the nation. They avoided hate-mongering and using racial labels to characterize the enemy, preferring instead to show how different were the values of fascism from those of democracy. For example, a film might use captured footage of Leni Riefenstahl's *Triumph of the Will* to demonstrate how in Germany the individual was indistinguishable from the collective whole, while street scenes from everyday life in Canada were matched to narration which affirmed that the individual was of paramount importance in the collective totality. Military victory was a goal, but the great strength of the Allied cause was each individual's commitment to the struggle under his or her own free will. Viewed today, the inspirational propaganda is obvious, though one might ask why there was no analysis of fascist ideology. Tom Daly, who learned his craft during these years and on these films, has explained that such analysis was not necessary since he believed that everyone knew what the Nazis were all about. He stayed at the National Film Board to become one of the most respected producers in the world of documentary film.

Daly has described the typical policy of not being afraid to show the military might of Germany. The image was visually powerful to the point of frightening some people. This at times led to accusations that the board was aiding the enemy by showing them so strong. He explained why the technique was used: 'If you did not show the Axis with the strength they actually had, you would never rise to meet that with enough strength of your own and you would be bound to fail.' The politics were left to Grierson and Legg. Most of the young Canadians' hands were full just learning the art of filmmaking. As Daly put it, 'If Grierson and Legg had left in the middle of the war I don't think there would have been anybody who would have known how to carry it on.'[4] One incidental Grierson practice was to not indicate the extent to which enemy films had been seized or used – as custodian of enemy property, he did not think it was in the public interest to know.[5]

In the summer of 1942, in its annual report, the National Film Board specified its purpose. Its films had been 'designed deliberately to promote a sense of national unity and a national understanding between the many groups which go to make the Canadian nation. They are designed to interpret the interests of each section of Canada to the others, and to integrate sectional interests with the interests of the nation as a whole. Many of them serve also in an important way to interpret Canada to the world at large.' This statement has remained the philosophy and credo of the Film Board to the present and has earned Canada substantial international recognition over the years.

As film commissioner, Grierson enjoyed remarkable freedom to write and speak. He had grown accustomed to his freedom as a result of his long experience as a public servant in the United Kingdom, and it had been confirmed verbally between himself and the Film Board's first chairman, W.D. Euler. When Major-General L.R. LaFleche replaced Euler in October 1942, he asked Grierson to prepare a draft outline of the film programme Grierson wanted to produce on national morale in the workplace. LaFleche added that he thought some sort of religious inspiration should be added to the morale programme. Grierson must have thought this an unusual intrusion into his own quasi-religious crusade. It was stranger yet when a month later LaFleche insisted that he review all press releases and public statements before they were published. Grierson balked and reminded LaFleche of his earlier agreement with Euler. Board members T.A. Crerar and Donald Cameron agreed with Grierson that he should continue to exercise his freedom; Grierson was vindicated. LaFleche had lost his first test of authority, though a month later he circulated a note which warned Grierson about taking too much liberty. It said, 'No employee is a free agent whether it be Government, a business concern or any other properly organized body. It is really a matter for care by all and understanding by all of his proper position in the scheme of affairs.'[6]

Specifically, the *Canada Carries On* series was effective in its treatment of wartime strategies, especially Canada's expanded geopolitical role *vis-à-vis* transportation and communication. Some twelve films developed variations of this theme. Production was the leitmotif in another six films which devoted themselves to organization for war in

'Bren Gun Girl' Miss V. Foster operated a rotary miller in *Women Are Warriors* (1942). 'Two years before she was just a girl wondering what to do,' said the narrator. The remark must have irritated many then too. (PAC 129380)

Joyce Campbell becomes a private in *Proudly She Marches*. The vital role of women in the war was a regular NFB propaganda message. (PAC 130049)

factories, mines, and farms. Nine films in the series addressed themselves to the inspirational subject of war aims and the changed world to
come after the war. These stand in contrast with the eight issues which
were filled with 'shot and shell,' as they dealt specifically with the military aspects of total war. Four films were devoted solely to women and
were far ahead of their time in their progressive attitude. Probably the
weakest group of films in the series was the dozen films which portrayed and often dramatized Canada's 'playing' at war, that is, training
for combat and preparing to hit the enemy militarily.

Before examining how these films succeeded or failed in purpose, it
might be useful to establish the link which existed between the series
and its senior American counterpart, *The March of Time*.

INFLUENCED BY 'THE MARCH OF TIME'

As the guiding creative force behind *Canada Carries On* in its first
years, Stuart Legg admitted that he was profoundly influenced by his
1939 exposure to *The March of Time*. 'I think possibly one of the more
exciting moments of my life was when I saw the first [1935–6] issues of
the *March of Time*. ... I think that these issues were the best they ever
made, particularly when they had two and even three stories in one
issue of two reels because then they really had to concentrate and some
of the things that came out were remarkable pieces not only of reporting, but of film making ...,' he acknowledged.

He borrowed for Canada a *March of Time* technique of telescoping
several stories into a single number, though there was usually only one
theme. And as in the American series, narration became the essence of
each film. The Americans stated that if the script did not fit the picture,
'We'd make the picture fit the script.' Legg tailored his script to fit the
picture, which is a significant difference. Neither series filmed heads
talking to the camera and the American series depended more upon
static shots for effect in rapid cutting than did the Canadian. *The March
of Time*, especially in its early years, relied predominantly upon staged
live-action shots to manipulate the audience; *Canada Carries On* shot
some original Canadian footage but mainly used stock shots. These
came from commercial and non-commercial sources, from state and
military units of allied nations and neutrals as well as from captured enemy material. Film Board employees, soon called 'pirates,' also

became proficient at locating material from the Pathé and Fox Movietone libraries in New York City. Grierson, it was said by Richard Griffith in Jay Leyda's *Films Beget Films*, described the propagandist's job in this context: 'This isn't a documentary war, it's a newsreel war.' Because the visuals were shot by anonymous cameramen around the world, the writer and editor emerged as the controlling figures. *The March of Time* took advantage of the power of the narrated word and became grammatically eccentric with its use of 'Time-speak' or 'Timese.' This included the use of powerful adjectives preceding a personality's name. *Canada Carries On* avoided editorializing in this fashion and kept the English crisp, concise, and direct. *The March of Time* did not try to realize a political or economic line, though its point of view was pro-British, anti-fascist, and interventionist, which in prewar isolationist America was controversial. The series' historian, Raymond Fielding, claimed it stood for uncomplicated American liberalism, general good intentions, healthy journalistic scepticism, faith in enlightened self-interest, and pride in American progress and potential.[7] *Canada Carries On* was less the cinematic *agent provocateur* and was more reminiscent of the British documentary in being didactic, earnest to the point of seriousness, and personal in its appeal. Quick cutting techniques gave substance to Legg's single commandment of documentary film production, 'Thou shalt not be dull.'

Sound was another important element in both series. One *March of Time* employee believed that Canada's use of sound was better than the *March of Time*'s. Stirring music, veritably martial in quality, almost always accompanied the visuals and narration in *Canada Carries On*. Describing the music, composed predominantly by Lucio Agostini, Tom Daly has remarked, 'Agostini always started with a crescendo and went on up from there to the end of the film. ... Legg always wanted to have something strong to bring up in between his phrases of narration so that no matter where they fell there had to be something strong going on behind.' In this way when the most important point of a sequence was being made by the narrator, the mood was upbeat and strong. By the last visual sequence, when the theme was reiterated and underscored for the last time, the music would build to a stirring crescendo and climax on a major chord. The confluence of visuals, music, and narration, by appealing to eyes, ears, and mind, could not leave a viewer unmoved. Of this approach Daly has said that the technique was right in principle, but it left the viewer breathless. 'Our own pace as young Canadians would not have been so fast – it was like having to run to keep up all the time.'

Legg was responsible for weaving these three complex factors into harmonious unity. It took time to find the right formula, as demonstrated by Legg's experience with the series' first number, *Atlantic Patrol* (April 1940). The film used prewar British naval footage and scenes which Legg shot on a Canadian destroyer on patrol outside of Halifax. He simulated an attack on a U-boat to make the film's earnest point: 'today, tomorrow, till the peace comes again, they will be on Atlantic patrol.' David Coplan, sales manager for the series' Canadian distributor, Columbia Pictures of Canada, mindful of the paying theatrical audiences, claimed the film was too long and told Legg to cut it to eighteen minutes. 'Stuart,' he allegedly told Legg, 'I've got to sell this crap.' In an interview years later, Coplan was more refined in explaining that he had the right to reject any film which he did not deem suitable for theatrical exhibition. In fact, he claimed that never again did he have to exercise this power, though he convinced Grierson not to fire Lorne Greene, about whom Grierson had doubts for some unexplained reason. It could not have been for reasons of proficiency; Greene recorded the narration in its entirety, live, without stopping and almost always without error.[8] Legg has acknowledged that in the field of theatrical presentation, he learned more from Coplan than from Grierson.

Raymond Spottiswoode, himself one of the early producers and teachers of documentary technique at the board, became responsible for the 'National Six' in 1942. He explained in 1944 how smoothly the arrangement worked between the commercial industry and the Film Board:

The Film Board acknowledged the fact that each distributor and theatre manager must stand behind the product he exhibited, and could not accept films of lower standards than those set by the commercial production centres of Hollywood and New York. It was therefore agreed to distribute the two theatrical series through two of the regular distributors, Columbia Pictures and United Artists, whose sales representatives normally see their pictures each month before recording, so that they can advise on titles, release dates, and other details of exploitation. In this way a very cordial relationship has been built up between the Film Board and the trade, which has resulted in the distribution since early 1940 of nearly 75 pictures, most of them two-reelers, not to mention more than 200 newsclips.[9]

Coplan's main concern was that the films should have theatrical appeal to audiences and thereby avoid unpopular associations with non-theatrical film. He and Grierson had also agreed to an important financial arrangement. In Britain, the Ministry of Information distributed films for free, but the *Canada Carries On* (and later *The World in Action*) series would be sold commercially like de Rochemont's *March of Time*. The theory was that if a theatre paid for a film, it would screen it rather than leave it in a corner of a projection booth. In practice these films often acquired marquee billing along with the feature attraction. The contracts with theatres for the *Canada Carries On* stipulated the same rental price as *The March of Time* ($125 per week in first-run theatres) and the government shared profits 60-40 with the distributors. Once the distribution network went into full operation, a film would have been screened in a total of 300 theatres in the first thirty days, a total of 600 theatres in the second thirty days, and a total of 900 theatres in the third thirty days. There would also be exhibition in sixty French-speaking theatres in that period. By the end of 1941 the films were being shown in training camps after their theatrical runs.

Where the filmmakers were unable to shoot what they wanted, they were able to control finely the image in the cutting room. This did not lessen the heavy reliance upon Lorne Greene's stentorian voice-over narration. Words had to give purpose to visuals which could have meant many different things, and this explains why Greene's voice became such a unifying element in the series. The words he read, if reminiscent of the 'talking book' aspect of Nazi propaganda, defined the cause, gave information, and repeated the general points again and again. The filmmakers probably took a page from Goebbels' primer on propaganda technique. The Nazi minister of propaganda wrote that propaganda had to be simple and repetitious. He elaborated in his diary, 'In the long run, only he will achieve basic results in influencing public opinion who is able to reduce problems to the simplest terms and who has the courage to keep forever repeating them despite the objections of the intellectuals.' His cynicism about intellectuals extended to a belief that they would always yield to the stronger, to the man on the street. For the Nazis, arguments had to be crude, clear, and forceful and to appeal to the emotions and instincts, not the intellect.

Legg and Grierson, themselves in a deadly chess game with Goebbels, rejected the dark side of the Nazi method. Canadian propaganda contained arguments that were simple, clear, and forceful, but which also appealed to the intellect. Grierson explained how this was done to young Sydney Newman: 'Don't tell the people of Canada what to do because you demean them, you insult their intelligence. Cite examples of what they are doing. Give them a reason why they are doing it, on their own impulse, then they'll understand it.' The propaganda then was decidedly paternalistic. It was tempered by respect for and sensitivity to the individual being addressed. Newman only half listened to his boss. His films tended to favour a visual rather than verbal barrage.

Grierson wanted propaganda to carry out a dual purpose. First, it was to mobilize film and give the news and the story of a great historical event. This would secure the present. Second, film was to secure the future by showing the everyday things of life, that is, the values and ideals that make life worth living.[10] That this approach worked is proven by the series' immediate popularity. Let us now turn to some of the main *Canada Carries On* themes and profiles.

PROFILES OF *CANADA CARRIES ON*

Organization for war, especially production strategies, was a common theme of the series. Such subjects were invariably linked to the coming peace in the postwar world. *The Front of Steel* (July 1940) was the first *Canada Carries On* to use captured Nazi film to describe Adolf Hitler, 'demagogue and warlord,' as the man who had convinced a nation to choose guns instead of butter. There followed an account of the brutal Nazi blitzkrieg into Poland and other parts of Europe. The narration explained the sobering effect of all this on Britain: 'Overnight the British tradition of muddling through vanished forever.' Now the British had a new phrase, 'Go to it!' The film then cut to Canada and factory scenes. The narration informed viewers that Canadians were making Bren guns, warships, and vehicles for mobile warfare. And science was now working with industry. The film concluded that the people of Canada saw the promise of victory in supply trains going to the coast and drew new strength from the calm efficiency of the soldiers in dunga-

Grierson consults with art director Harry Mayerovitch (left). Poster propaganda advertised both film and ideas. Grierson said, 'You can't sell the war as you would sell corn flakes. You may have at times to make people believe what they ought to believe rather than what they want to believe.' (NFB)

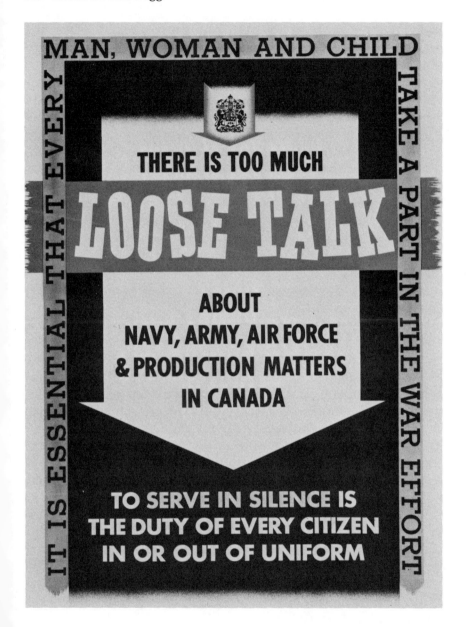

A 'total war' psychology was perpetuated by print and film without promoting hate.
(PAC 87426)

rees fighting on the front of steel. The viewer could conclude that, despite the military disasters in Europe, everything was under control and victory would come one day.

In *The Strategy of Metals* (July 1941) the audience learned of Canada's role in producing metals for the war effort, especially aluminum. To scenes of mines and industries at work, the narrator explained how the opening of the North meant new cities, new jobs, homes, and better pay for thousands. And the importance of Canada's resources would grow in the postwar world. The film cut to interiors of a Canadian factory. To excellent overhead shots of a moving assembly line, the narration stressed how important Canada's contribution was to the worldwide forces of democracy and how Britain knew that 'night and day from Canadian production lines are coming the tools to finish the job. Such in modern warfare is the strategy of metals.' In a rare attempt at humour, the last sequence showed a worker driving a new vehicle off the assembly line shouting, 'Get the hell out of the road – you're holding up the war!'

Thought for Food (May 1943) dealt with the importance of food in the war effort and explained why, because of armed forces needs, there were shortages for civilians. Canadian scientists were shown experimenting with vitamins and the narrator explained truthfully how nearly one in three North Americans suffered from malnutrition because of lack of vitamins. (The visuals cut to scenes of poverty-stricken children as the music became somber.) With up-tempo, the scene switched to Britain, where 'they know that wars can be won over the battle for food.' Against a backdrop of factory scenes of workers in cafeterias, the narrative stated that the employers must look after the nutrition of the workers. There was to be planned abundance for all after the war – a promise of plenty for peace. This optimistic conclusion was stated over visuals of a farmer ploughing his fields: 'Under the threat of war the people have agreed that from the yield of our farms each man shall have no more than his fair share. But over the harvest of peace we shall write a new charter – to each man there shall go no less than his fair share. Out of the thought we take for food today shall come the health of our nation tomorrow.'

Coal Face Canada (October 1943) used the theme of coal production to tell the largely dramatized story by Graham McInnes of a returning veteran who resumed his early career as a coal miner. The documentary footage of miners at work underscored the importance of civilian war jobs with the slogan 'We miners fight with coal!' There was a strong pro-union bias as the miners claimed how much better things were with the union. Bosses now had to think of the men. A local cooperative housing project demonstrated how community activity and cooperation drew the town more closely together. From the words 'there's almost no limit to what you can do when you're together,' the audience was supposed to conclude that Canada would win the war and build a better world. It is interesting to note how, in this and the previous film, the distinctions between worker and boss were blurred. The narration suggested paternalistically that the boss, portrayed sympathetically, must be concerned for the welfare of his workers. This film was part of the national industrial morale-building programme instituted under the Wartime Information Board especially to ease tension in the troubled coal industry. This and films like it were to be joint labour-management presentations during company time, promoting the positive while ignoring the negative issues which divided labour and management.

Target Berlin (January 1944) described construction of the first Lancaster bomber in Canada. Superb overhead crane shots of construction inside the aircraft plant concentrated on how, to the workers, the plane was a living thing and a symbol of Canadian unity. The plane was finished and then flown across the Atlantic to England where it was met by the Canadian high commissioner. British officials also commented on how important Lancaster production was to the Allied effort. Final staged sequences showed the plane on the way to a thousand-plane night attack on Berlin, with footage of actual barrages and bombing. Using a similar treatment with much less effect, *Mosquito Squadron* (October 1944) demonstrated how the plywood bomber, the Mosquito, was being built in Canada 'just as fast as we can train crews.' The film ended with planes taking off for a run on Germany and the rather pedestrian comment, 'And so they go, day after day and the enemy feels the sting of the Mosquito!'

Responsibility for choice of subjects lay partly with Grierson and Legg and partly with the sponsoring body, the Bureau of Public Information (later, the Wartime Information Board). There were also general thematic suggestions from the prime minister's office and from a number of ministers, both those responsible for the Film Board and those sitting on the board's directorate. Other times, requests could be imprecise, like General McNaughton's wish in 1943 to show more films to Canadian forces to keep up and improve troop morale. Grierson and Legg would lay out the themes for the coming year's series. Legg relinquished his duties in 1942 when with the original *Canada Carries On* team he began a second theatrical series, *The World in Action*. Raymond Spottiswoode and occasionally J.D. Davidson then made films for *Canada Carries On* on a rotating basis, but after Legg ceased being its producer the series suffered from lack of single purpose and style. Legg believed that the series became a 'sort of grab-bag into which films made by other Film Board units were pushed in order to fill the monthly theatrical spot.' Sydney Newman and Guy Glover became co-producers of the series in 1944 and 1945, but by that time Legg regarded it as a 'latter day hodge-podge.' It is difficult to know who produced which films from 1942 because there was a policy not to give credits. As Tom Daly has explained, 'Grierson often told us young Canadians, "You are not at it for your own blue eyes," meaning that Board policy discouraged *auteurs*. Ours was always a sense of working as a team.' Daly and Gordon Weisenborn became Legg's assistants, then editors. Daly began by collecting stock shots in New York from Pathé and Fox Movietone for expansion of the board's stock shot library. Daly's prodigious memory for all kinds of shots served Legg's purpose well, for Legg would lay out a plan of material and images he needed to support the essay on a particular subject. He would go over this with Daly, who with Margaret Ann Adamson (Lady Elton) would spend the next month collecting the shots in New York. Daly then returned to begin cutting. During this time Legg was free to write the general outline of the commentary. Legg spent the second month editing and negative-cutting the film while writing the narration and incorporating the music. It usually took eight to ten days to add Agostini's music, then sound effects were blended and finally Legg would have Greene record the commentary. Daly described how, in this critical operation, Legg did not lay down a quantity of words, but 'fit them like a vine' to the object. Then the last two weeks would be used to polish the final version. Work would then begin immediately on the next issue due in two months. For two years Daly watched Legg and learned his profession well. And Legg, ever the patient teacher, would think out loud for Daly's benefit as he edited. By the end of the war, Daly, with a group of other young Canadians trained during these years, was producing films on his own at the board.[11] Gordon Weisenborn had become a highly skilled editor of both picture and sound and a thoroughly practical artist.

About all that can be said about the production-oriented films we have mentioned above is that they brought the urgency of war home to the Canadian public and, as morale-boosters, tried to inspire self-sacrifice. More broad in theme and scope were the *Canada Carries On* films explaining the various geopolitical strategies which defined the nature of total world war. *The Battle of Brains* (April 1941) used stock footage to demonstrate how different the First World War of position was from the present conflict, which was dependent upon mobility and mechanization. The Second World War was also a war of brains. While Canada's factories supplied many of the mobile vehicles, Canada's scientists also stood beside the strategists. United with the soldier, science was working for maximum performance.

The Battle for Oil (September 1941) concentrated upon showing the strategic importance of oil, from Venezuela to Russia to 'all important Persia.' (Here an adolescent Shah Reshid Pahlavi stood nervously next to his towering militarily-uniformed father.) Oil fuelled the Royal Navy and gave it its power from Liverpool to Southeast Asia. Oil made mobile warfare possible, and as the visuals showed German advances, the narration remarked that it took Germany twelve million gallons of oil to conquer Europe and had taken three times that much so far on the Eastern Front. The Battle of the Atlantic had become Britain's battle for oil, the film concluded, and North America understood its duty to provide this crucial substance for the war effort. Canada too had a contribution to make – the tar sands of Alberta promised a rich yield once they were developed. (This was a few years before the giant 'conventional' discovery at Leduc would cause people to forget tar sands for forty years.)

Wings of a Continent (December 1941) explained the importance of air routes to the new strategic geography of war and stated that Canada's airways were crucial arteries for a commonwealth at war. The prime minister had requested development of this theme. It concluded with a glance at the future in which the Canadian North would be the gateway both to the East and to the polar routes to Europe. Three years later, a rather aimless *Flight Six* (December 1944) tried to revive this theme with stress on the importance of air mail; it dramatized several 'stories behind the letters' and failed to convince that Flight Six brought 'the promise of a future, the future of a world in the air.'

Food – Weapon of Conquest (March 1942) was a very strong propaganda piece which addressed itself largely to Americans, who had begun seeing National Film Board theatrical shorts regularly in December 1941. Its theme was that, while food was needed by the people of the United States and Russia as well as their fighting men, the Germans were using food for weapons, from fat for high explosives to apples for alcohol and milk for lubricating oil. The Nazi blueprint for conquest was that whatever part of Europe was not used for Nazi industry would be used to supply the 'master race' with food. To chords of sombre music and pictures of hungry Europeans, the narrator described how French and Polish workers were encouraged to emigrate to Germany: 'Hunger is the instrument of fulfilment to create a modern form of medieval slavery.' The narration mentioned Jews and Gypsies as sufferers under this policy, though there was no footage of either group. The Nazi blockade of Britain was the means to wage the battle of starvation. To shots of u-boats sinking Allied food ships on their way to Britain, there were sounds of sea and wind, guns booming, and ships sinking. Silence fell as a few survivors were picked out of the icy sea. An old man with a tea cup symbolized the suffering British as the narrator remarked bitterly, 'Even their beloved cup of tea became a luxury.' This depressing sequence was compounded by a dark admission that naval experts declared that shipping space devoted to food must be slashed to one-third its prewar volume.

From this low point the narrator began in a new and hopeful tone, 'Today in Britain a nationwide activity is underway to improve the produce of the soil.' Stock shots of allotment gardens, pigs at the London Zoo, and clearing scrub land followed. But, the voice-over continued, Britain can supply only half its food and still needs to import food from North America. American farmers, it was asserted, should cut back on wheat and produce more nutritive foods like pork, bacon, milk, cheese, vegetables, poultry, and eggs to raise health to battle strength. To visuals of farmers, the film concluded hopefully that the future would be one of planning and cooperation, not competition. There would be 'the inevitable approach of a concerted plan in which the American farmer, finally freed from the glutted markets and surpluses of former days, will devote his land to the *real* food needs of his fellow men ... a new world will arise out of these dreadful days ... in the hour of danger every American turns again with a new faith to his native soil, the soil that will win the war and write the future.'

The film was distributed in Britain as part of the series called *Front of Action*. There, in December 1942, the high commissioner for Canada in Britain, Vincent Massey, stopped its distribution because he felt that the film implied that Canada's part in food production was negligible and that the United States should be the main recipient of the United Kingdom's thanks. He wanted the Film Board to revise the commentary. Norman Robertson, answering for Prime Minister King, agreed with Massey, and asked Grierson to revise the film.[12] Here was one example of how 'education,' no matter how non-partisan, strayed into the very realm of politics which Grierson was trying to avoid. He revised the commentary.

Battle of the Harvests (November 1942) continued the theme of the importance of Allied food production. Stock shots of Russian farmers accompanied the narration which praised Soviet Russia for its farming achievements. The word 'collectivization' was avoided by substituting the purposely imprecise descriptive phrase, 'Russia saw the progress of the most violent experiment in farming history.' A brief section on the depression years in the West followed with stock shots depicting frankly that era of wasted production and dumped surpluses. The final sequence boasted that with new farming techniques and bumper harvests the dark days were gone forever. Land and industry were now closely intertwined; artificial oil and rubber were extracted from crops. For Canada, the film concluded optimistically, there was a harvest battleground.

Trans-Canada Express (April 1944), co-produced and co-edited by Sydney Newman and Guy Glover, stressed the importance of the railway in Canada, especially how it was the mode of getting war materials and troops to their destinations at seaports. There was a historical dramatization of how Canada was united by a bond of steel; scenes from an early Buster Keaton film showed how railways are fun; and contemporary scenes filled the screen with freight yards, turntable, and locomotives. Women, the film stated, had come to join the thirty thousand railway workers in Canada, replacing men who had gone into service. To footage of women at work, the narrator remarked cheerfully and innocently how 'they sure do brighten things up!' A dramatization followed of the urgency of getting troops from Vancouver to an Atlantic convoy via the Trans-Canada Express. The film not only borrowed scenes from the classic British documentary *Night Mail*; to visuals of racing locomotive wheels, there was a chorus unashamedly reminiscent of the chorus chanting the Auden poem in *Night Mail*, now chanting, 'Day or night, cloud or sun, the railroad's job is never done.'

The examples of films of strategies mentioned above were didactic and even occasionally inspiring. But the strongest of the *Canada Carries On* films were those which dealt with war aims and descriptions of the new world to follow war and victory. In these issues it seemed that the propagandists wore their hearts on their sleeves while urging audiences to prepare for the future. The films enunciated the following themes: the people were fighting to save democracy, to wipe tyranny from the earth, to affirm the worth of the individual free spirit in the era of 'mass man,' to achieve worldwide neighbourliness, to enjoy material abundance for all, to undertake resource development, to acquire knowledge, and to offer service to the community. Here were war aims that differed from the Nazi goals of victory and heroic sacrifice and, later, victory or death. These were goals which went much further than Churchill's cautious hope for victory for its own sake. If these Canadian goals of a 'brave new world' merited criticism, it was because they were indefinite and imprecise. Undeniably, they were stirring, imaginative, and morale-boosting, though in the quiet aftermath of war they were also unrealistic.

Prime Minister King had explained Canada's war aims in November 1939 in terms of wanting to stop Hitler.[13] That was hardly the stuff of good film propaganda. The Film Board's first attempt to explain war aims was in *Everywhere in the World* (February 1941). The theme was based upon President Franklin Roosevelt's renowned 'Four Freedoms' speech, which itself became the cornerstone of America's war aims once that nation entered the war in December 1941. The film showed Roosevelt enunciating those four freedoms: 1 / freedom of speech and expression, everywhere in the world; 2 / freedom for every person to worship his own way, everywhere in the world; 3 / freedom from want, everywhere in the world; 4 / freedom from fear, anywhere in the world. The narration proceeded to describe how with the fall of France the battlefields were everywhere in the world. The film then cut to war preparations in the commonwealth nations of Australia, New Zealand, South Africa, and Canada. Shots of Gibraltar, Egypt, Singapore, and Hong Kong demonstrated the global nature of the conflict. The United States too was contributing war *matériel* and building its army. Final shots of Canada in preparation for war accompanied a statement that Canadians and all men of the free world looked forward to a world founded on the four freedoms, which the narrator reiterated. This theme was crowned with a concluding authoritative statement: 'So speak the young nations of the earth now marching with fixed and single purpose to win the supremacy of individual rights for all men.' It was not until October 1942 that Prime Minister King formulated Canada's war aims of social security and human welfare.[14]

The Voice of Action (July 1942) demonstrated that the role of radio in the war was to gather the will and momentum of the whole nation. Its stirring climax went much further than describing radio as a voice of action. 'We of Canada fight today not to preserve an uncertain past but to lead in creating a future where the earth and its wealth are the common heritage of all. Today we speak through the voice of radio but ... the voice that will build the future is the voice of action: Canadian troops and airmen in battle – these are but the first pledge we give to make the future a reality. This is the message *we* of fighting democracy send out across a world at war. Let all hear it who may, for we speak with a voice of faith in action and in this faith we build our world of tomorrow.' The visuals which accompanied this narration were of troops on the move – this may have also confirmed subconsciously that action spoke louder than words. At long last, Canadian troops were about to be committed to battle under a united command. The disaster at Dieppe occurred the next month.

Five months later, in December, *Inside Fighting Canada* pursued a variation of this theme by showing Canada's Commonwealth Air Training Plan, the rural mobilization of farm production, urban workers at their factories, construction of the Alaska Highway, and armed forces preparing. The narration then turned to the Canadian people themselves, 'uniting their energies not just as a temporary war measure but to build for the future, a worldwide faith in neighbourliness.' The visuals depicted women at work in various jobs. The voice-over described the 'secret weapon of the democratic nation: the tremendous power of ordinary people working together of their own free will.' Here followed footage of street scenes across Canada, of people walking, troops marching, planes flying, and surf rolling into shore. 'The simple weapon that has turned the Canadian landscape into a gigantic arsenal and sent fighting men into every theatre of war around the world ... Canadians may well feel today that they are fulfilling the destiny they once marked for themselves. They indeed build a nation from sea to sea and from the rivers even to the ends of the earth.' The film was making an important point. Audiences had seen in earlier films how the Nazis were building their empire upon a modern form of medieval slavery. Democracy built its defences with the voluntary effort of people exercising their own free will. Here then was the implied comparison between the two systems and democracy stood supreme. Characteristically, no mention was made of conscription, which had split the nation badly in the spring of 1942. A national plebiscite in April had released King from his no-conscription pledge. He would find it 'necessary' to introduce it nationally in November 1944. Film Board propaganda would promote enlistment tirelessly, but conscription, the most divisive social issue of the war, was a film subject no Liberal government would tolerate. Grierson and Legg never touched it.

Inside Fighting Canada was held up by the Ontario Censor Board. Premier Mitchell Hepburn's hand was again not far from the action, though he disclaimed any responsibility for the banning and stated that the board rejected the film on the ground that it was purely political propaganda paid for by the Film Board out of national funds.[15] There was a single assertion in the film that the Ottawa government was running the country efficiently. Grierson tried to downplay the incident publicly but confided to the Film Board's directorate that the publicity given the film had been of great value to the work of the board.[16] But that Hepburn and his friends had no use for the Film Board is witnessed by a letter of Leo Dolan, the head of the Canadian Government Travel Bureau. Dolan had not got along with Grierson since a meeting in July 1941 at which Dolan had said he had little use for tourist films which Grierson had offered to produce for him.[17] Dolan's undisguised racism was applied to information about Grierson he hoped to use to embarrass the government. He wrote to his friend and King's foe, Premier Hepburn in December 1942:

This guy Grierson is the smoothest Limey to come here in years. He has had the inside path with your pal Willie King. ... I know that these New York Jews are always with Grierson and I am convinced the little bastard is an English Jew. This whole film board setup should be investigated. I know that they have had some queer dealings but of course I can't get the dope as I would want it. If the right kinds of questions were asked in the House, some enlightening information would be forthcoming. There were some returns filed last year that should make interesting reading. More of that for the new year and always,

Sincerely yours,

Leo[18]

So if Grierson was making headway orchestrating various schemes for film propaganda, he was making enemies all the while.

Reminiscent of *Thought for Food*, whose inspirational message had been that sacrifice today will mean plenty tomorrow, *Tomorrow's World* (November 1943) put an interesting twist on the theme of food shortages and rationing. Frank descriptions to visuals of food burning and starvation during the depression emphasized the changed attitude in the contemporary world. There could never be a return to the old days; in the postwar world there would be a total use of resources for total production, wisely planned. The industrial might of Canada would be used for purposes of peace. The key to the future was the conservation of natural resources and salvage. The narration gave credit to the intelligence of the audiences by asserting how important the individual was: 'We are living in a period when men's minds are fertile and dynamic beyond the norm.' The film concluded with scenes of wounded Allied troops, then cut to shots of industrial Canada on the move, and finally cut to huge jets of water shooting through a dam's sluice-gates hundreds of feet high. The inspiring narrative matched these visuals and ended bravely, 'The fighting men are demanding that out of their struggle to rid the earth of fear and want the foundations of this new order of the people shall be in perpetuity laid. ... The promise of that order is rising clear and bright. An order in which the great new forces of human and material energy, freed from the timid hesitations of the past, will build to the people's plan with all the people's wealth. ... And to the oft repeated question, "What will be the state of the postwar world?", men and women whose eyes have seen the vision of our times are making this simple answer, "Look around you, it is taking place already." The tide of man's creative world is flowing once again. Tomorrow's world is here!'

Behind this film one can sense the moral influence of the Grierson and Legg credo, to make peace as exciting as war. If the brave new world was not described specifically, there was a strong hint that it would be the people's world, one which planned its use of resources and one which promised a collective society different from anything the world had ever seen. This was daring propaganda, a courageous escape from banal platitudes, and was probably changing public ideas about the postwar world scene. Significantly, the federal government, since the Marsh Report of 1942, had been moving steadily if reluctantly toward a wide-ranging national scheme of social security, including family allowances, so the propaganda was not contrary to the developing political tide. But King was upset with Grierson that July for pushing too fast toward reconstruction. He wanted Canada under his direction and timing to move cautiously into the postwar world. His government promised family allowance legislation in January 1944 and introduced it in mid-year.

The theme of a closely knit postwar world was touched upon in *UNRRA: In the Wake of the Armies*, a March 1944 number produced and edited by Guy Glover, which was devoted ostensibly to explaining how this international agency was planning to help a shattered Europe rebuild and re-establish law and order. Following scenes of battle-scarred Europe, the narration warned that Allied charity was not desirable; rather the people should be helped to help themselves. The visual example of Russians emerging from their tent city to rebuild Stalingrad implied that such activity was to be emulated by others. The film ended with the notion of a more closely interlinked postwar world. For the people of Europe, the narration asserted, 'Prosperity, like peace, is indivisible. Their future is ours.' The implication was that international rivalry and enmity were gone forever and a new world demanding mutual material well-being had already arrived. The message was political and, to some critics, even pro-Russian in form: they would later decry these pro-Russian biases. UNRRA officials, however, were impressed and asked Grierson to help plan the UNRRA film programme.

By February 1945 the coming peace signalled the return to Canada of some fifty thousand veterans who planned to become students. *Univer-*

sities *at War* demonstrated the link between science, universities, and the war, but, more important, pointed to the relationship between knowledge gained at universities and service owed to the community. The concluding words accompanied visuals of students in and out of uniform, leaving a campus building. 'As more and more of every age and class are seeking the fruits of education, our universities have assumed a broader responsibility. Looking beyond the classroom walls they are pouring out their sons and daughters into the service of all man, for knowledge and service, like peace, are indivisible. And as Canadian youth return to the familiar university scenes of campus lawns and lecture halls, they see in these quiet symbols the meaning of knowledge. For knowledge is power and youth is its guardian in the coming task of peace.'

In this as in the above-mentioned 'brave new world' issues of *Canada Carries On*, the viewers were encouraged to look at themselves and their relationship to the fast-changing events of the world and to see themselves as having a positive role to paly, whether in attitude or in action. These films encouraged a sense of participation which was not predicated upon geography or profession but upon an understanding that the individual, as part of the larger group, was a significant figure who was not invisible and who owed the community service in constructing the new world of peace.

If the war was the all-pervasive element in most National Film Board propaganda, the films which addressed themselves to women stand as examples of how the war was changing traditional attitudes in a positive fashion. It would be easy to use contemporary feminist values to criticize the films for not being more aggressive in making their points, but, given the context of the times, the films were progressive without preaching. Having replaced tens of thousands of men, working women were vital to the functioning of community and democracy. In the June 1940 release, *The Home Front*, these ideas surfaced as the film tried to underscore the importance of women in the total war. If women in wartime had historically provided relief from suffering, now there was a new generation of women learning nursing and secretarial skills, now also doing men's jobs, from driving trucks and making munitions to instructing pilots. The film concluded that the Canada of tomorrow would depend to a great extent on the work of Canadians today. An August 1942 number, *Women Are Warriors*, reiterated this theme, but placed it in the international context, showing first how the women of England were doing important war work and then how in Russia (labelled a 'cooperative state') women had taken over 75 per cent of work in factories and worked with pick and shovel next to men. Canada, the film asserted, profited from the example of these two allies and its women had learned to turn domestic needle and thread into the tools of war; thus, deftness learned at home had application in war industries. Unfortunately the effect was spoiled when the film identified with a Canadian woman who 'two years before was just a girl wondering what to do.' The tone and remark were unnecessary. The film ended with a superb montage moving from shots of women in factories to a plane in action, to factory, to plane to factory and plane to demonstrate how important women's roles were to the war effort.

A more forceful statement of women's importance was made in Jane Marsh's September 1943 number, *Proudly She Marches*, which began with a female narrator's condemnation of man's traditional prejudice about women either belonging in the home or serving as ornaments. The dramatized story which followed showed how a number of women joined the Canadian Women's Army Corps where they pursued new careers – from jeep driver to radio technician to photographer to aircraft recognition expert and teacher. This film, made ostensibly to encourage female recruitment, concluded with positive observations about women in the present and future. Unfortunately, the female narrator was replaced by a male to make the points. Jobs once the property of men were now served equally by women. 'Our women are marching shoulder to shoulder with their brothers in arms,' he declared and concluded that behind the troops are the women of our nation. The last words implied that the changes in status might be permanent, since women had realized in their day-to-day work both personal fulfilment and development and a fuller sense of participation and pride in the very life and destiny of Canada.

Another Marsh film, *Air Cadets*, was completed, but never shown. Guy Glover has claimed that unknown persons destroyed it to spite her. There is no record of the film in the Film Board Archives.

Of immediate interest and attraction to most theatre-goers was the progress of the war itself, the aspect which Grierson referred to as 'shot and shell' and usually with great reluctance. Battle and the hell of war made for splendid action in film, but they were to Grierson 'the biggest bore on earth.' So when the *Canada Carries On* issues addressed them-selves to these themes, Grierson hoped that they would be about more than victory for its own sake. Mercifully, most of the films restrained themselves from showing the dead, since the two theatrical taboos of the day were nudity and death. And when corpses were shown, they were most often enemy dead. Somehow watching a city being obliter-ated from the sky was not as sickening as a single dead man. Probably the best of these 'shot and shell' films was *Churchill's Island* (June 1941), which won the first-ever Academy Award for best documentary film. It succeeded because of its insistence that the air Battle of Britain was won by the RAF above and 'the people's army below.' Amidst the continuing scenes of destruction the viewer learned that the men and women of England 'have brought about the silent wartime revolution which demands that nothing shall hinder the fulfilment of the nation's needs. Willingly they have faced sacrifices, discomforts, hard rations, long hours. ...' Reminiscent of the documentary theme of the 1930s, the narration declared that the worker has a dignity which derives from an 'inner strength' which was described as 'a stubborn calm which iron and steel and bombs can never pierce.' With great effect, if not bravado, the narrator's last words beckoned the German enemy, 'Come – if you dare!' A subtle element lay at the core of this film – it was to convince the Americans that though Britain was down militarily, her spirit was strong. The hope was that the United States, six months away from its own plunge into the melée, could feel assured that the united British spirit and resolve were as important in winning the war as was the force of arms.

Warclouds in the Pacific (November 1941) is discussed in a later chapter, but it remains significant both as a 'shot and shell' and as a geopolitical film which portrayed aggressive and militaristic Japan as ready to strike at will in the Pacific. It was released on the eve of the Japanese attack on Pearl Harbor; Legg's foresight was rewarded by both North America-wide theatrical distribution and more acclaim for the National Film Board.

A less convincing film with plenty of shot and shell was *This Is Blitz* (January 1942), which did not attempt to hide the depressing European military picture from the Canadian people. However dark the truth, films like these insisted on ending with optimism and confidence. Bri-tish and Russian citizen fighters, the film concluded, were prepared to fight for every inch of their home soil. For men like these, it declared, 'The Blitz can hold no terrors.' Distributed in the United States as part of the new *World in Action* series, *Time* magazine praised the film for being dedicated to the principle that the way to kill the fear of Blitz is to show people just what a Blitz is.' What the Film Board was doing, *Time* said, was making major aspects of the war clear to Canadians and 'may perform the same service for Americans who badly need it.'[19] (The Film Board suspended the rule of truthful reporting, however, in its failure to cover the ill-fated Dieppe Raid until a year had passed.)

Forward Commandos (February 1942) explained how guerilla warfare was having a telling effect on the Germans. Russia trained her men in the spirit of 'all for one, one for all'; Canada trained her commandos to strike effectively too. The final minutes of the film showed actual footage of a Canadian commando raid on German-occupied Norway and the withdrawal of these forces; it ended with a strongly worded commitment to return again. In light of the fact that Canadian troops were doing little militarily at the time, the film distorted facts by giving the impression that they were more active. Similarly, *Fighting Norway* in March stressed the strategic importance of Norway and, by using actual and staged footage, demonstrated how Norwegian guerrillas, in their democratic will to win, continued the fight against the Nazis.

There was military success to report in January 1943. *Pincer on Axis Europe* spoke of how the Allies were successful in their invasion of North Africa and their capture of Casablanca and Algiers. (Canadian troops were not involved in this operation.) Visuals of shot and shell accompanied the description of how the 'giant Allied nutcracker was now closing on Rommel's retreating forces.' The double pincers of Allied attacks from England and from North Africa would inevitably follow. As the film ended with footage of mobile and marching troops, the narrator predicted confidently, 'Germany has had her day of triumph and now across the rolling hills of Africa the United Nations are marching forward to launch their massive spearheads at the heart of Axis Europe.' Demonstration of the pincer effect was the subject of the unusually violent *Trainbusters*, a July 1943 chronicle of the RCAF's air war on the Atlantic and against enemy-held Mediterranean ports, 'bombed into useless ruins under the bombs of our air fleets.' Ground strafing, it was explained, was used to paralyse the German communications network. Using captured German footage with telling effect, co-producers and editors Glover and Newman portrayed a German munitions train being strafed and destroyed. Glover has said that the violence and action made the film work for the audience; they ended the film with the promise that 'the wings of a continent sweep on to the day of victory.'

The Allied landing at Normandy was the subject of *Breakthrough* (August 1944), with a special emphasis on Canada's contribution. To footage of captured German soldiers, the narration gloated, 'Their world dissolved in bewilderment and fear.' The film did stress once again the theme of the citizen's army and, to visuals of Allied soldiers, the commentary continued, 'For another kind of army was beating them, a citizen's army of men and women, resolute and cheerful, an army whose discipline did not destroy its soul; an army where military rule could sanction friendly and democratic feeling among all ranks. [Here the visuals showed soldiers playing a ball game near a tank.] A new army, well aware of its strengths and high spirits, was eager to meet and build the future once they had won the war.' To sounds of happy music, the film concluded, anticipating that with the end of the 'shot and shell' a brave new world would be born.

One of the least successful of the shot and shell numbers, *Fighting Sea Fleas* (November 1944), told the story of Canada's motor torpedo boats. These sleek speedy craft fought against German raiders of a similar type in actual and staged sequences. Notable in the film was its mention of Canadian officers and crew by name as they went through their routines aboard ship. The oft-used technique of identifying the personnel and their home towns was appreciated by Canadian audiences who could identify with the region if not the individual. This once again made people feel able to identify with individuals who comprised the citizen's army.

The weakest of the wartime *Canada Carries On* films were the ten issues which addressed themselves to 'playing war,' that is, portrayed Canadians training for battle or readying themselves for hard times on the home front. Six of these films were made in 1940, starting with the above-mentioned *Atlantic Patrol*. As Britain's garrison, the Canadian Corps remained largely inactive while awaiting the Second Front. The Sicily landing in August 1943 was the first real chance to boost public morale in view of the facts that General Eisenhower's initial communiqué forgot the Canadians and a Washington press leak announced the news before Mackenzie King could.

Letter from Aldershot (May 1940) showed the arrival in Britain of sixteen thousand Canadian troops and a day in the life of recruits. A soldier from each major region identified himself. The rather weak conclusion stated vaguely that what Canadians were preparing to fight for was the spirit of common decency. *Wings of Youth*, a September release, showed how training for the air war was multi-faceted and dependent on the individual skills of young pilots. Theirs was to be the battle for individual rights. Without quoting the inspirational source or referring to the raging Battle of Britain, the narration concluded, 'You who are young, we salute you, for never in the field of human conflict was so much owed by so many to so few.' In November, *Letter from Camp Borden* identified three recruits who were being initiated into the routine of becoming a soldier. Scenes of war games played at this Canadian base led to an indefinite conclusion which asserted that the recruits now had new confidence and were bound together by comradeship. There were visuals of soldiers on the move while a stirring background chorus of singing troops boosted the tempo, though not the film.

Another war preparation film, *Guards of the North* (January 1941), told of Canadian Forces' peaceful occupation and fortification of Iceland, where a German attack was expected. Now, it was stated, Atlantic convoys would be protected on their way to Britain. *Heroes of the Atlantic* (May 1941) had scenes of freighters and tankers taking on cargoes, about to form a convoy and make their way into the Battle of the Atlantic. Uncharacteristically, the film ended with a subdued narration in the form of a prayer. 'God protect you from the dangers of the sea and the violence of the enemy, that you may return in safety to enjoy the blessings of the land and the reward of your labour. God speed you.' In August 1941, *Soldiers All* described how Canadians in London were living through the Blitz, how soldiers were becoming accustomed to their rural English billets, how Canadian cadets at the Royal Military College at Sandhurst fared, and how the Commonwealth Air Training Programme was training Australian pilots. 'We're all having a lot of fun here,' stated one smiling trainee. The narrator's 'Godspeed your wings!' ended the limp document with visuals of planes flying in the clouds. *Up from the Ranks* (August 1943) was another training-oriented film aimed ostensibly at recruitment of platoon leaders. It was also one of the few *Canada Carries On* films not narrated by Lorne Greene, and after going through the endless dramatized litany of training, the narration concluded weakly, 'Radio announcer, teacher, farmer – citizens all, you have graduated to the high school of being a leader. Now your team is waiting.'

The *Canada Carries On* series treated the subject of Quebec several times, though in a very general manner. The first such film was the November 1940 release, *Un du 22ième*, also the first ever *Canada Carries On* with a French script. (Quebec normally saw French translations of the series, called *En avant Canada*.) This film was made to encourage recruitment and to show somewhat idyllically that the French Canadian way of life was respected in the army training camp at Valcartier, Quebec. A young French Canadian, Gilles, after bidding adieu to his sweetheart, was then portrayed going through the rigmarole of training. He maintained a close relationship with the camp's priest, then was shown enjoying the spirit of *bonhomie* as he and his fellow recruits drank beer while singing traditional songs. It was significant that producer Gerald Noxon had to get permission from the archbishop of Quebec before shooting the film, which may in part explain the film's focus and stereotyping. The film ended unconvincingly with troops marching at camp into the sunset.

In *Quebec, Path of Conquest* (September 1942) there was no desire to raise the very hot and divisive conscription issue or to identify the various political currents in Quebec which tended toward fascism. Rather the film played on the traditional stereotypes the English share about Quebec, though there was acknowledgment of modern industrial Quebec and its important wartime role. The narration spoke of the French-speaking Canadians of Quebec, 'whose steadfast tradition of independence does not take kindly to the ways of tyrants.' The viewer was told that 'the real strength of Quebec lies ... in the land, in the deep strength of men whose lives are governed by the seasons of the soil.' This 'spiritual approach to life' (described with the accompaniment of visuals of *habitants* in their fields) came from hard work and simple living. Thus, the narration continued, the pattern of French Canadians is to maintain faith in themselves in order to achieve all things. Quebec's path of conquest, its river, was a path stretching forward to the

Nazi stronghold, down which supplies and rare metals were funnelled to the Allies. And so, the film concluded, the men of Quebec have trained to become the fighting troops for freedom everywhere in the world. To strains of O Canada, the last words attempted to promote national unity and sacrifice, which was obviously good propaganda for both founding peoples. In these times of peril, it was said, the people of Quebec were determined to preserve that spirit which interprets freedom first and foremost as the opportunity of each man to contribute to the common good. Here could be seen another theme often repeated by Grierson and Legg, the moral obligation of citizens to serve their communities. Grierson thought that the prime minister especially was grateful for these Quebec films, which 'had done more for Quebec than the other information services.' He thought this support from the top might come in handy some day.[20]

The series was cautious in its treatment of the sensitive subject of the Soviet Union. Once that nation became an ally in the global conflict, the public's mind had to be conditioned to accept the changed reality of erstwhile godless foe now become an invaluable ally. Curiously, in all the references to the Soviet Union in the years of the series, the words 'Communism' and 'Communist' were never once mentioned. Rather, the visuals of Russians were usually accompanied by chords of Russian folk music and comparisons to the 'citizen's army,' and on numerous occasions there were references to Russia's watchwords, 'all for one, one for all,' instead of more specific Marxist statements. A reference to Russia's collective farming methods (Battle of the Harvests; see p. 131) was disguised as 'the first example of a modern state integrating its whole resources of land for the essential food needs of a growing people.' Cooperation with Russia in northern development was mentioned in Look to the North (December 1943), while in Wounded in Action (July 1944) it was said that some Russian nursing skills were borrowed by Canadians. Political differences were totally ignored for the duration of the conflict; most references to the Russian people were in the context of international neighbourliness and friendship and continuation of this relationship into the postwar world. The propaganda was a matter of re-educating a public which had felt an almost pathological distrust of the Russians.

A last point should be made before closing this chapter. It is interesting that in all the Canada Carries On war issues, Prime Minister William Lyon Mackenzie King was practically never mentioned and only made three brief appearances for several seconds. In *Soldiers All*, he was photographed welcoming the prime minister of Australia, Robert Menzies, to Canada, but was unnamed. He was named but made no appearance in *Inside Fighting Canada*. 'Behind the spires of Parliament and the leadership of the prime minister, William Lyon Mackenzie King, stands a people disciplined for war.' Nor did he appear in *Pincer on Axis Europe* where he was heard to speak significant words: 'To Canada, the coming year will see all our armed forces in action. We shall need to muster all our courage as well as all our strength.' These 'significant words' were mere platitudes characteristic of King's difficulty in inspiring the Canadian public. These examples also reflect how the series steered wide of partisan politics in its various propaganda crusades. Hence opposition charges in 1943 that the prime minister benefited from a substantial amount of publicity both from still photos and in Film Board productions were groundless on the latter count. The opposition must have been referring to still photos when it claimed that the National Film Board had taken pictures of Mackenzie King 'as numerous as the posterity of Abraham, as the stars in the sky or the sands in the sea ...'; the facts did not bear out the allegations. Grierson's propaganda crusade would have become diluted had the films been caught up in bald partisanship. Yet in trying to portray government as good he could not fail to do the Liberals a service. The several specific references the series made during the war years gave the King government less to complain about than the opposition.

In the final analysis the *Canada Carries On* series succeeded by concentrating primarily upon trying to place Canada in relation to world events and the global struggle of war, and avoided falling back upon nationalism and parochial issues. Legg set the standards; the films urged an aggressive total strategy rather than tactics of local defence. Themes were less concerned with individual bravery or even military teamwork than with elucidating the level of cooperative and corporate energies possible in the context of total war and its aftermath. Years later, Legg's own evaluation of the series seems remarkably objective: 'All the time we were concerned in making these films, not with the surface events of reporting but with why things were happening, what was likely to result from things which were going on in the world. In that way we tried to foresee what would happen in this country after the war, and I think we did with some accuracy. ...'[21]

It can be concluded too that Legg, a practitioner of and collaborator in Grierson's philosophy of propaganda as education, put flesh on the bone of Grierson's permanent national propaganda conception. The nation was coming to assume more and more powers over its citizens in everyday life during the national emergency of war. Grierson and Legg anticipated the continuation of the government's role after the war; its collective planning and conservation would usher in a world that would allow the individual his or her place and recognition within the national collectivity. It was strong stuff and was underscored by the Film Board's activities in non-theatrical propaganda film. Grierson and Legg found another clientele outside the theatres, in community halls, schools, and churches across the country receptive to messages of inspiration and willing to accept a national image of Canada fashioned by the National Film Board.

5 | Non-theatrical Film Propaganda and Rural Circuits

Distribution of films became as important a component of the whole wartime film set-up as production. Canadian and American commercial interests had provided some eight hundred Canadian theatres as part of their wartime duty, but the non-theatrical film and distribution network could reach a larger audience. And so Grierson had the National Film Board turn to the unglamorous task of orchestrating the various information campaigns to inspire public will and active citizenship in all other walks of life where people were likely to congregate. As he was often fond of saying, there were more seats outside of theatres than in them.[1] Fortunately for him, by 1939 there was already a non-theatrical network in place which could be extended. During the heyday of the Canadian Government Motion Picture Bureau, the use of educational films, especially in urban areas like Toronto, was not an uncommon occurrence; nor was it unusual for them to be shown in select areas of Alberta and Nova Scotia. By 1939, the bureau offered between two and three hundred sound and silent 16-millimetre films for non-theatrical use.

Rural circuits had been used for non-theatrical film exhibitions by showmen, cooperative movement fieldmen, farm machinery representatives, university extension officers, and representatives from the departments of agriculture and various community associations. One such individual was Donald Cameron, who was regional agent for film circuits for the Department of Extension of the University of Alberta and also sat on the directorate of the National Film Board. Also, from 1934 there appeared a number of urban film societies across the country. The National Film Society was organized in September 1935 under

Dr Sidney Smith as chairman. Donald W. Buchanan, the secretary-treasurer, became one pivotal figure in the organization of wartime non-theatrical distribution.

It might be presumed that the combination of Buchanan's talent and drive, his family's extensive media holdings, and an illustrious father, Senator W.A. Buchanan, provided him with invaluable contacts to promote the very successful non-theatrical circuits across Canada. By January 1940, Buchanan had organized the Central Government Distribution Services, while the Canadian Film Committee had undertaken responsibility to develop the use of films by schools, educational bodies, and specialist organizations. Soon Buchanan found himself stationed in Bermuda to collect captured enemy film footage, which he sent on to the National Film Board for the filmmakers to re-cut for their own propaganda.

By the summer of 1941 Buchanan was back in Canada where he helped Wesley Greene and Janet Scellen to expand the non-theatrical distribution system. Grierson and G.H. Lash, director of the Wartime Information Board, agreed to pool resources to institute a system of travelling film circuits for a six-month trial period. Grierson called them 'Lash Film Circuits.' Each circuit would bring 16-millimetre programmes once a month to twenty rural communities, villages and towns without theatres, as well as to an equal number of schools. Attendance averaged 2,200 per week per circuit. As Grierson described it, Buchanan built up this distribution system by going out to communities across Canada, making contact with chambers of commerce, Kiwanis clubs, and other such organizations, and finding the 'fastest men,' that is, those who were going into politics or were going to be community leaders. These men in turn created a community organization around themselves which would handle non-theatrical distribution. Also, Buchanan appealed to existing 16-millimetre film distribution agencies, university extension departments, and audio-visual bureaus in departments of education. The heads of such agencies often became National Film Board regional agents who were authorized to hire projectionists and direct the rural circuit operations. In the early days of rural circuits, Film Board projectionists reported that on their first round, one-half or more of the people in the audience were seeing a sound film for the first time. By January 1942 some forty-three travelling theatres in collaboration with the Canadian Council of Education for Citizenship were serving remote areas in every province. By 1945 there was a total of eighty-five.

The programmes were seventy to ninety minutes in length and always contained one or two films about the war (usually a *Canada Carries On* or, later, a *World in Action* release) no longer in theatrical circulation. The rest were entertaining or educational. The films were selected at the national level and distributed through provincial regional agents in eight cities. A typical film programme would be composed of films, selected from a 'bank' of seven: *Churchill's Island, H.M. Mine-layer, It's the Navy, Northwest Frontier, Peoples of Canada, Ottawa on the River,* and *Letter from Camp Borden.* In addition, the projectionist might add one comedy or sing-song per programme. (Norman Mc-Laren's and Alexander Alexieff's animated *Chants populaires* were popular.)

A few other non-theatrical films which were released from July 1941 to early 1942 demonstrated how Grierson was using film at war to permeate every aspect of Canadian life: *Tools of War* was Canada's answer to German industrial might, *Fight for Liberty* was a half-hour recap of the second year of the war, *Call for Volunteers* was about Winnipeg women organizing, *Our Soviet Ally* was a ten-minute item on Russia as one of the United Nations, and *Song of Liberty, Blue Horizons,* and *Those Other Days* were five-minute musicals.[2]

The local communities were in control of programmes in schools and community halls. Rural schools and community groups usually took advantage of the opportunity each month to bring in other films for use in classrooms and to supplement evening programmes with films about credit unions, recreation, or other topics of local interest. In order to be welcomed in the community, the projectionist had to contact a local leader to secure his endorsement and support for the film programme. Such a person might be the school principal, mayor, or chairman of the local War Savings Committee. The projectionist, ferrying his own equipment around himself by car, tugboat, dogsled, or other transport had to make his circuit once a month on the same day from September to June. He would try to organize local luminaries to speak on local community activity possible to support the war effort. As to the effect of these shows, if the topic struck a positive chord, there was often a measurable response. For example, a film on rural electrification led to an immediate post-show organizing committee. By the following year, an entire town had become electrified. The net effect of these wartime circuits was that they built a wide public support for the Canadian war effort in rural areas. They may also have been creating a sense of national purpose and national image. Especially useful in bringing the rural element to centre stage was the Film Board's practice of using and naming in films local young people with whom the audience could identify, whether they were from that community or lived a thousand miles away. Finally, the habit of using 16-millimetre film led to schools' and community groups' proliferating this mode of communication after the war.

By the end of 1941 the network of mobile circuits was both respectable and expanding. Non-theatrical films reached nearly a quarter of a million a month. British Columbia had three circuits, Alberta had eleven, Saskatchewan six, Manitoba and Ontario five each, Quebec six, New Brunswick three, Nova Scotia and Prince Edward Island one each. Attendance figures attest to the attraction to children. Quebec had four French-language circuits serving 76 centres. In a month there were 146 shows with average attendances of 310 at afternoon children's showings and 326 at evening adults shows. The total per month was 24,000 adults and 22,000 children. Manitoba with one French- and three English-language circuits had 149 showings in one month with attendances of 202 per children's showing and 257 per evening showing, for a total of 31,000 a month.[3] At evening showings discussion trailers and discussions followed films; one field representative reported that five to seven local citizens took the platform with him during a half-hour intermission to have a round-table discussion. 'Criticism was not lacking,' he admitted, 'but was usually quite intelligent and the discussions always took a decidedly positive direction. Very constructive consideration of social issues came to the fore.'

Helen Watson Gordon, who helped coordinate the rural circuits from Ottawa, said each projectionist had to send in a detailed monthly report which she usually posted on a wall under the photo of the individual. In this way she kept track of the personnel and the entire operation. This method also allowed the Film Board to take the pulse of the country's population at will.

Evelyn Spice Cherry, who made a great number of agricultural films during the war for the Film Board, has given credit to Watson for making the two-way communication process so effective. Cherry described a splendid flow of enthusiasm and ideas for films coming from the people. 'We didn't sit in committees or consultations and decide what the films would be. The film ideas came in and then we sat and talked about how we could do it. We'd say, "Those people out there ... have sent in ideas. Now how can we get this done in order to send a film back to them?"' Cherry's account illustrates how the Grierson philosophy of listening to the people as well as communicating to the people was more than rhetorical cant.[4]

In January 1943, a system of industrial film circuits reaching factories, munitions plants, shipyards, and other large enterprises began to operate under the Film Board's Gordon Adamson. He also developed the idea of discussion trailers, which were attached often to non-theatrical films. He formed these circuits carefully and slowly with the cooperation of labour, management, provincial governments, and education agencies. There were on average 1,116 shows a month reaching 132,712 workers. Films were shown to factory workers between shift changes or at lunch hours in cafeterias. A typical programme might show English and French copies of *Forward Commandos*, *Controls for Victory*, and *Tools of War*; another might contain *People's War* and *Great Guns*; a third could feature *Battle for Oil* and *Quebec Path of Conquest* in French and *Battle for Oil* and *Smoke or Steel* in English.[5] These programmes lasted from twenty to thirty minutes and, besides the information film, might feature a travelogue or comedy. There were short film clips too on safety in the plant and at home, on recruiting, on increasing production, or on morale. Other clips had messages such as 'Buy Victory Loans,' reminiscent of the film tag from First World War days. A typical Norman McLaren animated film devoted to preventing loose talk was *Keep Your Mouth Shut*. It depicted the enemy as a talking skull which said he was grateful for the information overheard in public chatter. The film showed troop ships sinking and war plants being sabotaged as a result of information being heard by the wrong people. In demonstrating the workers' relation to the war effort, the film frightened, but it did not provoke hatred, only caution.

Adamson worked with boards of trade, chambers of commerce, and sponsoring government departments like the Wartime Prices and Trade Board, Munitions and Supply, the Department of Labour, and the National War Services. When Stanley Hawes took over non-theatrical production from Adamson in 1944, there were sixty-six representatives

During a factory work break in Montreal, an NFB projectionist screens an industrial short for these workers. (No date) (NFB)

employed by the Film Board in an industrial film circuits programme. They reported almost 3,000 screenings and an attendance of 385,000 a month, including civil servants who saw films on a regular basis. If Montreal can be cited as an example of how the industrial film circuits succeeded, it was reported that during the war bond campaigns there were as many as seventy-five showings a month in local industrial war plants.

In 1943 and 1944 two publicity agencies were set up within the Department of Labour: the Information Branch and the Industrial Production Cooperation Board. The former was supposed to keep the public fully informed about legislation the department administered and the latter was to promote the growth of Labour-Management Production Committees (LMPCS). An assortment of films would help these agencies fulfil their purposes. After the war and the end of the Industrial Film Circuits, the Information Branch gave financial assistance to the Film Board to set up the Industrial Film Preview Library, consisting of films chosen by the Information Branch and distributed throughout the country 'with a view to encouraging the formation of community industrial film circuits.'[6]

Midway through 1942, with the approval of top union management, the Film Board organized the trade union film circuits. The circuits were sponsored by the Workers' Education Association and the labour congresses in Canada. The Department of Labour had the Film Board make films for specific campaigns. The sponsors selected the programmes which were shown each month to unions across the country. By 1945 there were 300 union locals in eighty-four districts attending screenings from September to May. Average monthly attendance was 26,426. Many of the films dealt with labour laws, the duties of shop stewards, and the responsibilities of union members, these being specialized subjects for a specialized audience. The government was particularly keen to promote films encouraging formation of Labour Management Production Committees, which were in effect company unions. In principle this was an application of the 'corporatist' idea to Canadian society where industrial and professional corporations served as organs of political representation, exercising some control over affairs in their ken. Even with compulsory collective bargaining, LMPCS were useful vehicles to pre-empt confrontation, and numerous Film Board films helped to promote government labour policy. Coinciden-

To stem industrial labour strife, the Department of Labour promoted the growth of Labour-Management Production Committees. A number of NFB films followed this theme. (PAC 87500)

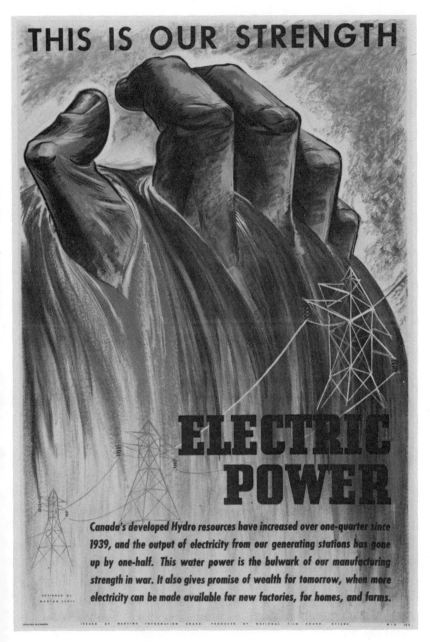

The Wartime Information Board encouraged the idea of a brave new postwar world. This poster for national electrification helped create rising expectations nationally. (PAC 87493)

tally, they fit neatly into what Grierson would call educational propaganda. Stanley Hawes went to Britain to do the research on this useful film subject.

The non-theatrical network justified the Film Board's intensive production of educational films on myriad social subjects, from rural health services to agriculture to consumer-oriented themes with practical purposes. Most of the films were about twenty minutes long and were deposited in film libraries both in the United States and across Canada.

Using 1944 as a sample year, the following National Film Board films were available in 16-millimetre in at least twenty film libraries across the country besides the board's own film libraries. The theatrical series, *Canada Carries On* and *The World in Action*, were also available and have been described earlier. The films were divided under the headings Agriculture, Consumer, Education, Social Planning, Sport, and War. The titles demonstrate how information extended to every corner of national life. The significance of the non-theatrical films becomes evident if one realizes that the films reached countless thousands who otherwise would not have been directly touched by the war. There were also a few American and many British films available under these headings in the catalogue but we shall omit them for reasons of expediency.[7]

Under Agriculture, there were *Hands for the Harvest*, which described how farmers overcame labour shortages on the farm, and *Plowshares into Swords*, which explained how farmers can make the best possible use of existing equipment. There were films too in the Farm Improvement Series, plus *Farmers of the Prairies*, *New Plans for the Land*, and *Windbreaks on the Prairies* in less than ten film libraries.

The following Consumer films were available on a wide basis as part of the 'Knife and Fork' nutrition series: *Children First*, a film about the importance of milk in the wartime diet, *Coupon Value*, which explained to housewives how the food coupon system could be best used, *The Main Dish*, advising how to buy wisely, *Make It Over*, which demonstrated how the clothing shortage should be faced with a pioneer spirit, *The Plot Thickens*, showing the dos and don'ts of community gardening in wartime, *Vitamin Films*, four shorts on vitamins A, B, C, and D, *Vitamin-Wise*, a film warning against waste by careless cooking, *Voluntary vs. Involuntary Savings*, explaining payroll deductions, and *What Makes Us Grow*, which dealt with the problem of child nutrition.

The 'Knife and Fork' series was a response to what Grierson referred to as the necessity of harmonizing producers' and consumers' viewpoints. It was sponsored by the Wartime Information Board and the Wartime Prices and Trade Board.

For Education there were a number of health films from Britain on inoculation, contagious disease, and the Red Cross, available in at least twenty film libraries. *High over the Borders* was a popular nature study film about the migration of birds from Alaska to Argentina. A sizeable number of ethnographic films were listed too, though they were available mainly through the Film Board libraries across Canada. Also through the Film Board and a few libraries one could obtain *Chants populaires*, a series of ten-minute cartoons of Quebec popular songs, produced by Norman McLaren and Alexander Alexieff. These delightful morsels of Quebec folklore were entertaining to French and English adults and children.

The heading Social Planning contained a number of films which were available in at least twenty film libraries. *Film and Radio Discussion Guide* was a three-minute trailer dealing with the use of film in connection with radio forums, especially on the subject of postwar problems. *A Man and His Job*, produced by Dallas Jones, presented the story of a typical Canadian working man from the depression to wartime and showed how the Unemployment Insurance Act was a positive development. Being laid off was no longer such a hardship because, as the film concluded, 'Ahead is the security that comes when all men look toward each other in their vision of the future, the security that makes living rich.' The point of the film was that unemployment insurance was not a wage substitute but a guarantee of freedom from fear and want for all workers. Significantly, it appeared at a time when labour shortages were a greater social concern than unemployment. *Partners in Production*, a film about labour-management committees, demonstrated the importance of total democracy during total war. *The People's Bank* described the growth and expansion of credit unions all over Canada. *The Voice of Action* described how radio helped draw together Canada's widely scattered population.

There were only two films made during the war for Sport, *Hot Ice*, about hockey, and *Ski in the Valley of the Saints*, about a Laurentian ski holiday. The first was available in eleven film libraries, the second only from the Film Board.

Under War there were a number of non-theatrical items. *Before They Are Six* was the story of Canada's day nurseries. *Canadian Mail* was about the postal service during wartime. *On Guard for Thee* was a chronology of Canadian development from 1914 to 1944, and *Ottawa, Wartime Capital* explained how thousands of government employees were doing their part to keep the war machine going. *Handle with Care* pictured life in an explosives plant; *Radio Front Line* described how a radio front line report was given; *Smoke and Steel* and *Tools of War* were films about supplying war matériel; and *When Do We Eat?* encouraged workers to improve their eating habits. *Not Peace but a Sword* explained how the war began in 1939, and *Under the Cross of Lorraine* gave an overview of Free French and Allied activities in the Middle East.

There were several non-theatrical ethnographic films during the war years which deserve mention because of their anthropological treatment of minority groups in Canada, to the almost complete exclusion of politics. *Eskimos of the Eastern Arctic*, produced and directed by Laura Boulton in 1944 with consultation by Robert Flaherty, described the gentle Eskimos and their severe struggle against a harsh environment. With good reason the film portrayed the Eskimo hunter as 'master of his severe world who acknowledged no superior.' There were seal- and walrus-hunting sequences and scenes of communal feasting along with excellent recordings of women singing and chanting. Reminiscent of *Nanook of the North*, this film reflected the Inuit way of life with accuracy and sensitivity.

People of the Potlatch, another of Boulton's films in 1944, did not succeed as well. The potlatch was not really described in detail, nor was the imposition of modern life on the Queen Charlotte Islands treated with anything but praise. The viewer might have wondered if smiling Indian children at the Canadian government school were so perfectly adjusted or if indeed 'economic and spiritual needs were satisfied by basket-making.' The last words underscored the unreality of the film: 'The Indian's life gives him leisure for living in this beautiful mist-laden land.'

The March 1941 issue called *People of Canada* was an Associated Screen News Production, directed by Gordon Sparling. Legg was associate producer. The film touched on Quebec briefly as it described nine ethnic components of the Canadian population and their usual employment. Forgetting the thousands of city-dwellers, the film portrayed the

The NFB recorded Inuit music for *Eskimos of the Eastern Arctic* (1944) in a series of ethnographic films by Laura Boulton in consultation with Robert Flaherty. (PAC 129913)

A.Y. Jackson sketched the village of St Tite des Caps, Quebec, for *Canadian Landscape* (1943). Grierson wanted Canadians to understand that what they were fighting for included art and culture. (PAC 129918)

Quebecker as a farmer whose church was at the centre of community life: 'And so today, as yesterday across the landscape of Quebec, stand the stable deep-rooted communities grouped around their Church. On this soil abides from generation to generation their culture, their tongue and their civilization.' The film's other depiction of ethnic types across Canada, the Scots, Dutch, Germans, Scandinavians, Dukhobors, Hutterites, Mennonites, and Chinese, was in the context of 'Canada is becoming strong because of its tolerance for others.' Humanitarianism was underscored as the film closed showing a teacher telling his class that they must have respect for other people's beliefs.

Northwest Frontier, a 1941 film edited by Stanley Hawes and James Beveridge, similarly tried to capture the essence of Indian and Inuit life, though its depiction of modern white values also seemed to gloss over the natives' difficulties of adjustment. The future promise of opening the North to resource development was integrated visually with the Indian way of life, implying that growth and assimilation would be simple. Unfortunately, no quesions were asked.

Jane Marsh had more success with her lyrical, ethnographic film of 1943, *Terre de nos aïeux*, a study of a Quebec farm family in Charlevoix County. This film was constructed around the cyclical patterns of rural life dictated by the seasons, and the omnipresent St Lawrence gave the film an almost classic literary characterization. Folk songs were woven throughout as was the presence of religion and church in the daily lives of the family members. The film avoided most references to the contemporary mechanized world.

This brief treatment demonstrates how non-theatrical film production and distribution were an integral part of the Film Board's wartime activities. Many of the films, if in response to public demand, were also sponsored in conjunction with government agencies. Marjorie McKay, who played an important role in the early administration of the Film Board, described how some ideas became films. Grierson would initiate discussions with a cabinet minister. He carried the idea for the film (an idea which came usually either from the field reports or from the filmmakers) directly to the cabinet minister. If the minister agreed, the Film Board's liaison department made official contact with the information departments or heads of sections in other government departments. And once the film had been decided on at that level, the producer in the Film Board met with the corresponding person in the department and the project took shape.

The whole non-theatrical network held together because of fairly tight supervision from the top. From the central office in Ottawa there came a concerted effort to proliferate non-theatrical exhibition to the furthest corners of the country. The establishment of the Volunteer Projection Services was aimed at serving the needs of urban community groups not covered by the Industrial or Trade Union Circuits. Projectionist training classes were held in most Canadian cities once or twice a year and screenings were organized by local civic bodies and service clubs. The projectionists were first trained by a Film Board field representative. Later those who had become skilled projectionists trained others. From this scheme there grew a sizeable pool of qualified projectionists, many of whom were women who showed Film Board films to hospitals, hotels, chambers of commerce, libraries, and churches, and to youth and women's groups. The distribution mechanism across Canada at its peak included 600 films councils and 660 voluntary film circuits. The Film Board had supported the loaning of projectors and the depositing of blocks of film in local libraries and community centres. By the end of the war there were a hundred Film Board staff in the field and eighty-five representatives across Canada.

Finally, both non-theatrical and theatrical distribution of newsreels should be mentioned because they reached an astounding worldwide audience of forty to fifty million a week by 1944, most of it theatrical. The non-theatrical newsreel series, *Eyes Front, Canada Communiqué*, and *Pictorial Hometown News*, came nowhere near gross newsreel figures, but were important because they reached the troops. *Eyes Front* was for camps at home, the others for troops abroad. The Newsreel Co-ordination Unit, established in September 1942, was producing twelve newsreels of forty-one stories by 1944, comprised mainly of film shot by the Canadian Army Film Unit. These were incorporated into eight issues of *Front Line Reports*, the Film Board's regular newsreel for industrial and rural circuits. *Eyes Front* usually lasted ten minutes and would have several items, such as how soldiers who needed economic help could apply, how dogs were trained for the army kennels, and how to guard against malaria. *Canada Communiqué* was a semi-monthly newsreel distributed through the Auxiliary Services to fighting forces overseas. There were, in addition, four other series developed for rural and industrial non-theatrical circuits: *Rural Newsreel, Industrial Newsreel, Front Line Reports*, and *Screen Magazine*. A number of these were shortened adaptations of the two theatrical series, *Canada Car-*

ries On and *The World in Action*. Other Canadian newsreel material was made available to United States newsreel companies who paid for and distributed it to 4,700 theatres there.

To conclude, the non-theatrical distribution system reached the far corners of the country and the world. By 1944-5 there were some 3,112 prints of 761 films that were being shown on urban and rural circuits to an average monthly audience of 465,000. Rural circuits then numbered 92 and reached a quarter of a million people a month in 1,700 community and school shows. French distribution in industrial and rural circuits totalled 896 shows to an audience of 133,000. In addition to these impressive statistics, National Film Board film libraries drew over 400,000 viewers a month at home, 1.5 million a month in the United States, and a half million a month in the United Kingdom. Their films were also available in distant world capitals, dubbed in that country's language, from Mexico City to Singapore. There was also a special effort to cover eleven countries and territories of the British Empire. In all, by 1944-5 there were 1,948 prints circulating in thirty-one countries, including fourteen Latin American nations; the number of prints does not include the 4,138 prints of 446 films in the United States. Distribution was effected generally through twenty-five Canadian diplomatic and trade offices abroad.[8]

What non-theatrical distribution had done was to link rural and working-class Canada to global events, to introduce school children and the less literate to a national image and common purpose, and to teach dozens of countries about a young and confident Canada. At home, field reports claimed that people everywhere were learning by viewing and discussing these films. Abroad, Canada ceased being the best-kept secret of the United Nations wartime alliance. By 1945 the propaganda crusade had seemingly extended to its furthest limits. Film had brought Canada's citizens together and they were becoming part of the active democratic process. On the horizon lay television, a one-way information delivery system which would come to alienate these same citizens from each other. The technological advances which television heralded would diverge radically from the wartime information process. After excitement with the new gadget wore off, citizens would realize that they were receivers only. The two-way process Grierson and the Film Board developed was years ahead of the concept of 'global village' which media pundit Marshall McLuhan was later to develop in his explanation of the communications revolution. The Film Board's non-theatrical network evoked a sense of unity between the individual and his own environment and the world around him. And unity meant tolerance of diversity, not homogeneity, American-style. Most important, someone was listening to the individual while trying to inspire him. At the point of apparent success, Grierson had been experimenting with an ideological approach to film propaganda which involved politics and intrigue, the games he liked to play fast and free. He seemed to be vindicated by the success of the powerful theatrical series, *The World in Action*, and its orientation toward international theatrical audiences. But as he expanded his bailiwick from parochial Canada to the world, the calculated risks he took left him vulnerable to attack from many quarters.

6 | Focusing on World Events and the Destiny of Nations: *The World in Action*

After two years, *Canada Carries On* had become the bellwether of the National Film Board theatrical market and had demonstrated that propaganda, if approached maturely, could be positive and inspirational while promoting national unity. Propaganda without hate-mongering also gave Canada a new and respected international stature. After December 1941, the Film Board sought to break into a relatively closed United States market with those films which addressed themselves to international themes. There was hope too that they would qualify for and earn worldwide circulation. National Film Board propaganda was ready to play in the major league. The arrival of Film Board competition ruffled the feathers of *The March of Time*'s Louis de Rochemont. Grierson found himself embroiled in political intrigue against his erstwhile ally, who brought a lawsuit against the distributors of National Film Board films for the issue *Warclouds in the Pacific*.

The film was released in November 1941. De Rochemont entered an action in the District Court of New York because certain sequences of that film were given to Canada by *The March of Time* for use by the Film Board for exhibition in Canada only. In all probability de Rochemont wanted to prevent United States distribution of *Warclouds in the Pacific* because it was the first of the newsreels and documentaries of the day to anticipate Japan's involvement in war with the United States; it warned of the Japanese presence and strength in the Pacific a week *before* Pearl Harbor. The powerful narrative in Lorne Greene's authoritative voice warned ominously, 'Limited in cruising range to some fifteen hundred miles and mounting less than a hundred heavy-calibre guns, the tactic of the Japanese battle fleet must be to strike swiftly and hard before the combined strength of the United States and Britain can be massed against them.' Stuart Legg put the film's conclusion graphically and hopefully in terms of geopolitics: 'And so today, as we hear the roar of the patrol planes sweeping out in their ceaseless watch over mountain and sea, the people of the Pacific coast know that their defences stretch out across one-third of the earth's circumference and range unbroken from the icebergs of the North to the coral islands of the Southern seas.'

The film's uncanny prescience and mature analysis combined to demonstrate screen journalism at its finest and certainly matched, if not surpassed, *The March of Time*. A bitter de Rochemont resented too the intrusion of competition into what he thought of as his country's safe market. RKO Pictures supported him because Grierson had sold the film to a rival.

De Rochemont wrote directly to Prime Minister King, complaining that this competition seemed to be a serious breach of good faith and friendship, especially after his organization had instructed and paid Stuart Legg. His complaint was sent on to J.T. Thorson, minister of national war services responsible for the Film Board. Thorson told Grierson to handle it. He read and approved of Grierson's letter of response before it was dispatched to the plaintiff. He hoped this would dispose of the matter and avoid a debate in the Privy Council. Grierson's letter was polite but direct. The Allies were all circulating their films in each other's markets and Canada felt it wanted more publicity since it received only occasional notice in *The March of Time*'s thirteen annual issues. There was room enough in the North American market and the public would be demanding more films in this field of editorial war reporting. The two series, he argued, complemented each other. He wanted to work more closely with de Rochemont to do a great work for public information and enlightenment regarding the war. He thought 'our personal considerations have to be aligned with these larger considerations' and concluded that both men had a great responsibility to the war effort and should work together.[1]

Unwilling to yield, de Rochemont persisted in his legal machinations. Grierson knew that, in terms of the lawsuit, he was fighting on tenuous grounds. The best defence was offence. Planning his attack, the combative Scot first let it be known that he had obtained the New York lawyers for United Artists to fight for the Canadian government's right to use the disputed footage. Then he, McLean, and Legg arrived in New York to meet with de Rochemont, the bevy of lawyers from Time-Life Incorporated, and representatives of the National Film Board's distributors, Loewe's Incorporated and Warwick Pictures Incorporated.

According to Grierson, he and his counsel went to the Manhattan meeting of de Rochemont and the legal minions of Time-Life Incorporated with two weapons in their arsenal. First, his lawyer pointed out that the *March of Time* shots could be replaced by similar material from other stock-shot libraries. It would be easier not to tamper with the film and credit *The March of Time*. The second weapon was a bald threat by Grierson. He claimed to have said, 'Gentlemen, I have it from the highest authorities in Canada that if *The March of Time* insists on pressing this suit, Canada will revise the existing laws regarding importation of foreign films to Canada.' A moment of silence followed, then one of de Rochemont's attorneys allegedly spoke. 'Louis, you started something you can't finish. Drop it.' No one was prepared to jeopardize the entire American film industry's open Canadian market over a few feet of film. If the story is true, Grierson had pulled the rug out from under his adversaries' feet in the same way that Turnbull had disarmed Colonel Cooper the year before, by implying that Mackenzie King had given him the authority to make this statement. In later years, Grierson would never confirm that the prime minister *had* given him this authority; the knowing twinkle in his eye and absence of corroborative evidence make it seem improbable. This time reckless bluff and luck had carried the day. Grierson had demonstrated a tendency for political risk-taking, which was so integral a part of his professional career and success. He was also lucky.

The House of Commons account of the conclusion would read with deceptive simplicity. 'It was agreed that a subtitle in the following terms should be added to the film: "This motion picture was produced by the National Film Board of Canada with the cooperation of the *March of Time*." No money payments of any kind were involved in this settlement.'[2] The film received nationwide distribution in the United States, earned some $30,000 for Canada, and, significantly, inaugurated the regular distribution of National Film Board films there.

Most of the subjects in the *Canada Carries On* series were of parochial appeal to particular Canadian interest groups like farmers and factory and munitions workers. Late in 1941, Grierson and Legg were thinking of launching a new series for international audiences. The film commissioner went to Hollywood early in 1942 to obtain the agreement of United Artists' Charlie Chaplin, Mary Pickford, and Alexander Korda to distribute the first dozen films of the new series. It was to be called *The World in Action* and its first issue was in April. With American distribution guaranteed, Grierson thought these films might become powerful instruments of state. It was an opportunity beyond the mere question of dollars and cents.[3] His missionary impulse could barely be contained.

Grierson and Legg continued to use the now-familiar turning globe in the titles and kept the recognizable voice of Lorne Greene for narrator. The ambitious early issues identified each film as 'a screen editorial on great events shaping the destiny of nations the world over.' What they were attempting was to influence and direct the political attitudes of international audiences toward an internationally oriented postwar ethic. As Grierson put it to his British colleague, Basil Wright, a month after the series began, 'Canada is moving as swiftly toward a world viewpoint as England in recent years has been moving away from it.' Wright was struggling to keep the remnants of the ailing first documentary film school from being suffocated by a top-heavy British bureaucracy at the Ministry of Information. Grierson explained what he and Legg were trying to achieve:

... this is one time, we say, when history doesn't give a good goddam who is being the manly little fellow in adversity and is only concerned with the designs for living and dying that will actually and in fact shape the future. If our stuff pretends to be certain it's because people need certainty. If our maps look upside down, it's because it is time people saw things in relativity. If we bang them [films] out one a fortnight and no misses, instead of sitting six months on our fannies cuddling them to sweet smotheroos, it's because a lot of bravos in Russia and Japan and Germany are banging out things too and we'd maybe better learn how, in time. If the manner is objective and hard, it's because we believe the next phase of human development needs that kind of mental approach. ...[4]

So, from its first issues, the series assumed its internationalist orientation. While the conflict raged, Legg and Grierson enjoyed a relative *carte blanche* to preach utopian brotherhood. After having prepared the public for the brave new world, with peace imminent the United Nations unlinked and began to set the world up as a chessboard for the struggle between East and West power blocs. *The World in Action* would be the last casualty of the Second World War.

Many of the subjects in the series resembled those in *Canada Carries On*; they included themes like strategy (six films) and the new world which was likely to follow the war (eight films). There were three films which dealt with the Soviet Union, four which described the Japanese enemy, two on women, and one on labour. The new series avoided some of the weaknesses of its predecessor: hence there were only four films which could be described as having 'shot and shell' themes and only three of which, 'played war' in training films. The films showed respect for the intelligence of the audience by not condescending. The public's favourable response was attested to in box office success; to the chagrin of some American competitors like de Rochemont, a number of films earned their $15,000 average per production costs back for the Canadian government.

By the spring of 1943 the Film Board reported that its United States distribution was in 5,000 theatres. But receipts and expenditure figures reveal a less glowing, if still respectable, picture. The board's income figures tended to be kept confidential mainly because Grierson wanted to keep the commercial industry, his competitors, ignorant.[5] Therefore the following calculations were made on the basis of postwar aggregate figures and wartime Canadian marketing practices. What follows is a general overview, which admittedly comments on only the broadest aspects of the board's foreign distribution practices.

From 1942 to 1947, net receipts for films in the 'external' field totalled $265,000 against an expenditure of $610,000. In 1946–7, revenue from the United States was only $30,000, leaving an average annual income from 1942 to 1945 of $78,300. Let us assume that 'external' meant the United States alone (and it did not, because theatrical films were distributed in a thousand United Kingdom cinemas) and that the films were rented on terms similar to the Canadian market. In Canada they rented theatrically at $125 a week in first-run theatres to as low as $15 a week in last-run theatres. Twenty-three English prints and two French prints of each theatrical film were distributed to nine hundred Canadian theatres for six months.[6] If the same distribution procedure were used in the United States, about 140 prints of an issue would have to circulate to reach five thousand theatres over the same period. Renting at $125 per fresh print, each film should have generated $17,500 per first run alone. With twelve theatrical films a year, the income should have been $210,000 annually for the first run only, yet the actual amount was only 37 per cent of that total, including second-, third-, and last-run incomes. What the rough calculations demonstrate is that either Film Board films were not reaching five thousand theatres, or that not all the *World in Action* issues were being distributed in the United States, or that figures were being suppressed (see p. 225).

The answer probably lies somewhere in between. Some films received maximum distribution while others may have had shortened runs in newsreel theatres in key American cities, or in fewer cases, may not have been shown at all. What should be kept in mind is that *The World In Action* came to be regarded as the voice of Canada on the screens in both the United States and the United Kingdom and monthly films were seen with some frequency by thirty to forty million people.[7] The expenditure of $610,000 over five years surely was a worthwhile investment to the government.

Obviously the circulation of the *World in Action* films was having significant impact in the United States. *The March of Time* angrily accused the series of being a blatant counterfeit; yet though the *World in Action* films may have looked like de Rochemont's in structure, according to the *New York Times* they avoided nationalism, something which *The March of Time* insisted upon in so many of its issues. 'The secret behind the success in dodging political barriers,' said the *Times*, 'not only at home but abroad, is that the editorial sights of the *World in Action* subjects are raised high above the level of nationalism. They interpret the facts squarely and by doing so have earned the respect of audiences who are struggling to understand more clearly the world in which they live.' The *Times* also believed that the series demonstrated Canadian thought about the international scene and represented the viewpoint of the Canadian government. Even *Time* magazine, which shared the same parent as *The March of Time*, praised the series from the outset.

A few months later Grierson wrote to the under-secretary of state for external affairs, Norman Robertson, about how he had won a progressively larger amount of screen space for Canadian films in the United States. The films took the United Nations viewpoint and the Canadian war effort was related to it in due proportion where possible. He did not want Robertson (or Prime Minister King) to miss the import of the value of this propaganda for Canada. Here he was not thinking of the message but rather of the publicity boost for Canada, forgotten child of the Allies. 'Their publicity value for Canada lies in creating and holding a most powerful platform before the American public, from which the Canadian effort can in due proportion and relationship be discussed. No other country has acquired this integral place in the powerful propaganda machinery of the United States.'[8]

Before looking at specific films in the *World in Action* series, it might be useful to identify one of the most successful of the techniques applied, the integration of visuals and sound. Ernest Bornemann, who was in charge of instructional films, described the highly complex three-part counterpoint between visual, music, and effects tracks running side by side. Since the visual itself skipped constantly from place to place over the world,

... it became doubly important for the commentary to draw the two other tracks and the visual together into a single continuity, and this had to be done in such a manner as to make its points through the subconscious as well as through the conscious of the spectator.

Aside from active verbs and pseudo-quotations ('the experts say that ...') the most important innovation here was the use of metaphors and similes drawn from an incidental aspect of the visual into an incidental aspect of the commentary so that both of them became permanently but, to the spectator, quite imperceptibly welded to each other, as in the following examples:

War for Men's Minds (R. 4)

Pix Oil covered survivors, airman rescued from sea, comes toward camera and *smiles as he sees it.*
Com. 'The people are everywhere marvelling at the bravery of men faced with horrors beyond belief. And in these men, who can *laugh in the face of death,* they perceive not strangers, but their own brothers, fathers, sons.'

... These examples were mainly meant to impart their meaning through the spectator's sub-conscious rather than through his conscious. In other words they were to exert their effect without being noticed. Other examples, how-

Captured German footage showed starving people clamouring for food in *Food, Weapon of Conquest* (1942). But there was little or no footage of deportations and 'resettlement' of Jews, so the NFB said little about the plight of European Jewry. The King government ignored the subject because there was nothing to be gained politically. (PAC 129916)

A clever and frightening publicity poster for the NFB's major film on propaganda, *The War for Men's Minds* (1943). (PAC 130041)

'The people of the earth march forward into their new age, march forward in the certainty that the gates of hell cannot prevail against them,' concludes *The War for Men's Minds*, here uniting visual, verbal, and musical elements in a stirring climax. (PAC 129919)

ever, made use of conscious irony, and still others of contrast rather than of similarity in word and visual.

Here are two examples of ironic simile, the first one particularly remarkable because of its use of direct quotations:

Gates of Italy (R. 2)

Pix Sequence of Mussolini trotting around turning the soil, heaving a pick, laying a brick, scattering seeds, kissing babies, being cheered, and ending with *baby clinic.*
Com. 'Already I control the forces of Politics and those of Economics. Soon I shall even control *the great forces acting in Nature.*'

Balkan Powder Keg (R. 1)

Pix *Ox scratching ass with horn.*
Com. 'Hungary, the country whose rulers have *gazed irritably backward at the past.*'

... And here, finally, is one of the most dramatic uses of contrast rather than simile:

War for Men's Minds

Pix Chinese refugees and woman crawling on hands and knees.
Com. 'With such proof of their own towering strength, the people of the earth march forward into their new age – march in the certainty that the gates of hell cannot prevail against them.'[9]

But as in the *Canada Carries On* series, narration provided the essential cohesion to each film because newsreel stock shots and anonymous Allied and enemy film clips still predominated. Control was best achieved with the spoken word and by skillful editing. Legg mastered control of the footage in numerous ways. If, for example, there was a shot which was too dark, Legg would make the connection by narrating, 'In those dark days ...' or he would make a boring shot dramatic by using commentary to develop a new meaning with a phrase like 'Unseen eyes watched ...' Lucio Agostini's music of inspiring crescendos was still permeating the background but it was an editor's and writer's medium. Years later, Legg described his task as trying to put meaning to the dramatic world events which unfolded before him daily on celluloid:

One could sit in the theatre in Ottawa sometimes and run let's say forty or fifty thousand feet all day, of a Tolstoian panorama of what was going on in the world. It was incredible. I've never seen anything like it before. You had this vast sense of global upheaval in which millions and millions of people were involved and you would be trying to take hold of the growing points around a given subject or given theme and organize it. It was a remarkable operation and I think it was probably the thing I most enjoyed in my film career.[10]

To digress momentarily, Legg and Grierson's pursuit of inspirational propaganda was a role model for the old General Post Office film unit which in wartime Britain became the Crown Film Unit. Unfortunately the British creative talents could not succeed in raising their propaganda much beyond patriotic verse about the Home Guard and the moral superiority of Britain. They must have envied Grierson and Legg's *carte blanche* while they were hamstrung by their government's insistence that there be a 'no war aims' policy.

Britain's unsuccessful attempt at inspirational propaganda left the Crown Film Unit somewhat flat by the end of the war. The films of Humphrey Jennings stood out as exceptions. They communicated the emotional immediacy of the national mood and morale. Rather than trying artificially to create inspiration, Jennings' films like *London Can Take It* (1941), *Listen to Britain* (1941), *Fires Were Started* (1943), and *A Diary for Timothy* (1945) were personal interpretations of the uniqueness all around him. The device he used often was associative and non-narrative, using combinations of visual sequences of public images (like St Paul's Cathedral) to elicit national feeling. In the opinion of film critic James Agee, his films had the sinister freezing beauty of an Auden prophecy come true. In Canada, filmmakers faced a more difficult challenge in a country lacking Britain's abundance of public images and a great number of national traditions. The Film Board had to rely on inspirational words, not images, to build morale.

A Diary for Timothy reflected a national mood in England of doubt and despair, illustrating Jennings' associative style at its best. A helpless baby, Timothy, was, like the people around him, trying to cope with a complex world he had not made. The narration, by E.M. Forster, pinpointed the fact that with the danger of war over, life was going to become more dangerous than before because 'now we have the power to choose and the right to criticize and even to grumble. We're free men. We have to decide for ourselves. And part of your bother, Tim, will be learning to grow up free.' The final question asked whether his greed for money or power will endanger the world, or whether he and all the other babies will make the world a better place. The film touched cursorily the old documentary theme of social problems, but Jennings refused to promise a better world to come. His film posed questions from a point of view which promised nothing. Perhaps Jennings' refusal to use inspiration as a documentary film theme was anticipating a new direction for postwar documentary film to explore. The Italians would find it in neo-realism while the Canadians would not discover it until the 1960s. Jennings' untimely death by accident in 1950 extinguished a great talent which might have assumed a leading role in reshaping the British documentary film tradition.[11]

THE PROPAGANDA OF GEOPOLITICS

Legg's interest in using film didactically can be seen in all the films related to strategy. It was not enough to urge victory for its own sake; everything had to be seen in its geopolitical context. Thus, *Geopolitik – Hitler's Plan for Empire*, the second film in the series (May 1942), set out to explain the racist and imperial designs of Germany. If the masses generally had little interest in or knowledge of world politics, they could at least see graphically what the war was about. The cleverly animated map of Evelyn Lambart portrayed continents and oceans as they might look from space and described visually how the Nazis would stop at nothing less than world domination. The film explained the science of geopolitics, or the military control of space, through the maxim 'He whose guns command the seven seas commands three-fourths of the earth.' Applied to Hitler's plan this meant Nazi control of Europe, then Africa, then Turkey, land-bridge to Asia, then Iran and India. North Americans had to beware of a possible German thrust into South America and the Panama Canal via Africa. Using Nazi battle footage for his own purposes, Legg turned the Nazi doctrine of invinci-

Norman McLaren and Evelyn Lambart were responsible for much of the wartime animation, from trailers promoting Victory Bonds to the animated 'wook' map which explained geopolitics graphically. (NFB)

This 'wook' map describes simply and graphically Nazi geopolitical objectives. (PAC 130051)

bility and victory into a powerful tool of counter-propaganda. With subtle manipulation he coaxed the audiences to believe that their will could prevent the Nazis from succeeding. Though the stock shots were often unspectacular, the film ended powerfully because its narration was near poetry. It concluded that for North Americans,

The first line of hemisphere defence lies no more along their own coast, but in the sandswept tracks moving forward to battle lines in the sun-scorched shores of the Mediterranean; in the gleaming wings of fighters keeping their unceasing vigil upon the very cradle of mankind, where the proud ramparts raised by conquerors of the past write their lesson for the would-be conquerors of today – the stern lesson of empires born of vanity and greed and swiftly brought to dust.

Disaster on the Eastern front in 1943 altered the German strategy from attack to defence. It became clear that the Allies would soon try to assault Hitler's Europe. *Invasion of Europe* (April 1943) tried to guess where the Allied invasion of Europe would come. (It would, in fact, come fourteen months later.) The suggestions, pinpointed on animated maps, included Norway (too far from England), the coast of France opposite England (one of the most heavily defended German bastions), the shores near Dunkirk, the Mediterranean route from North Africa, the southern shore of Europe, defended by mountains, and the Balkan peninsula. In fact, the only part of Europe which the film did not mention as a potential landing zone was the Normandy coast, where the actual landing was to occur. Whether Legg had drawn the same geopolitical deductions as the Allied commanding staff is hard to say, but had the Nazis studied the film closely, they might have drawn inferences from what had not been said. As the film concluded its map lesson, the narration warned that not only had German confidence turned to fear but also the Germans had earned the lifelong hatred of their neighbours. Visuals of dead and suffering children (as unusual in this series as in *Canada Carries On*) were accompanied by one of the few references to a disturbing moral question of the war – will the German people be held responsible for the mass deportations and killing and wounding of children? Nothing specific was mentioned about the Jews.

A little over a year later, despite the grisly news trickling out of
Europe about what was happening to civilian Jewish deportees, Canada's information policy (and therefore film policy) as enunciated by
the Cabinet War Committee was to remain silent and keep Canada off
the hook. Public antipathy to Jews, especially in Quebec, was shared by
the government, which continued an all but closed-door policy toward
them. In 1944 it spurned the idea of providing temporary asylum for
refugee Hungarian Jewish children with a neutral catch-all remark that
barely disguised cynical rejection: 'In view of the confused situation in
Europe no further action has been taken in this matter.' Further, the
Cabinet War Committee ordered all atrocity stories held up until they
could be verified.[12] Another year would pass before 'verification' was
made. By then, the war was over, as was the immediacy of the refugee
issue. Canadian civilian morale had been spared while most of the
abducted European Jews had been murdered.

Failure of the print and film propaganda agencies to take up or to try
to turn public opinion on the question of wartime refugees casts doubts
over Grierson's 'progressive' handling of information. Long-standing
Canadian anti-Semitism, however, was a powerful force by itself, and
Canadians were not likely to be receptive to pro-Jewish refugee propaganda. Canada, like all the dominions, feared to be awash in a sea of
Jewish refugees. A wave of 'accidental immigrants,' almost two thousand Jewish males who entered Canada in 1940 as German prisoners,
was one of the few large influxes during the war. By 1945 Canada had
allowed a scant 3,500 of the refugees it had accepted during the war to
remain. One may conclude that on the refugee question the government allowed itself to be led by public opinion rather than tried to
change it. Grierson could not have been ignorant of the fact that Prime
Minister King sensed politically that there were more votes to be lost
than won if Canada took up refugees as an issue. In the generous postwar atmosphere of victory, refugees became a respectable information
theme.[13]

On the question of atrocities and mass murder, the Canadian print
and film propaganda machines were also silent. Reliable information in
late 1941 and 1942 about mass murder, about the use of poison gas and
the manufacture of soap from corpses was generally disbelieved. Mis-
reading one lesson of history, many people remembered how the First

World War propaganda had often contained atrocity stories which had been invented or exaggerated. Jews both inside and outside Europe were reluctant to believe the information about the Final Solution, as was most of the non-Jewish world. Then, too, the magnitude of a world at war seemed to eclipse the Jewish catastrophe, film of which was rare. Most nations saw it as a marginal issue before the Herculean Allied task of winning the war against Hitler.[14]

That geopolitical problem demanded imagination, especially when it came to the ticklish question of welcoming a defeated Fascist Italy back into the Allied fold. The film *The Gates of Italy*, shown in Canada just four days before the invasion of Sicily in July 1943, was to all intents and purposes a 'scoop.' But Grierson and Legg found themselves in hot water with certain segments of the public and press who, accustomed to thinking negatively of Mussolini's Fascist corporate state, mistakenly thought the Film Board was going soft on Fascism. Under pressure, the Film Board confessed that it was possible that the line between the humanist and Fascist principles was not drawn sharply enough. In fact, the film interpreted wisely Allied strategy to reintegrate Italy quickly into the democratic fold without punishment or malice. The film tried to demonstrate that forty million Italians were sick of war and short rations and had been confused by Mussolini, who had made them into an unhappy junior partner of the Axis. Italians had made a historical contribution to western civilization and were anxious to rejoin the mainstream. As victims of Mussolini and the Germans, the film concluded, the Italians had been chastened.

For three years they have seen the hated Germans returning yet again. And helpless in the hands of one invader they have been watching, waiting for the coming of another. ... And with Allied convoys heading for the gates of Italy, Italians everywhere are remembering the words spoken four centuries ago: 'Italy shall find her liberator. It is our common hope that the true banner of this people will once more be raised among the nations of the world.'

The film also made waves in the United States and did not receive wide distribution there. In Canada it caused concern in a committee in External Affairs. Grierson promised to have continuously closer contact with the committee in respect of distribution of films abroad. Though the Film Board had been enjoying a certain independence since 1939, it was clear that when it was straying into the realm of politically sensitive matters it needed to exercise great caution. And Grierson was not known for his great caution. Early in August, John R. Baldwin of the Privy Council asked if the members of the Privy Council could be invited to attend some of the private screenings at the Film Board.[15] It was probably becoming clear to the government that it should see more of the film propaganda than it had seen before. Major-General L.R. LaFleche, the minister responsible for the Film Board, asked Grierson a week later for a memo on this plan for closer contact so he could discuss it with the prime minister.[16] The furore all died down in a month, but Grierson had unsettled his superiors once again. They wanted to keep an eye on him.

The Fighting Dutch (December 1943) was a much less powerful statement of strategic goals. It contented itself with describing how German occupation of the Netherlands had turned the peaceful Dutch into a fighting force committed to return with the Allies to occupy their homeland. Legg also showed the geopolitical importance of the old Dutch empire of the East Indies, whose staples were now coveted by the envious and probing Japanese eye. The film did not speculate what would happen to the postwar East Indies once the Japanese were expelled.

When the Allied invasion occurred in June 1944, Legg's uncanny timing ability was demonstrated: just three days after the invasion had begun, *Zero Hour – The Story of the Invasion* (July 1944) appeared in the United States and Canada. The film's premise was that Germany could never hold its conquered territories. As a land power, it could not follow up its invasions with amphibious warfare. The British, who had had the greatest amphibious empire of all, had used the first three years of the war to perfect techniques of amphibious assault. The final result depended of course on the common infantryman who understood Napoleon's maxim, 'March separately, strike together.' The film had plenty of shot and shell, while its emphasis on the Allied strategy of 'attacking the enemy's main basket' made it didactic and useful in explaining geopolitics. It ended hopefully, promising that from their dugouts the enemy's long-sheltered troops must venture out to do battle. The beachheads of Europe were but the beginning – the main job was yet to come.

Spotlight on the Balkans (December 1945) was another exercise in geopolitics focusing on how the six Balkan states had always been a storm centre of history. The editing in this film was unusually rough and even fragmented. Descriptions of the Balkan states were followed by a geopolitical lesson that asserted how important they were to contemporary Britain because of their proximity to the Suez Canal; they were also important to Russia, which desired a warm-water port and closer ties to Turkey. The task of rebuilding the Balkans, the film emphasized, was a gigantic endeavour. Then it jumped to the conclusion that all eyes were turning to Czechoslovakia as an example of a state to emulate, for 'it shows what can be done if you build for the future.' The final stirring words allegedly came from 'a great Balkan statesman: "You have nothing in the past, for history belongs to kings and nobles who were once your masters. You have nothing in the past. Yours is the *future!*"' The unevenness and lack of centre of the film can be explained by the fact that it had become a political football, and was censored and cut twice. We shall discuss it in more detail later (p. 211).

WOMEN AND WORKERS

In the fall of 1942 Grierson met with representatives from the Department of National War Services, the Department of Munitions and Supply, and the National Selective Service. The discussions indicated the urgent need for a large-scale educational campaign among those employed in war industries. The rationale for the films was to create a deeper understanding of civic responsibilities and to secure a readier participation by individuals in the common national effort.[17] There would follow a number of films on women and labour in response to these discussions and a progressive note was sounded in each. *Wings on Her Shoulder* (February 1943) was like *Canada Carries On* films of the same genre. This film demonstrated how important the Women's Division of the RAF was to the air offensive. It portrayed women in training, 'shaking off the leisure of civilian life, ... asking no feminine favours' and emerging as 'polished professionals.' The narration then indicated how this change in women's roles had generated an insistence for equal opportunity in a cooperative life. 'They will tell you that in the satisfaction of cooperative efforts and in the spirit of cooperative life that inevitably goes with it, they have found an answer to a long-felt demand – the demand for direct participation in the shaping of their nation's destiny.' The now-familiar statement about the cooperative world to come followed this and brought the film to its climax. Women were in the front line with Canadian squadrons in critical support positions overseas. 'Thus are the women of Canada's Air Force the women who wear wings on their shoulders that men may fly.' If contemporary feminists sense omissions and patronizing in the film, one must at least acknowledge that *The World in Action* expressed a positive attitude to working women and was conditioning audiences to become accustomed to new and permanent women's roles in the working world.[18]

The Labour Front (October 1943) dealt ostensibly with the world of working men and women. Manpower shortages, caused by wartime urgencies, had ushered in a new age of full employment. Women needed to be relieved of domestic chores and provided with better transportation and housing; labour-management committees were an innovation on the domestic scene, a harbinger of a better era to come in labour-management relations; Allied production was being boosted and community action was opening a new career to many women. 'All along the labour front,' the narration asserted, 'the realization is dawning that of all the revolutions wrought by war, none has been so significant or irrevocable as that which has swept away the scourge of unemployment and opened the floodgates of human energy that are the working capital of the people.' To a final visual of a dam's sluice-gates being opened and water surging out, the narration claimed that all of this demonstrated how men and women were releasing the floodgates of victory. (The same visual analogy would be used the next month in the *Canada Carries On* film *Tomorrow's World*.) Its message was based on more than blind optimism, since by this time in the war there was military certainty that the Allies would crush the Nazi foe. There was also a feeling (at least in Grierson's and Legg's minds) that, in a progressive postwar era, capital and labour, and perhaps even capitalism and socialism, could live side by side in peace and prosperity.

SHOT AND SHELL, WAR GAMES AND FILLERS

There are four 'shot and shell' films which deserve brief mention. *Corvette Port Arthur* (May 1943) was made by the well-known Dutch progressive documentary filmmaker, Joris Ivens. Grierson was glad to get Ivens, whose technical skills he thought would give a boost to the young Canadian filmmakers. The film demonstrated how important the corvettes were in keeping the convoys safe. Shots from a convoy captains' briefing were followed by an exciting, well-paced staged encounter with and sinking of an enemy U-boat by a Canadian corvette. After Ivens had been working for some time, Grierson brought the reluctant director of Royal Canadian Navy security to Ottawa to show some rushes which happened to include that officer. The promise of fame and publicity was sufficient incentive to the officer to give the National Film Board whatever men and ships it wanted. Unfortunately, the officer did not know the difference between rushes and the edited final print, from which the sequence would be eliminated. Later, however, the officer would receive an 8 by 10 glossy print of himself from the excised material, signed by the film commissioner. Grierson would have thought this wily stratagem not at all irregular but part of a day's work in terms of getting the job done.[19]

Letter from Overseas (July 1943) began by showing Canadian troops and a ridiculous training item on the platoon's mobile washing machine in England. It next had Canadians preparing for 'a special task' in August 1942 – Dieppe. Visuals of carefully edited German battle footage intercut with stock shots of Canadian manoeuvres on the Scottish coast were accompanied by a claim that the Canadians had achieved their objectives the year before. The narrator quoted some unnamed soldiers: 'And when we sailed away we left the littered beaches to remind the Germans that we had punched one hole in Hitler's fortress and that it wouldn't be the last.' Considering that the Canadians at Dieppe suffered a casualty or captured rate of more than 57 per cent, this sequence was brazenly misleading the audiences. Explanations of the truth about Dieppe would be decades in coming. The National Film Board had cooperated with Associated Screen News to produce a newsreel item in September 1942 headlining the 'Return to Canada of Heroes of the Dieppe Raid,' but remained mute at the time because the whole truth about Dieppe might have triggered a widespread collapse of public morale. Propaganda was supposed to build the faith, not undermine it. The press across the country cooperated in the cover-up. Sample headlines from 15 to 22 August read, 'Dieppe Raid a Second Front Dress Rehearsal,' 'Canada Rolls Drums of Death for Hitler,' 'The Dagger's Thrust,' and 'Young Canadians Rank with Their Fathers.'[20] *Letter from Overseas* concluded 'Back in Britain Again,' and showed

This shot of Canadians landing at Dieppe was in fact old stock footage of manoeuvres on the Scottish coast. (NFB)

The NFB withheld this captured German footage showing the true picture of what had happened at Dieppe. A brave narration concluded, 'We had punched one hole in Hitler's fortress and it wouldn't be the last!' (NFB)

Dutch documentary filmmaker Joris Ivens (right) directs a sequence from *Action Stations* (1943). A shortened version, *Corvette Port Arthur*, appeared in theatres. Weeks later the corvette engaged and sank an Italian submarine in the Mediterranean. (NFB)

shots of tanks and troops on manoeuvres. It was obvious that the filmmakers had no qualms about ignoring the military debacle and kept looking straight ahead until the military tide turned favourable.[21]

The previously mentioned *Zero Hour – The Story of the Invasion* (June 1944) offered plenty of shot and shell and showed the Allied forces attacking Europe. Six months later, *V-1*, adapted by the Film Board from the British Ministry of Information film, demonstrated the appalling devastation visited upon England for three months by the flying bombs. Despite the depressing scenes of ravaged Britain, the narration affirmed that the British could endure because their sons and daughters were the future of that nation.

In all, the four *World in Action* films of shot and shell were exceptions to the regular series which attempted the 'world theme message' and inspiration wherever possible. Happily there were only three series films depicting training or playing at war. They must have seemed like little more than 'fill' at the time. *Paratroops* (November 1942) gave a short history of paratroops and portrayed contemporary rigours of training for that service; the above-mentioned *Letter from Overseas* was mostly a record of Canadian preparations for combat, with the Dieppe raid slipped in about one-third through. Finally, *War Birds* (November 1943) described training and using carrier pigeons to help locate downed pilots and staged a rescue.

There were four non-National Film Board productions which were included as 'fillers' in the *World in Action* series and were not part of the master plan as conceived by Grierson and Legg. *New Soldiers Are Tough* was a British Ministry of Information film which staged a hunter-hunted story of a British and German soldier, with a predictable outcome for the British Tommy; *Five Men of Australia*, edited by Tom Daly to half its original length, portrayed in story form how that country's men were training and fighting in the global conflict; *A Harbour Goes to France* (May 1945) demonstrated the Allied use of floating piers in military operations, and *Dover's Cliffs* (December 1942), produced by the British Army Film Unit and narrated by Edward R. Murrow, was an optimistic look at a Britain prepared to strike back at Europe. As part of the stiff-upper-lip syndrome of the day, the audience was supposed to feel confidence when it heard the British warn, 'Look out Jerry, here we come!'

INTERNATIONALISM FOR A BRAVE NEW WORLD

In its first months, the *World in Action* had made a broad and successful impact upon North American audiences as well as in Britain where
it was called *Front of Action*. Positive press responses from various
United States newspapers were read into the minutes of the Film
Board's monthly meeting in November 1942. A typical review might
read, 'Films of the Grierson type contain no whimsy, no soft tones and
little, if any, make believe. They bring a new punch to the screen that
only the free minds of free people can absorb.'[22] It became apparent that
the series' screen journalism was the kind of propaganda that responded to a perceived need of the audiences. It will be recalled that
Grierson's own idealistic assessment was that he and Legg were embarked on a propaganda crusade whose aim was the greatest mobilization of the public imagination since the churches lost their grip. His grip
on that imagination tightened when he became general manager of the
Wartime Information Board in January 1943. He began thinking of the
possibilities of planning groups of films on current public questions to
facilitate coordination of common programmes.

Inspirational propaganda would be applied to mundane issues like
youth problems, manpower, work power, morale, and conservation
(mainly for *Canada Carries On*), while a series of eight films was
planned for the far-reaching and politically significant postwar international world. These eight films would follow a theme of the 'brave
new world' to come and were significant for their attempt to shape
public consciousness to expect a postwar internationalism without
defining it in any precise detail. The films came very close to encroach-
ing on Prime Minister King's jealously guarded initiatives in foreign
policy. He either was not aware of them (they appeared sporadically
from 1943) or left Grierson alone to get on with his national morale-
building propaganda. In the final analysis, King did not like them.

Battle Is Their Birthright (March 1943) began as a film which was
dedicated to the youth of the world who were shaping the destiny of
this century. Canadian youth were portrayed at basic military training,
'getting ready for a life of discipline, ready for the responsibilities of a
new age, the responsibilities of leadership.' Visuals showed how Japan
and Germany had prepared their youth for war and aggression before
1939. In Russia, the leaders of the Soviet Union had encouraged youth

to contribute to their communities, seeking not a greater share of production, but a greater production to share. In China too youths were shown seeking new knowledge in anticipation of a brighter future. Canada's children were next portrayed on salvage drives, picking vegetables, repairing fish nets, and serving their communities. The narration asserted, 'Where there is a will to action there is no limit to achievement.' The film concluded that now young men were pledging their lives to the service of the people and that 'beyond the devastation they must create in the image of youth itself, another and braver world.'

The film had attached to it a three-minute discussion trailer entitled *Any Questions?*, showing four panellists questioning the film's premises. One asked, 'Will people who come back from active service be committed to collective action?' Another wondered, 'Is the film itself not an exact replica of our vague ideas?' A third panellist insisted that postwar Canada must not struggle for a nationalist society but a better society in which the people dedicated themselves to a cause like Canada and the common people. 'All this begins with education itself,' asserted the fourth. The trailer ended with one anxious individual pronouncing that the whole problem of Canada's future had to be tackled before the war was over. 'One step at a time,' was the final indefinite response.

The film's propaganda message had been plain enough – Japan and Germany would be defeated while Russia's cooperative society, encouraging service to the community, shared a common goal with Canada. The internationalist slant of the film was vague enough to escape direct sanction. Dedication to Canada and the common people should have raised no eyebrows – yet the thrust of all this was to stress internationalism at the expense of nationalism.

One of the strongest films in the *World in Action* series and probably the most personally satisfying effort of Grierson and Legg's wartime career was finished early in 1943. It was a film about the very battle of words and images the propagandists were fighting, the psychological war of propaganda to win the hearts and minds of a world in upheaval. Provisionally titled *Triumph of the Will*, then *Not the Gates of Hell*, Grierson and Legg finally called it *The War for Men's Minds*. Originally forty-three minutes long, it was intended for the leaders and officials of the day who would be responsible for setting the policies of the postwar world. In an obvious reflection of the Grierson propaganda mission, it anticipated that government would play a significant role in providing information permanently through the media. The now-familiar internationalist message was a secondary theme.

Grierson was especially glad that it had such a positive influence on the prime minister in February 1943. Then again, King could only have been pleased to have been linked to Roosevelt as being one of the two voices of North American leadership, despite the fact that the Canadian army, idle so long in Britain, was not yet engaged in full-scale combat. Grierson also planned a private cabinet screening and wrote about it to his old mentor Sir Stephen Tallents, in 1943:

... Legg and I recently did a piece on our political faith which excited him [the prime minister] a great deal, and he was more than generous about it. He has already seen it twice and is sending a personal copy to Roosevelt. It's a 45 minute film, a film on the Lincoln theme: 'When the common people rise to find their liberty, not the gates of Hell will prevail against them.' For once we wear our heart on our sleeve and it's as near Goya, in film, over the last passage, as makes no matter. ... It's one of these luxury films, so personally satisfying – for the moment – that it does not seem to matter whether it's shown or not. But there is at the same time the likelihood that it will command a good deal of attention in the States as a fiercer statement of the progressive democratic outlook than any government source has publicly attempted. I can't think of what the reactionaries will say, but I imagine that they will stumble into all sorts of healthy trouble over it. ...[23]

The film was shortened by half for the *World in Action* series and released in June. Its emphasis on propaganda was diminished while the internationalist message could have come from a church sermon. It emphasized that the strength of the Allied cause was its commitment to human brotherhood; in the new world order the people would come first, before all. The Allied armies, the narration preached, being citizen's armies, had a purpose – that the meek shall inherit the earth. There is a new spirit of universal comradeship, it continued, forgetting the call for rights and remembering the spirit of service. Standing on the threshold of their own century, it vaunted, the people have a new spirit, and their eyes are fixed on the world of tomorrow.

Yesterday we were afraid that the propaganda of Fascism might infect us with its philosophy of despair. Today, we fear no more. For the people are moving forward with their might and power; no force, no trickery, deceit or violence can stop them now. And if we of the new world prove to our comrades in arms in every land that we fight with them in spirit as in combat, then indeed we shall have won our struggle for men's minds and we shall see the separate anthems of the nations become the single united marching song of all mankind.

The film now became messianic in its narration as it cut rapidly to scenes of soldiers and people the world over:

All previous sufferings will be seen as the birth pangs of a new age, as triumphant proof of the strength of the human spirit, the very strength upon which tomorrow's world will rest. ... Standing on the threshold of a new world, this, the people's century, the peoples are marvelling at the bravery of men faced with horrors beyond belief. And in these men, these who can laugh in the face of death, they perceive not strangers but brothers, fathers, sons. ... The people of the earth march forward into their new age, march forward in the certainty that the gates of hell cannot prevail against them.

The film was a perfect crystallization of Grierson's philosophy of propaganda. It was convincing too. *The War for Men's Minds* exposed Nazi propaganda for its poisonous lesson that might is right. The film extracted shots from Leni Riefenstahl's *Triumph of the Will* which it identified as Hitler's speeches on propaganda. Germany's spiritual defeat had already occurred in the face of the Allies' commitment to a world formed on the Four Freedoms. The message, so smoothly delivered in this film, extolled the Allied cause. As for its content, among the Allies few seemed to want to take issue with the playing down of personal rights and the call for service to the community. As a whole, the propaganda seemed acceptable in a general context, though in fact it militated against the spirit of fierce individualism which lay at the core of North American belief. But few would refuse to rally behind selfless generalities during world crisis.

The next 'brave new world' number, *Global Air Routes* (April 1944), was much quieter in tone and dealt with the necessity of establishing international understanding and agreements about global air routes in the postwar world. Polar flights would become a peacetime phenomenon and the cooperation of the United States, Canada, Britain, and Russia was essential in that endeavour. As the narration stated, 'And so, our whole conception of the world we live in has changed,' a flat map of the world became animated, cut, and reassembled as a globe. The last words reiterated the need for international cooperation to organize it: 'Along the global air routes of tomorrow lies a great adventure of peace.' Tom Daly had said that the idea for this film came from the prime minister's office and Legg followed through with the film. This kind of geopolitical thought was obviously on many minds. A month later one of King's post-hostilities advisers, perhaps anticipating the real world to come, pointed out that the polar projection map made it clear that 'Canada is the air highway and the land route for attack on the United States either from the east or west. ...'[24]

Inside France in September had a specific purpose in its brave new world theme: to convince public opinion to welcome France back into the fold of the Allied cause and to explain why, historically, France had succumbed to 'a clique of feudal-minded men' who had signed away the country. The narration asserted that France had been divided before the Nazi invasion; but the Allied response to Nazi aggression had led at least one Frenchman to say, 'Better to live free in ruins than with a tyrant in the house.' This attitude confirmed the belief that France would always be a vital link in the defence of the western world. The film ended with strains of the *Marseillaise*, 'which sends forth to France its thrilling battle cry of human hope.'

The coming peace and future of Britain were the subjects of the sobering *John Bull's Own Island* in April 1945. The film was more realistic than idealistic in its anticipation of Britain facing the hard realities of a changing world. Historically the industrial might of Britain had rested on industrialization, investment, and building in far-off lands. But the effects of six years of war were such that Britain had lost much of its capital investment overseas. There was doubt that Britain would regain the lost export markets and the narration supposed that the government might have to take interest in industrial and commercial policies in the postwar world. A statement followed that government and industry might work with labour to make a better world, especially with the promise of the Beveridge Report to provide more social service to more people. In a peculiar way the film was almost anticipating the rise to power of a Labour government, an event which was but a few months away. The film concluded optimistically that the British were a determined people who would rise to re-establish their overseas trade. Improvisation would work until Britain was able to rebuild. The narration ended with optimistic words accompanying visuals of workaday Britain unashamedly interspersed with shots from the classic 1930s documentary, *Industrial Britain*: 'They have seen dark days before. Indeed they seem to see a little better on a cloudy day and in the storm of calamity they have a secret figure and a pulse like a cannon.'

The essence of the postwar international dream was spelled out in the May 1945 issue, *Now – The Peace*, a film requested by the US State Department on the future of the new international peace organization. Using historical footage, the film tried to explain the lessons of history and answer the question why the peace of the First World War had failed. The League of Nations' only weapon had been words. (Visuals of bombings and burning cities followed.) Now collective security would not fail again. 'The foundations of tomorrow's peace will rest upon preventative military power. ... Such are the stern realities of history.' There followed an explanation of the structure of the new United Nations Organization. Then, reminiscent of the frequent allusions to Russia throughout the series, the narration continued, 'In tomorrow's world, there cannot be prosperity for one unless there is prosperity for all.' The film then juxtaposed shots of starving people with intensive agricultural activity. It turned to a theme anticipating a postwar world of collective action and stated that two-thirds of the human race has always lived on the verge of starvation, while in the postwar world there was a plan to pool the world's land so that production would be best suited to particular lands. There were plans too for an international bank to enable nations to buy food. The hopefulness of the film was reflective of Grierson's and Legg's optimism and Canada's commitment to a global security organization as the war was drawing to a close. The Department of External Affairs cooperated closely with the Film Board on this production.

It might seem incongruous, but the discussion trailer (for non-theatrical audiences) which followed the film, called *Getting the Most Out of a Film*, challenged this optimism realistically and took issue with the film's assertions. Different people in a 'sample' audience arose to express doubts and fears. One said a third world war would mean world destruction; another feared that if such a catastrophe happened, Canada would be in the centre of it. The moderator tried to explain how the structure of the United Nations was more realistic than that of the League and quoted from the world charter. Another member stated bluntly that the problem of war was an economic one and that wars were made in sales offices and counting houses. Canada was beginning to think internationally, said another, but he was reminded by someone else that the world charter would do nothing to solve domestic issues. Another critic complained that labour had not yet been consulted by the international body. With all these criticisms brought out after the film, the moderator turned to the camera and said, 'There are many more angles to it than we have had time to suggest, but you can carry on the discussion from here.' What was remarkable about this example of a 'brave new world' film was the filmmakers' willingness to provoke audience response, negative as well as positive, in the belief that such a discussion was at the very least a healthy exercise in democracy. It could be argued too that the propagandists felt so sure of their cause that critical observation could not shake the truth.

Shortly after this film, there appeared *Food – Secret of the Peace*, which dealt with the phenomenon of food scarcity in Europe while reiterating the brave new world theme. The narration explained that war-torn Europe could not feed itself because of the collapse of its transportation network. The United States and Canada could produce the food for Europe, it continued, and their engineers were already helping to repair the severed distribution arteries. The internationalist message came through strongly in the film's conclusion: 'For so closely are fates of nations bound together in these crucial times that only with the friendship of a new Europe, strong and hopeful once again, can we build a new world, strong in peaceful purposes. This new Europe of tomorrow is part of our world today.'

Just how close to official policy was the brave new world theme? Where Grierson had been warned off specificity in his reconstruction ideas in 1943, by 1945 Canada emphasized officially the international aspect of much reconstruction planning. Canada was to support international arrangements independently to ensure a lasting peace. Prime Minister King, as secretary of state for external affairs, insisted on taking virtually all initiative in foreign policy. What Grierson and Legg achieved was to state in the most general terms the international aspects of that policy. The great enthusiasm King expressed for *The*

'... Only with the friendship of a new Europe, strong and hopeful once again, can we build a new world, strong in peaceful purposes' were the concluding words of this 1945 theatrical issue. (NFB)

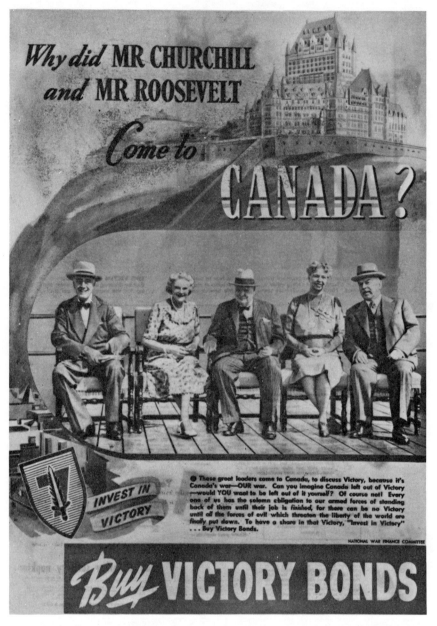

Prime Minister King was on the outside for most of the meetings at both Quebec Conferences. This picture's symbolic unity made both good political and victory bond propaganda. (PAC 93606)

Prime Minister King poses with President Roosevelt, happy to appear to share the limelight at the Quebec Conference. (No date) (PAC 130025)

War for Men's Minds may have convinced the film commissioner that he was making headway in his crusade and was winning important converts to the concept of permanent government propaganda. King was probably more impressed with Grierson's portrayal of him on an equal level with Roosevelt than with any notion of subscribing to the film's philosophy of propaganda.

Canada's policies on postwar international organization were designed principally by Hume Wrong. Lester Pearson, in Washington from 1942 to 1946, was the principal agent in the attempt to convince the Great Powers of their merit. The 'international' themes in Film Board propaganda were not far from Pearson's ardent and compelling support of collective security as the basis for the postwar international order.[25] External Affairs may not have been following consistently Grierson's propaganda activities, but Pearson sat on the directorate of the National Film Board from January 1942 until December 1943; thus Grierson could not have been out of touch with the direction in which External Affairs was developing its policies. The board's propaganda tended more to complement than contradict those policies. King's own inclination was to adopt a 'middle of the road policy' between extreme nationalism and exaggerated internationalism. Canada must support international arrangements independently to ensure lasting peace, he thought. The internationalist line stressed that Canada's position was that of a 'great mediator' between the United States and Britain on the one hand and then briefly, in the uncertain months following the war, between those Allies and the Soviet Union. The former position seemed hollow in light of King's exclusion from both Quebec City conferences and the latter proved impractical as Truman marched the English-speaking world into the cold war. Where Film Board propaganda began getting into stickiness was in its enunciation of a messianic internationalist line predicting a new world order without national rivalries. There were a few films which treated the Soviet Union positively and a few references in others to anti-imperialist sentiments, referring to Britain. The King government became discomfited, then annoyed, and finally hostile to the Film Board for dabbling in foreign affairs.

TO RUSSIA WITH LOVE

The theme of international brotherhood came through subtly though effectively in the two *World in Action* releases devoted to the Soviet

Union. Both films' oversimplification was likely intentional; rose-coloured glasses were necessary to accept the former atheist enemy as a lifelong friend. The very first *World in Action* issue, *Our Russian Ally*, also entitled *Inside Fighting Russia* (April 1942) was ostensibly a demonstration of the indomitable inner spirit of Russia's peoples. By interpreting favourably 'young and vigorous Russia' and by omitting the word 'communism,' the film attempted to promote toleration of the Russian system and the new Russian ally. Archival footage of Lenin accompanied the statement that he replaced the life of poverty under the tsar and made Russia's watchword 'All for one, one for all.' The film's only recognizable Marxist phrase, 'From each according to his ability, to each according to his needs,' was stated in reference to the nation's five-year plans and without mention of Marx. In the only reference to socialism, the narration maintained that Soviet leaders made a *Blitzkrieg* against ignorance, for it was the children who were to become the rulers of a new socialist state.

The Soviet system was portrayed concisely, if too simply: 'Workers struggle now not for a greater share of the production but for a greater production in which to share.' Legg's narration pronounced Russia's new message of hope to Europe: 'Our task is to pull poverty and darkness and slavery out by the roots. Herein lies our strength.' The film paid homage to Russia's people and was commendable in its positive portrayal of women, who, it declared, 'talk on equal terms with men and officers and in the factories.' The message of the film was summarized in its final reference to Russia's 'Red Badge of Courage,' a visual montage of Russians hard at work in all walks of life:

... Russia knows that her true warpower lies not alone in arms and equipment but in the *inner* spirit of her peoples. And today, across the vast spaces of steppe and tundra the men and women of the new Russia are reading the message which the Red Star, shining from the smoky windows of giant munitions plants sends forth into the night: 'We are strong because we have the faith.'

Legg has admitted that perhaps the conclusion was naïve, for it did give opposition critics in Parliament cause to decry Film Board propaganda as communist. He has explained his position in geopolitical terms:

Symbolic of the hope for continued friendship in *Tomorrow's World* (1943), this American soldier blots out the US insignia and paints the Red Star over it as a Russian soldier watches. (PAC 129920)

'The new Russia sent a message of hope ... one for all, and all for one,' stated the narration in *Our Northern Neighbour* (1944). The NFB avoided the word 'communist' as it attempted to link the average Russian and Canadian citizens. (NFB)

Inside Fighting Russia (1943) became a political football when Legg's narration referred to the message of the Red Star which men and women there were reading: 'We are strong because we have the faith.' The film was not shown in the US because it was considered 'communist propaganda.' (PAC 130050)

A female work force from *Inside Fighting Russia*. (PAC 130037)

... One has to remember at that time that Russia was an ally and an ally of enormous importance in holding the main German forces for several years from Western Europe and I think there was a good deal of cause to be friendly to Russia ... we might not approve of their politics, but we approved of their soldiery. We didn't really know about the terror, the Stalinist terror, and though it didn't negate the whole film by any means, I think if you look at it now I think you'll find that the end looked rather naïve.[26]

Inside Fighting Russia was withheld from distribution in the United States by United Artists. They said it was 'communist propaganda.' They were pressured to reconsider and at last released it to one lesser-run New York theatre for a week or so. It was not distributed elsewhere.[27] When the film was shown to the Soviet and Chinese ambassadors in London, they expressed great satisfaction. High Commissioner Massey obviously had no problem, for he commented that he felt the film 'reflected great credit' to the National Film Board. Such conflicting responses should have been adequate warning to Grierson and Legg to be cautious about Russian themes. A similar effort in 1944 would bring controversy too.

The message about the Russian people's strong inner spirit occurred again in a December 1943 release in the *Canada Carries On* series, *Look to the North*. The point which was reiterated in these films was how much the average Russian citizen was like the average Canadian. In the January 1944 *World in Action* issue, *Our Northern Neighbour*, a new dimension was added, propagandizing for an effective and long-lasting peace to come. It would be nearly fifteen years later that the phrase 'peaceful coexistence' would enter international jargon, but the core of its meaning was already being enunciated. The purpose of this film was made clear as the narration explained that the United States and Canada were pondering their future relationship with the 'powerful and mysterious' Soviet Union:

... And now, with the Red Armies' offensive everywhere approaching their titanic climax, the western democracies are realizing that the effectiveness of the peace will greatly depend on how well they grasp the viewpoint of the Kremlin, on how well they understand the background and the memories of past events that live in the minds of those who guided the Soviet state through its early contacts with the outside world.

In a skilful adoption of footage from Eisenstein's *October* and other Russian newsreel or actuality footage, the film explained with great sympathy the historical evolution of modern Russia. Its strong pro-Russian bias was evident in its interpretation of Soviet home and foreign politics. The Comintern, it was said, openly supported working people everywhere 'so that any nation willing to make war on Russia will be prevented from doing so by its citizens.' To the revolutionary, Trotsky, were attributed the words, 'We must provoke world revolution or we are doomed,' and then the commentary compared him with Joseph Stalin. 'But now there spoke a quieter voice, Joseph Stalin – the man of steel.' Stalin's plan was to build a pattern of socialism for all the world to see. 'And for Trotsky, all that remained was the leisure to contemplate in exile his shattered dream of world revolution fomented by his own conception of the Comintern.' Here visuals portrayed Trotsky in exile among some ancient ruins, looking into the sun with his hand shading his eyes.

The film's treatment of Russian foreign policy in the thirties was oriented to an identifiably leftist position and also to a geopolitical viewpoint. Norman McLaren's cleverly animated 'wook' map showed how it would have felt to be a Russian with German expansion coming so frighteningly close to home. The narration stated that Russia joined the League of Nations hoping it could prevent an attack by Germany. However, Russia had been purposely excluded from the discussions of the democracies and fascist powers in that decade. And the policy of appeasement made it appear as though fascist aggression to the East was being countenanced. Hence the German-Soviet non-aggression pact counteracted the 'enemy' marching east and allowed Russia to occupy lands to its west to make its frontiers secure. This reasonable explanation, accompanied by appropriate newsreel shots, certainly must have been an eye-opener to audiences long accustomed to seeing the voracious Russian bear everywhere. But its gross oversimplification of internal Soviet politics must have been difficult for critics to swallow despite its avowed attempt to create a postwar world free from international rivalry. To quote the film's optimistic conclusion:

But now as the dawn of a new era breaks across vast Russia, a new figure is coming forward on the stage of world affairs – the Soviet citizen. For the common man of Russia is thinking hard and soberly of what awaits *him* when

victory is won. He is thinking first of the years of labour he will spend rebuilding the appalling devastation visited on his land. But he is thinking too of the
giant resources that lie ready for the task, resources which the efforts of government and people have increased ninefold in less than thirty years. He is
thinking of the contrast between a listless Russia of bygone times and the
youthful forward-looking Russia of today, a Russia that endured the ordeals of
war because of its people's faith in the future of their nation. ... He is thinking
of what that future holds for himself and for his children, of a promise of
ultimate freedom and good living which he believes now at last is to be
fulfilled. For all around he sees the signs that the State is relaxing the discipline
of the lean years that have passed, opening the way to a brighter world and a
broader view of life.

Today the Soviet citizen knows that his labour and his valour have placed
his nation among the great powers of this earth. ... And as together with our
Russian neighbours, we say, as it was said at Teheran, 'We seek the collaboration of all nations, large and small, for the elimination of tyranny and slavery,
oppression and intolerance.' We met in determination, we march on, friends, in
fact, in spirit and in purpose.

Such heady optimism was followed immediately by the non-theatrical discussion trailer, entitled Getting the Most Out of a Film. The moderator, addressing a 'typical' audience, claimed that Canadians had
much to learn about the Soviet Union in order to diminish the chances
of a World War III. Stanley Hawes, who directed some seventeen
discussion trailers in all, arranged for the recording of a series of un-
scripted but rehearsed questions (with no answers) which were supposed to stimulate audience discussion. The questions were specific,
though uncritical of the film, and included such subjects as Russia's
five-year plan, women and maternity benefits, why unions must exist,
and common Russian-Canadian interest in northern development. The
moderator replied that he would not try to answer any of the questions;
rather, 'If you want to remember the film and get something out of it
you must discuss it yourselves.' He then referred the audience to literature supposed to accompany the screening of the film: Films for Freedom was an educational sheet prepared by the Workers' Educational
Association; Canada and the USSR was published by Canadian Affairs
(whose editor, hired by Grierson, was named in 1945 as an agent for
Russian intelligence); and Organized Labour in the Soviet Union was a

book published by the National Council of American-Soviet Friendship.

If audiences were encouraged to react to this film, it is difficult to know just how it struck them. The Department of External Affairs approved it, with or without the trailer, though members of the board's directorate had not seen it by February 1944. In the minds of the parliamentary opposition, the Film Board was perceived as drifting onto dangerous political seas. Opposition MP A.R. Adamson attacked the board in March 1944 and undoubtedly caused the government discomfort by his charge: 'There has been a growing suspicion that the film board has become a propagandist for a type of socialist and foreign philosophy,' he began. 'Heretofore it was merely an instrument of propaganda for the government.' He complained that he opposed a national instrument of government that was 'obviously putting out Soviet propaganda.'[28] It is possible that this negative response was linked directly to the fact that the Quebec Censor Board held the film up, believing that it was strongly pro-communist in its interpretation of Russian history.

Major-General LaFleche, the minister responsible for the board, tried to defend his agency for showing the situation as it actually existed. He claimed defensively in the same debate that the sixty-odd rural circuits were not being used for government propaganda. He then tried to take the offensive by claiming that there were always people who felt it necessary 'to be fearing this or that.' He said that Canadians were capable of thinking and dealing with matters themselves and warranted having the member's confidence. But the intractable Adamson concluded, 'I still do not think it is the duty of a government body to put out films concerning the foreign policy of any country.'[29] The Privy Council discussed the Adamson complaint, supported LaFleche, and noted both that members of the House could see films on Tuesday and Thursday nights and that members of Parliament tended to defend the Film Board.[30] Grierson was flippant about the criticism. In a letter to a newspaper friend he remarked that the principal complaint came from the Soviet legation in Ottawa. He had expected it. 'They do not hold my particular form of objectivity in veneration any more than they like my memory of Dostoevsky,' he wrote lightheartedly.[31]

But the *World in Action* series, in its attempt to prepare audiences for international brotherhood, was straying into a realm of practical politi-

In 1944 Prime Minister King ordered *Balkan Powderkeg* withdrawn because of its anti-British bias. A year later it raised opposition in Parliament, was withdrawn again, stripped of its British references and this shot, and released as *Spotlight on the Balkans*. King grew annoyed with Grierson. (NFB)

The depressing European military picture was not hidden from audiences in *This Is Blitz* (1942). Citizen fighters, British and Russian, would fight for every inch of their homeland, insisted the brave conclusion. (PAC 130026)

A citizen points out his tormentor in *This Is Blitz*. The image and narration reinforced a general sense that there would one day be a reckoning for this war. (PAC 130027)

Mussolini's posturing could be turned against him with some clever NFB commentary and an assertion that he had confused Italians and made them an unhappy junior partner in the Axis. *Gates of Italy* (1943) (PAC 130046)

cal orientation which could cost the government politically. Despite his vow to dodge political labels and ideological positions, Film Board commissioner Grierson was being a bit too careless and glib in his own defence. He explained to another newspaper friend how he maintained his precarious balancing act of being a government propagandist and one who was influenced by the significance of Marxism:

Yes, I allow the significance of Marxism – deeply – and I also allow the significance of Alyosha and of Dostoevsky. [CCF parliamentary leader M.J.] Coldwell asked me plump one day what my politics were. I said I stood one inch to the left of the Liberal party in power and would stand one inch to the left of a C.C.F. party in power – which would be easy – and would hope for an inch to the good even if a Progressive Conservative party were in power.[32]

The problem was that despite his caution in keeping within the realm of government sanction, he was making waves and even enemies. There would be no more *World in Action* films on Russia, but the damage had been done. In the attempt to be progressive and to keep Russia as a postwar ally, the National Film Board's propaganda had become both political and a political football.

Grierson was not alone in left field. King had been committed to a policy of developing publicity as a means of avoiding dependence on force in the postwar world since the conclusion of the November 1943 Moscow Declaration. The prime minister wanted to see machinery developed for 'letting in the light' to the nations concerned. Such machinery could provide for the formation of an intelligent public opinion and a means of impartial investigation of existing wrongs.[33] Grierson and Legg's sympathetic treatment of the Soviet Union surely was in line with King's policy. In 1944–5, some eighteen Film Board films were circulating in Moscow through the Canadian embassy, including a one-hour theatrical entitled *This Is Canada* which the Soviets had requested be made. It showed how Canadians lived, Canada in war, and the potential for trade, industry, agriculture, and air transport.[34] Obviously the trusting sympathetic approach was doing Canada no harm in Moscow. The damage was occurring in parochial Canada.

SITTING ON A POWDERKEG

The *World in Action* may indeed have been moving toward daring and innovative screen journalism as the postwar world was beginning to take shape. But the political implications of Grierson and Legg's propaganda as it applied to foreign affairs roused the prime minister at last. The January 1945 film *Balkan Powderkeg* went an inch too far into the realm of foreign affairs, the prime minister's own special domain.

It was feared that the film was fraught with considerable consequence for Canada's wartime relationship with Britain because in dealing with the historical background of the troubled Balkan peninsula, it portrayed Britain in an unfavourable light. That fall, the prime minister had been hard pressed by Churchill to commit the Canadian Corps in an operation against the coast of Yugoslavia. Churchill planned this action in spite of the fact that he was still stinging from criticism, especially from the United States, of the British forces' recent intervention to prevent the Greek Communist ELAS army from seizing control of Greece. King's ever-cautious position had been that Canadian troops would not be employed outside of Italy without the Canadian government's concurrence. To make that event unlikely, he had given a public assurance in Commons on 6 December that his government had 'no wish to interfere in the internal affairs of liberated countries where that can possibly be avoided.' Churchill was furious with King for these remarks and noted frostily in a telegram that Canada's reaction was a 'marked reflection on our [British] credit and honour.'[35] It was at this inopportune moment that *Balkan Powderkeg*, with its anti-British innuendo, was about to be released.

Lester Pearson, Canadian ambassador to Washington for only a few days, phoned after he and a group of UNRRA officials previewed the film prior to its public release. They had all commented favourably on the film's forthright and 'liberal' editorial attitude, especially as it held to the sympathetic presentation of working-class resistance movements then in conflict with British troops.

Arnold Heeney, still clerk of the Privy Council, offered his advice to King. He commented that he expected the American reception to be good, but that there might be trouble with London: the film's wide circulation in the United States would make it hard for the British to explain and justify a difficult Greek policy. He then turned to the Film Board's handling of current and controversial political topics. His remarks indicated that Grierson and Legg were operating with great freedom. The Liberal in him probably led him to admit that he was 'reluctant to press advice on the Film Board,' which 'scrupulously refrain from consulting us about their work in hand or future plans. This absence of prior consultation gives the Film Board a sense of independence and gives us a limited freedom from responsibility.' But he admitted that where the board was embarking without consultation on a new programme dramatizing aspects of Canada's external policy, he had misgivings despite the fact that the fresh and lively outlook of the board made up for minor gaffes in their films. In the final analysis, he thought that *Balkan Powderkeg* should not be held up, as it would cause more fuss and embarrassment.[36]

Norman Robertson, the under-secretary of state for external affairs, tried to give a balanced view of the film and the Film Board. The latter agency, he reminded the prime minister, reflected enterprise and initiative which were usually lacking in government agencies. One reason for this was the fact that it had been relatively free from the restrictive controls exercised by more cautious government departments such as Treasury Board and External Affairs. It was, in the last analysis, he concluded, an agency of the government of Canada. If the prime minister desired it, he would be willing to work out with Grierson some *modus vivendi* which could ensure Film Board consultation with External Affairs on their treatment of questions likely to affect Canada's external relations.

King deliberated, then called in Major General LaFleche for a meeting with himself and Robertson. If the question was about the film, beneath the politeness the real issue at hand was Grierson. Robertson pointed out the difficulty of objective treatment of the subject and the potential for embarrassment if it were shown in the United States. Though he was grateful to the board for the wide and favourable publicity Canada had received, he was concerned with the problem of providing 'appropriate methods of consultation in relation to films such as that under discussion.' In short, the government was saying politely to the minister responsible that the board had been let alone too long in its propaganda crusade.

The prime minister was more direct. He felt that steps should be taken to formulate carefully the policy which should govern the production of films for release by the Film Board. In general, emphasis should be placed upon Canadian subjects and controversial themes should not be dealt with by a government agency. 'Arrangements for prior consultation in such matters should be carefully considered with a view to satisfactory definition.' He decided to withdraw the controversial film.[37] Significantly, this was the end of Grierson's freewheeling activities, though the general policy had yet to be spelled out. King, who spent his public career avoiding controversy, wanted to stop this man Grierson who spent too much of his public career attracting it. King would not soon forget this incident and would recall it in his diary the next time he assessed Grierson's overall value.

It was, however, typical of King not to reveal the full depth of his feelings to those outside his closest circle and often not even they knew what he felt. So when the prime minister called in Ross McLean, he dealt with the film alone and ignored the policy question. He explained to McLean why he had decided to withdraw *Balkan Powderkeg*. He pointed to several telegrams on his desk and said they were from Prime Minister Churchill, who was unhappy with the government's reluctance to support British policy in the Balkans. King explained to McLean that he felt the British government would be justified in resenting the Film Board's distribution of *Balkan Powderkeg*. Since the prime minister wanted to avoid worsening relations between Britain and Canada, he asked if the film could be withdrawn without much trouble. Grierson had already flown to New York the day before to cancel the film personally. McLean replied that as the film had been released to only three theatres in Canada, it could be withdrawn easily. The prime minister then told McLean that if anyone asked why the film had been withdrawn, the prime minister's name could be used. Shortly thereafter, a bright reporter from the *Ottawa Journal* found out about the film's deletion and wrote a story for *Time* magazine about the prime minister banning the film. The New York editor of *Time*, himself a Canadian (probably Robert Elson), called Grierson in Ottawa and asked if the prime minister had indeed banned the film. Grierson said yes and explained some of the circumstances. Then an extraordinary thing happened. The editor asked if Grierson wished *Time* to withdraw the story.

McLean, who was in the office with Grierson at that moment, concurred with Grierson that it would be better if the story did not come into print. The public never learned about the first withdrawal of *Balkan Powderkeg*.[38] If this incident demonstrated the rather special relationship and unwritten agreement which the government, the press, and Grierson enjoyed during these years, it also planted permanent suspicion in the prime minister's mind about Canada's crusading propagandist who had nearly upset King's self-appointed role as conciliator/mediator between the United States and Britain.

The Film Board's relationship with External Affairs was essentially the issue. Nine months before, Arnold Heeney had noted in a confidential memo to Norman Robertson that there was a problem of keeping in touch with the Film Board at the 'policy' level in some continuous way that would have the necessary practical effect on production.[39] Now, on the heels of the *Balkan Powderkeg* conundrum, Grierson had a talk with that department. He reviewed his idea of the necessity of a quasi-independent unit which could provide information 'of a general type not limited by Departmental considerations.' As a 'trusted agent' of the government, he continued, the board could exercise freedom and initiative in its production. He believed that External Affairs should have little to do with production. There could be no such thing as 'production under a committee.' A brazenly independent Grierson feared a board of reviewers and would not agree to any system under which Film Board scripts would be examined by External Affairs or discussed in detail. He would, as a compromise, accept a 'father confessor' there to whom he or McLean could outline plans or outline problems and general considerations. He did not think that the board should be restricted seriously in its freedom in order to achieve complete accuracy of detail.

With remarkable candidness, the film commissioner reiterated his philosophical stance, 'one inch to the left of the party in power.' This was confidence of the sort that missionaries might reflect; others might think it impudent. He said that he did not wish to return to Britain because the possibilities for film developments in Canada were as great as Britain's and had been well begun. He concluded that too restrictive or elaborate an arrangement had to be avoided. With general discussion in advance of particular plans, he noted, 'we should have an adequate opportunity to make our views known and sound such warnings as seem to be necessary.[40]

Grierson was sticking tenaciously to his perceived independence. Admirable though that was, there would be a ripple effect spreading from the whole affair. First, the government did not encourage him to remain at the Film Board. Second, a new minister, Dr J.J. McCann, described by King as a bit dour and not very pleasant, was appointed to head the Film Board in April. He found himself at loggerheads immediately with Grierson, questioning films and film policy and generally making life difficult at the board. Finally, the decision by Grierson to recommend a shift in film themes to dominion-provincial relationships as part of its next step in development may have reflected the changes in the air.

And the troublesome *Balkan Powderkeg* would still not go away. In May Grierson had the audacity to raise once again the question of its withdrawal before the Film Board's directorate. The members agreed it was an excellent film and suggested the possibility of re-editing it for subsequent release.[41] It was reissued that fall. A member of the opposition in Commons complained in December 1945 that the film appeared to be anti-British and pro-Russian. He claimed that the film engendered real opposition in the minds of the people of Toronto. Because of these protests, and because the government was increasingly sensitive to National Film Board criticism, the film was withdrawn from circulation. It was then cut to ten minutes, stripped of its British references, given the innocuous title *Spotlight on the Balkans*, and shown to External Affairs on 26 February 1946. The only powderkeg left was the one which Grierson and Legg had lit and were sitting upon.

THE ORIENTAL PUZZLE

Lest it seem that *The World in Action* never backslid from the messianic line, there were four films devoted to militaristic Japan which tarnished the series' progressive image. One came close to being racist, while the others could barely disguise their heavy-handedness. In the context of the times, the films may not have seemed baldly offensive. But in contrast with the rest of the series' films, they were incongruous.

Inside Fighting China (July 1942) began inoffensively enough in its attempt to explain why Japanese aggression in Manchuria in 1931 was ignored by the democracies. Stock shots followed of depression-ridden Britain and the United States, both preoccupied with their respective crises. Then, to old newsreel footage of Japanese troops invading Manchuria, the narration described how the Japanese army went through Manchurian streets 'butchering civilians and soldiers alike.' To this statement there was a sequence of two bound Chinese soldiers shot dead before the camera's neutral eye. Japanese ferocity was thus portrayed with frightening impact. In no other *World in Action* or *Canada Carries On* film was the enemy's barbarism portrayed as so vicious. Nazi brutality had been as bad and worse – yet such footage of the Nazis had been studiously avoided. Even with the 'shot and shell' films there was hardly ever a face-to-face encounter with death. Bombs would rain on cities, guns would blaze ceaselessly, but the personal identification factor was missing. For the Japanese there seemed to be application of different rules of propaganda.

To visuals of appropriate battle footage the narration described how Japan planned to use Manchuria as a stepping-stone to China. The Japanese employed the scientific use of liquid fire, gas, and bacterial warfare. The Chinese, under Chiang Kai-shek, were fighting back and were building a new China, 'a democracy militant and activist.' And so, China, its Communist forces united with Chiang against the common enemy, destroyed the myth of Nippon the invulnerable along with forty thousand soldiers of the Rising Sun. The film concluded with the alleged words of nameless Chinese veterans: 'We do not ask for peace in our time, we seek only the high privilege of leading our people into their great future, the future which even now is rising from these bitter days. This alone is our understanding of militant democracy. On this alone is based the faith of fighting China!'

The militant Japanese enemy was portrayed as sinister and menacing in the highly inflammatory *Mask of Nippon* (September 1942). Its opening caricatured the Japanese soldier and minced no words: 'The soldiers of the Rising Sun are little men, quick and wiry; their uniforms are slovenly, their faces even in the heat of battle are tawny masks, black, expressionless. They believe that they have embarked upon a holy war, a war of liberation.' There followed a sequence of Japanese soldiers beating, shooting, and burying people alive and the grisly bayonetting of a child to a background chorus of women's shrieks. Tom Daly believes that this footage, extracted from a feature film, was

Described in *The Mask of Nippon* (1942) as 'individually honest and unselfish, collectively treacherous and greedy,' the Japanese caricature in several NFB films hovered on racist. (NFB still from *Warclouds in the Pacific*)

Inside Fighting China (1942) narration described how the ferocious Japanese army went through Manchurian streets in 1931 'butchering civilians and soldiers alike.' This was a rare example depicting death in NFB films. (PAC 129915)

staged and that the child was a doll. Still, it was sickening to watch the violence. The narration which accompanied it pretended to be the Japanese themselves speaking: 'It is senseless to seize an empire where wealth remains in the hands of the inhabitants. We must eliminate every element reluctant to cooperate with Japan.'

After this terrifying prologue the film tried to explain the cultural roots of Japan. It spoke of how godlike ancestors, who practised deceit and treachery as well as good, imposed similar values upon their earthly child. Medieval Japan, with its traditions of the *samurai* warrior class, also left its mark upon that society. The Japanese were ruled by ghosts which were at once beneficent and cruel. With the coming of industrialization, the narration continued,

The Japanese people bowed before the altars of a new god, the almighty yen, a deity whose symbol was the high collar and whose creed was competition. ... The new plants were but the stronghold of a modern medievalist, ... 13 million workers, little more than serfs, sweating their 100-hour weeks to the commercial glory of the great family trusts.

This select historical overview continued and revealed the origins of the film's title: 'Once friend and ally of the democratic nations, Japan turned to Germany. ... Thus at last, the double face of Nippon showed itself in its true light – individually honest and unselfish, collectively treacherous and greedy.' Territorial aspirations left no doubt of Japan's imperial designs. The narration reiterated its near-racist caricature: 'This then is the face of militant Japan. Some have said it is only an empty mask, others that it is the face of a savage; but of this we may be sure – that it is a face schooled through the centuries to hold all life in contempt believing that duty is weightier than a mountain, while death is lighter than a feather.'

At this point there was a statement of how the democracies would find the weakness in the armour of fanaticism worn by Japan:

The double character of the Jap, they say, will be his own undoing. In his hands are modern weapons, but in his head is a mottled faith, the faith of a man driven into battle by the gods of a ghostly and barbaric past. Strike him with a faith deeper and greater than his own. Strike him with a contempt for death that rings not of superstition but of fierce conviction and his spirit will surely break.

As the film ended to sound and visuals of guns blazing, the narration asserted boldly that all the Allies speak with a single voice: 'Convince the Jap that we also do not fear to die and the false mask of arrogance will fall forever from the double face of Nippon.'

This was the first appearance in any *World in Action* or *Canada Carries On* film of the word 'Jap.' The United States had become so accustomed to using this term in press and film that few would even raise eyebrows about its possible racism. It is interesting though that its use in the film was associated with what others said rather than with what the *World in Action* said. This in no way diminishes the fact that the portrayal of militaristic Japan remained a particularly disturbing one, which when compared with treatment of the other Axis powers hovered on the edge of racism.

In June 1944, the *World in Action* series again turned to the East in *When Asia Speaks*, a prediction and a geopolitical analysis of the post-war world in Asia. Skipping from one locale to another, the film described the widespread imperial collapse in Asia as national movements grew. The Japanese, now on the military defensive, were using propaganda to convince their subject populations that Asia for the Asiatics is a happy ending. Both India and China, the narration continued, were at the beginning of national development. If the old imperial dream was dead, there seemed to be a hint that a new system would develop, one that seemed to imply a decolonized Asia's desire to keep some tie with the West. But the specifics were fuzzy and the narration said just enough to please everyone and offend no one. The voices of Asia, it concluded,

... are telling us that our friendship and cooperation, adding secrets of our skills to the wisdom of the orient, can bring benefits beyond belief to one half of all mankind. Today the fighting nations of the western hemispheres are seeing in their Eastern allies future allies in another common cause. For like themselves, the colossus of the East is on the march, a thousand million people resolved to build their own new world in the coming times of peace.

The last film on the Japanese, *Fortress Japan* (July 1944), was a 'shot and shell' issue which gave an account of the Allied advance upon beleaguered Japan. There were two references to 'the Jap,' each of which accompanied visuals of dead Japanese soldiers. The film's purpose was to demonstrate how the Allies would not stop their drive to break the military back of Japan. In the closing moments of the film there appeared a typical and callous Western pronouncement on the Eastern mentality which was probably inserted to harden Allied resolve and deflate expectations of early victory. 'And so, a nation which has ever held life cheap prepares to practise once again its ancient arts of death. If our bodies are broken, they say, we shall fight on with the spirits of our forebearers until the Emperor calls "cease."'

The final words reiterated this theme:

The armies of Japan hope that the enemies, weary of strife and sacrifice, might offer terms of peace. But in the ponderous Allied fleets now heading out into Japanese home waters, they have their answer to their slender hope. They have it in the deep conviction of the whole Pacific world that none can turn their thoughts to peace while Nippon serves her present rulers. ...

Hence, it concluded, the Allies were upon Japan with all their strength. In part, the film was a psychological outlet for the United States and Canada, who, having felt the sting of the Japanese military whip, were now administering the punishment. The visuals of dead Japanese objectified as 'Japs' certainly would support this contention; and few could deny that by this point in the war the Allies, weary of strife and sacrifice, needed to strengthen their resolve.

Tom Daly has tried to put this in perspective and believes that, despite the few verbal slips, the films did not substitute an emotionally negative object for a true thing; that is, they showed that the Japanese existed as actual intelligent people. 'It wasn't the people and it wasn't the culture that we were at war with at all,' he said. 'We were against the way things were used and misused. We did not want to use terms that were against the people.' He admits too that lack of familiarity with these people was a limiting factor in making the films, though Legg was fascinated by the ceremonial side of Japan, especially its codification of rituals and the mentality of the Kamikaze. In all, the better films in the series reflected Legg's more balanced understanding of the European situation.[42]

THE WAR'S END AND THE SERIES' IMPACT

One film in particular stands alone in a separate category in the *World in Action* series because it tried to put an end to the war. Its dual theme was revenge and justice. *Guilty Men* was a late-1945 film which demonstrated how those who started the war had to pay the supreme penalty for their war crimes. The film's title, dripping as with blood, set the mood. As the film opened it explained how in Russia in 1943 a set of rules had been laid down to deal with those guilty of war crimes, which were defined visually by stacks of bodies and ovens. Visuals then cut to a gruesome scene of a war criminal being executed by hanging, followed by a quick cut to a lone bird in the sky. Then a brief historical account followed, of Kaiser Wilhelm in post-World War I Holland, having escaped international jury and trial and tossing split wood onto a woodpile for his punishment. The Allies would not allow history to repeat itself; hence they set up the tribunal at Nuremberg to try Nazi leaders. The key individuals were identified with their crimes. Descriptions of Streicher's and Rosenberg's crimes against humanity accompanied scenes of starving inmates at concentration camps, the first confirmation of years of rumours and the first reference to such atrocities in the series. Then the Nazi leaders were seen being marched into a courtyard where behind closed doors a firing squad was heard doing its duty. The film next turned to Japan whose leaders, it was asserted, would suffer a similar fate. The film's final message was that peaceful nations have combined to utter the solemn warning 'that those who bring tragedy to the peoples of the world must suffer the peoples' justice.'

This film was unusual for its dark message of vengeance and death, though in the context of the times it was quite justifiable. Tom Daly, who directed it, has remarked that there was a certain feeling of vengeance in it, though he believed its tone was not vicious. He explained the intention behind the hanging sequence and the visuals of the starving prisoners and the crematorium ovens. 'The picture of the image of what these people had done was used as a reminder that they had put to death so many people and now this one was being put to death by us.' He claimed that it was not revenge which motivated him, but a desire to put two elements together, the justice of killing mass murderers and the definite need to put an end to the war.

For the millions who had sacrificed for years there had to be a final accounting, both physically and emotionally. Thus, as an exercise in catharsis, the film was purposeful. What remains somewhat problematic is the film's reluctance to explain Hitler's policy of mass murder of the Jews. The enormity and the monstrousness of the Holocaust had not yet become sufficiently known publicly or understood. But it was curious that the pictures of the Jews were not linked to the narration. Even if it was obvious, it needed to be stated. Perhaps the words of one British statesman to Harold Macmillan might explain the horror dawning at that moment. These were the crimes, he had said, which had to be forever in our minds, but never spoken of. *Guilty Men* began tentatively to put the images and meaning into some focus. The war was over but its significance was not yet understood. Reflecting the government's new concern with Film Board propaganda, minister Brooke Claxton ordered that the film be checked with External Affairs.[43]

This leads us at last to some concluding remarks about the *World in Action* series. The consistent propaganda message had been inspirational and its context was one which explored a world theme with a Canadian element usually thrown in for good measure. Hatred of the enemy was not a propaganda objective – it was too crude. The aims were to build Allied morale and to inspire the collective will to action. Behind the constant bombardment of words and images lay Grierson's and Legg's belief that audiences were intelligent, capable of grasping the global patterns of world events, and able to feel that they were part of these events. During world crisis it was strong ammunition to defeat fascism and to sustain the democratic cause. One can only conclude that the often-repeated messages must have been having a positive impact nationally. There were, occasionally, troubles with delinquent exhibitors, those who had discontinued exhibition of Film Board films. In July 1943 Grierson had sent a field person out to visit forty-eight towns in Ontario to find out about the lapses. He reported that there were local booking problems, overbuying in short films and time limitations with double features, but that most of those contacted personally agreed to resume exhibition of Film Board films. A number of exhibitors of Italian and German descent refused to show Film Board or any war films, despite the pressure from the field person that their action might be termed sabotage of the war effort. Additional moral pressure was placed on them through the commercial industry and through local politicians.[44] The propaganda war continued on a national scale.

Tom Daly has cautioned, however, that he believed the impact of the messages was not as concentrated as it would appear from the extracts cited in the above chapters. The few lines, he felt, should be seen in the context of a whole fifteen- to twenty-minute film. None the less, the combined impact of word and image cannot be denied. The audience was watching and its collective consciousness was being manipulated toward a particular point of view. Over the months and years attitudes were being formed and strengthened in the context of a value system which the audiences shared. This then was the fundamental strength and mass suggestion appeal of wartime propaganda films.

One of the new attitudes which the war had fostered was the acknowledgment of the interdependency of nations on a scale never before realized. It was this new reality which both Grierson and Legg hoped would replace the old nationalism which had been partly responsible for both world wars. If people and governments could be convinced that an era of international brotherhood was to follow the war, there would indeed be a brave new world. Obviously the alternative was World War III and the end of civilization. As a reflection of propaganda which Grierson had once called totalitarian propaganda for the good, the *World in Action*, under Stuart Legg's deft narration and guidance repeated the simple inspirational message and took seriously its task of linking its messages to 'great events shaping the destiny of nations the world over.' As with every life crisis, the problem that remained after the crisis ended was to stop talking about the imaginary world to come and to begin living in the real and complex world of today.

Few could find fault with the ostensible purpose of these films during the war, but in war or peace, narrow nationalism and parochialism are the grain for the politicians' gristmills. With victory and peace on the horizon, Canada's opposition members of Parliament would look for means to boost their own political fortunes by taking the National Film Board to task for its 'political' orientation.

7 | Down the Greased Pole: Practical Politics and Igor Gouzenko Deflate Grierson's Triumph

The success which the Film Board enjoyed during the war years was attributed in part to Grierson's and Legg's luck and to a degree to their ability to shun government sanction. The non-theatrical series both educated audiences and united the nation's purpose on the job and in the community. The two theatrical series largely avoided displeasing or embarrassing the government because the propaganda message was, as has been demonstrated in preceding chapters, progressive and appealing in principle to Liberal ears. Grierson was insistent, none the less, that the Film Board was in no way serving as a bland apologist for the Liberal regime. Both he and the government deflected easily the few uncoordinated barbs that were hurled by the opposition. But all the while he was operating close to the world of practical politics ('one inch to the left of centre') and without enough influential friends within the government to shield him if he came under attack. As far as they were concerned, from 1944, when victory became increasingly assured, there seemed to be more reason to monitor his activities. In the final analysis, his independent style would cost him dearly.

Trouble was the last thing on his mind as he reached the crest of professional success in 1944. He was Canada's undisputed propaganda maestro. Home audiences for *Canada Carries On* numbered two and a quarter million a month, while the *World in Action* drew some two million in Canada and ten million a month in the United States. Another million a month saw French translations of films. The world-wide audience for Film Board newsreel material was a healthy forty to fifty million a week. Seeking to avoid private industry's wrath, Grierson wanted to keep confidential the $250,000 income from the sale of theatrical war films from 1943–4.[1]

Such success notwithstanding, by January 1944 Grierson was already beginning to contemplate leaving his government positions to prepare for postwar activities on an international level, possibly with UNRRA and ILO. Besides, there were some signs of strain between himself and those with whom he had daily contact. He wrote to John Bird, editor of the *Winnipeg Tribune*, in January, describing the reasons for tendering his resignation as general manager of the Wartime Information Board. He had undertaken the job of 'slum clearance' there and was pleased with the success of his efforts. He had turned a bad budgetary position into an excellent one; the team and teamwork were improved; the services were extended; and the reputation of the Wartime Information Board had changed much for the better, both with the press and with the public.

In short, the Augean stable job, for what it was worth, had been completed and, considered as a special assignment, a tour de force or an act of God or a bloody miracle – as you please. I could, with hand on my heart, say, 'Well, there's what you wanted, and I dood it.' As you know, in my business of public service there are only two strikes. Six months is one, twelve months is another; and thereafter you can only resign at somebody else's pleasure, which always causes speculation and does harm both to the organization and the resigned. Or you have to raise an issue, generally with political implications, and embarrass yourself into a political line. I prefer, as you might guess, to choose my own moments.

Grierson admitted that administration and paperwork were not attractive to him; lumping Wartime Information and the National Film Board together, '70 percent of the whole is just a dreary business of keeping things in Civil Service line. Seen ad infinitum, moving into the infinite space of next year and the next again, I began to wonder when I'd get down again to the more attractive business of kicking things around.'

He discounted rumours in the press suggesting that he would become the prime minister's political interferer in CBC business, though it is likely that he would have jumped at the opportunity, had it been presented. 'I thought I had amply demonstrated I was nobody's political valet,' he insisted. Besides, he suspected that General LaFleche (the minister to whom he was responsible) had had too much of him at the National Film Board to want him anywhere near the CBC. Yet he found it hard to see what might be one of the great Canadian institutions of the next decade go by default. 'Short of making myself Canada's most eminent goat, I would like to help.' No one asked him. On another level he was becoming attracted to UNRRA and ILO and concluded, 'My promotional nose twitches and something tells me they lead to the lemonade springs where the bluebird sings in the Big Rock Candy Mountains.'[2]

Grierson believed that he was no one's political lackey, despite the ever-sensitive political nose which seemed to anticipate the moment to act and to act correctly in terms of his benefactors. In day-to-day activity, he never hesitated to indulge himself in the attractive business of kicking things around. As he explained it to the Film Board's Controller, A.G. McLean, who resigned in a huff because he disagreed with Grierson's plan for reorganization of supplies and purchasing, 'All of us are servants of an organization and responsible to the Board. Any decisions I make are made in trust for the Board ... it is not therefore a question of you or of me, ... but of what benefits the Board.'[3] His objective remained one of revealing (figuratively) Hegel's incontrovertible Truth in a world of chaos and contradiction. He had no man to fear because public service was its own reward. Grierson had marched confidently far beyond his wartime assignment of reminding North America of its obligation to help and save a faltering Great Britain; he had propelled a reluctant Canada on to the world stage to perform an international role in the name of and for the good of all mankind.

But the political cost was formidable. With his eye on new horizons, Grierson did not realize the effect he had had upon some of his Canadian hosts. From the viewpoint of King's adviser and clerk of the Privy Council, Heeney, Grierson's decision to leave Wartime Information was a sound one. Grierson had been the right man for the job at the time.

On the other hand, I have felt for some time that Grierson's peculiar qualities have served their purpose and that the time has come when he should, if possible be replaced by someone of different capacities. Grierson is not, by nature, a manager or administrator. Now that his work is largely done it would be of advantage to have someone else in this category.

Heeney felt that A.D. Dunton, Grierson's recommended successor and assistant general manager at the Wartime Information Board, was a good choice.[4] Dunton, on loan from the *Montreal Standard*, would remain manager of the Wartime Information Board until 15 August 1945. Shortly thereafter, he became head of the CBC. Heeney concluded that Grierson would be a useful person to call upon for ideas and advice and suggested a special appointment be made for him as adviser on information. Subsequently Grierson was named special adviser on information but he resigned this title after he left the National Film Board in August 1945.

Concerned that the postwar National Film Board's employees might find themselves idle or without a crusade, Grierson wrote to King's secretary, Walter Turnbull, in March. He tried to develop a scheme which would appeal to Turnbull's old loyalties as public relations officer for the Post Office. He might have known too that Turnbull would be leaving the prime minister's office soon to become deputy postmaster General. The scheme was that the National Film Board undertake a public relations programme involving the Post Office on the same lines as the public relations film programme of the GPO in London in the thirties. Grierson argued that the change from wartime to peacetime footing would lead the public's attention to focus on the Post Office in the national picture. He suggested that a modest fifty or sixty thousand dollars be expended over the next year to develop such a programme.[5] Though Turnbull was somewhat interested in the scheme, he doubted the possibility of realizing that much money. He commented that Grierson tossed the sum around 'in a very light fashion when you have to run up against the penurious attitude of the Post Office.' Nothing would come from the scheme and Grierson continued to look around for suitable government departments with which he could involve the National Film Board. Shortly thereafter he talked about developing a series of films which would present the sociological as distinct from technological gains of the war.[6] That spring he thought it was time to develop and renew Hollywood contacts with a special eye to the resumption of the tourist trade. He also undertook discussions with an UNRRA official with the hope that he could help plan the UNRRA film programme.

If much of the film propaganda seemed to pass general sanction, there were disturbing undercurrents which Grierson ignored or hoped would go away. In May, the board's members found themselves having to answer criticisms that the Film Board was using its facilities to produce films that might be classed as Russian propaganda. 'The Board discussed generally the extent to which it should produce films dealing with foreign countries and extraterritorial issues. The consensus was that the Board had a special duty to the Canadian public in the matter of education in Canada's international relationships, but that great care should be taken in the presentation of foreign material, particularly when its nature was controversial.'⁷ The argument was obviously Grierson's, though the *caveat* was a political warning which most likely was being articulated especially for him.

Grierson could not have known that the Federal Bureau of Investigation had been keeping a file on him since 1942. There were only two items in his FBI file until 1945, one a negative report by an FBI informant who had been watching the *World in Action* films since 1942. He charged Grierson with being a 'communistic sympathizer.' The second was a negative newspaper article. Whether he wanted to admit it or not, Film Board dabbling in international themes was providing ammunition to the Opposition. For example, *Our Northern Neighbour*, a *World in Action* release we have discussed earlier, had become one such political football. Because it dealt with the Soviet Union as ally and gave a sympathetic treatment of Russian history, it was held up by the Quebec Censor Board, though it had been approved by the Department of External Affairs.

There were other enemies of the Film Board, like the head of the Canadian Government Travel Bureau, Leo Dolan, to whom we have referred earlier. There was also an unsigned memorandum on the Film Board which appeared in the files of Mackenzie King's resentful fellow Liberal, Mitchell Hepburn. Its nine points were: 1 / there was said to be sufficient waste and corruption in the Film Board to defeat King's government; 2 / someone should find out why Grierson was fired by the GPO in England; 3 / the Film Board's personnel had expanded from two or three to two or three hundred and expenditures had increased twentyfold; 4 / an opposition MP should ask Parliament to investigate the Film Board; 5 / the Canadian district manager of United Artists, David Coplan, was using his position as a dollar-a-year adviser to the board to his own and his company's advantage; 6 / the true picture of the Film Board was concealed by interdepartmental appropriations; 7 / Quebec's refusal to show the Victory Loan trailer and *Inside Fighting*

Russia conclusively proved Grierson's communistic leanings; 8 / Mrs John Grierson had contributed communistic articles to United States magazines such as the Nation and the New Republic. Question: how many conscientious objectors and draft dodgers are employed by the Film Board? There was enough in his memorandum to plant doubt in some minds, though it is not known if it received wide circulation. At the very least it proved that the Film Board could become fair game if information like this fell into the hands of the Conservative opposition.

A disaffected National Film Board employee, Douglas Ross Sinclair, wrote to Prime Minister King in October 1944 that the board had 'definite Fascist leanings,' proof of which was that the World in Action film Gates of Italy had been banned in the United States. Grierson immediately answered these specious charges in a letter to Walter Turnbull in which he stated that Sinclair, a desperately unstable boy, was under psychiatric observation in the Army. This rebuttal was subsequently sustained, but rumour, once started, is hard to quell. Inside Fighting Russia and Gates of Italy had received only limited distribution. And worse, the message of progressive internationalism was putting Grierson into a realm of practical political orientation. This made the prime minister nervous.

If he was drawing some political heat, Grierson seemed to retain outwardly his confidence and optimism. In September 1944, he outlined an expansive policy and future prospects for the Film Board. He seemed undeterred by criticism and claimed that the demand for information imposed on the Canadian government would increase in the field of cultural relations. Other countries were demanding to know about Canada. Because of Canada's increasing part in international organizations, there was a political necessity of presenting an account of Canada's national and international stewardship. There was also an economic necessity of presenting a background picture of Canada in support of foreign trade. He believed too that there would be expansion in health and welfare as well as in every phase of industrial and rural sociology. Finally the dawn of the television age promised a new lease on life for the board. Three months later he would favour a stillborn scheme where the Film Board would retain control of initiating and producing films suitable for television broadcast.

Grierson indicated that he was interested in remaining commissioner if the Film Board continued useful creative work in the educational field on a national and international scale. His blunt appraisal was that if government policy were so to alter as to diminish this opportunity, he would have to go where new work was to be done.[8]

A month later he claimed that the prognosis for the theatrical series *Canada Carries On* and the *World in Action* to continue in the United States after the war was good, since 'most of the principals in the industry see the advantage of continuing the policy of national service and, not least, the American principals who are gradually learning that trading into foreign countries involves obligations towards them.' Canada's cooperative relationship was keeping the Canadian landscape before the United States public and would become most valuable when Canada was providing a regular supply of tourist films.[9]

This was sheer fantasy on his part, but he could not be blamed for trying to plan sustained postwar activity for his nearly eight hundred employees. Besides the war information propaganda, the Film Board planned a national film programme for the year 1945–6 with films relating to the Canadian life, character, and resources that would provide the foundation for the development of postwar trade. Five films were to be on Canada for foreign distribution, other Canadian films were to be revised for foreign distribution, while six films were to be devoted to promoting national unity. They were to be on industry, agriculture, commerce, research, and welfare and the contribution of community groups to the building of Canada. The Film Board had also obtained a commission to produce $50,000 worth of films for the UNRRA.[10] In all, the Film Board would complete 310 films in the coming year, 101 under the national film programme, 109 under the war information programme, and 100 for other government departments.

Early in 1945, sanction was becoming an issue when the prime minister ordered the withdrawal of *Balkan Powderkeg*. The indomitable Grierson, seemingly unchastised by the prime minister's own intervention, felt that the principle of Film Board independence had to be respected. In mid-February 1945, he asked the directorate of the Film Board to approve his decision to suspend the film even though the original request had come from cabinet because the principle involved the authority of the board in the administration of a programme of information. Grierson had had the temerity to draw the prime minister's attention to this aspect of the question and the prime minister said he would look at the question in the future. More likely, King added another mental black mark after Grierson's name. Meanwhile the Film Commissioner informed the Film Board members that he did not want the agency to become a spokesman for the official view lest it be charged with being 'merely a propaganda agency of the Government.'[11]

The whole film propaganda crusade had been built upon the world crisis of war and threat to civilization by fascism. Propaganda which exhorted self-sacrifice, duty to the community, selflessness, and international cooperation could do no harm, whether or not it was 'one inch to the left of the government in power.' The big question, however, once the titanic struggle was over, was what place, if any, there would be for such inspirational film propaganda in the postwar world.

A POSTWAR FILM PROPAGANDA CRUSADE?

After nearly six years, it was almost inevitable that Grierson was finding himself in some political hot water. According to Ross McLean, his main foes were officials in the permanent public service. The reason for the enmity was not hard to guess. Grierson did not fit into the typical civil service mould, nor was he interested in seeking political office. Senior officials could not deal with someone who saw himself as a temporary employee or as one who was happiest knowing that impermanence rather than permanence was his professional signature.

As for the men in the 'inner circle' around Mackenzie King, they had always considered him to be, in Walter Turnbull's words, 'somewhat of a dreaming outsider' and kept their distance from him. A.D.P. Heeney, a formal and somewhat rigid personality, could not tolerate Grierson's one-man style of operating. Heeney was himself a 'take charge' person and scorned Grierson's independent attitude. Norman Robertson, under-secretary of state for external affairs, also questioned Grierson's style and would soon have real reason to doubt Grierson's political sense as demonstrated in his personal selection of an heir-apparent to the National Film Board. Grierson had also isolated himself from J.L. Ilsley, penurious minister of finance and receiver general, from A.D. Dunton, his successor at the Wartime Information Board, and, to a lesser extent, from Brooke Claxton, minister of national health and welfare, who in 1947 became minister of national defence and was from October 1945 to February 1947 the minister responsible for the Film Board.[12]

Perhaps, too, those close to the power centre resented the film commissioner's bluntness, especially if he was referring to themselves. A typical example might be his report to the board about adverse reactions by some two hundred exhibitors in the Prairies to booking war films. 'It was apparent that there was a feeling in the country that there was a lack of vision and inspiration in Ottawa, in spite of the efficient handling of administration matters,' he told the board members. No one wanted to hear the messenger's bad news. Perhaps more than one thought about finding another messenger.[13]

In April 1945, after spending some time in Washington helping the State Department with a film on the future of the new international peace organization, Grierson was the object of a rumour that said he was resigning his post in Canada to take over a film position for the United States government in Washington. Dr J.J. McCann, the minister of trade and commerce and new minister responsible for the Film Board, was not anxious for this kind of publicity. He denied officially that there was any foundation to that rumour. Before long McCann would resent Grierson for causing him grave political embarrassment. Apparently Grierson gave the prime minister some sensitive political information which exposed McCann to King's wrath and public rebuke at a Cabinet meeting.[14] McCann did not like his film commissioner's crusade and recommended that safety and health films replace peda-gogical films. Grierson would also soon lose a sympathetic friend in Walter Turnbull, who in June 1945 was to leave the Prime Minister's Office to become deputy postmaster general. A less accessible J.W. Pickersgill succeeded Turnbull as head of the Prime Minister's Office and special assistant to the prime minister. As one historian has put it, Pickersgill manifested 'that special blend of blind and competent devotion Mackenzie King demanded of his assistants,'[15] and was not enamoured of the Grierson missionary style.

With the surrender of Japan on 7 August 1945 and the end of the Second World War, Grierson tendered his resignation as film commis-sioner. He had said early in 1945 that he was planning shortly to leave his post, so there was no reason to believe he was being forced out. A leak to the press revived the rumour that he was joining the United States government. To discount this, with the Film Board's approval, he issued the terms of his resignation to the press. He apologized to King, after the fact, for what may have appeared to be a discourtesy to the government. The Montreal *Gazette* covered the story with due credit to Grierson, claiming that he had been encouraged in his policy of putting the Film Board on an international basis. In a backhanded reference to his enemies within the government, Grierson said that this had not been done 'without occasional criticism from unimaginative and isolationist quarters.' He concluded by voicing a hope that all parties of the Commons would continue to appropriate funds with 'the same largeness of view which they have so notably demonstrated in the years of my commissionership.'[16]

Behind his resignation, he explained to the prime minister, was a desire to do some pioneering in his own field before he slowed up. In the letter of resignation to the cabinet, he outlined the specific course he wished to follow in New York, 'to produce for international theatre circulation two monthly series of films: one dealing with international affairs, the other with scientific and technological developments in various parts of the world.' He also wanted to form an organization for the extension of documentary production in Canada for non-theatrical circulation at home and abroad. By November, he would organize and register International Film Associates Inc. in Ottawa and Washington, DC, with Stuart Legg and Mary Losey, sister of film director Joseph Losey. This company would be the forerunner of The World Today, Incorporated, which was to undertake actual documentary film production.

In the 10 August resignation letter, Grierson was especially grateful to Mackenzie King for the 'personal blessing' he had extended to the film organization which had become one of the strongest and most articulate anywhere. Grierson felt it could not have been done 'without the constant feeling that I understand your mind a little, had your personal confidence and could rely on your generosity. Under these unwritten but nonetheless decisive auspices we have, I think, done a progressive work for the war effort, for Canada and for internationalism.' He went on to discuss a successor, whom he thought should come from the National Film Board. He hoped the choice would be a young man, 'for this is a young man's medium and its work in the building of Canada is for the fresh eyes of a new generation.' He proposed three names: Ross McLean, who had been assistant film commissioner since 1939, Malcolm Ross, a competent administrator who had been in charge of distribution but who had had little production experience, and James A. Beveridge, a young man of twenty-nine who was a respected producer. Grierson's preferred choice was Beveridge, who he believed could hold together the Film Board's imaginative elements.

Beveridge seemed a curious preference. McLean should have been the obvious successor. Relations between him and Grierson were good, so there was little apparent reason for choosing someone else and a relatively unknown person at that. But Beveridge was Grierson's first choice if his plans for the postwar National Film Board were to be realized. Bizarre as it may seem, his plan was to marry the film agency to the Department of External Affairs.[17] In 1944 Grierson had outlined future perspectives for the organization and anticipated the following scheme: when the Wartime Information Board disbanded after the war its press liaison service should be carried out either by External Affairs or by the Bureau of Statistics. Those other educational and cultural information services which were then a matter of joint operation by Wartime Information and the Film Board would fall naturally upon the Film Board as the only organization equipped with the personnel, skill, and experience to undertake the complex technical work of production and distribution involved. Most of all, Grierson envisioned the Film Board becoming part of an international interchange, along the lines of ILO and UNRRA. Canada could present an image of its international achievement; its audience throughout the world was not to be a general one, but rather a great number of specialized audiences corresponding 'each to each' with the specialized interests and groupings of the Canadian population.[18] National Film Board propaganda would interpret government foreign policy and perhaps even constitute the vanguard of future foreign policy, with an emphasis upon the particular interests of groups all over the world, regardless of country, regardless of politics. This was to include such fields as education, public health, town planning, and the development of resources. As long ago as 1939, Grierson had written, 'When you see this from the international viewpoint, you will realize how much these specialized services could mean to international understanding and to the expression of the democratic idea.' As he saw it, people were interested in the same things, though they were divided into groups of specialized interests. To put it succinctly, he believed that 'The real internationalism is in the manias we share with each other.'[19]

All this was expansively optimistic. But why select the young James Beveridge? He was the logical choice as successor, thought Grierson, since he was first cousin to Norman Robertson, under-secretary of state for external affairs. Robertson had become King's closest adviser in foreign affairs in his thirties (the prime minister held the portfolio for external affairs); Beveridge's twenty-nine years were no greater a liability. Grierson had joined the Empire Marketing Board at that age, and perhaps in an indirect reference to King who had become the first deputy minister of labour at twenty-six years of age, Grierson reminded the prime minister that 'there is an illustrious precedent for the appointment of one so young in a new field of government endeavour.'[20]

Grierson had in fact blundered, even though much of the politicking was being done by word of mouth. Turnbull has no doubt that the scheme would have been rejected out of hand had it been presented officially; further, Robertson would have resisted the scheme because of the possibility of opening himself to charges of nepotism.[21] Pickersgill has put it even more bluntly: 'No one who was realistic would have given a serious thought to the Beveridge succession. Grierson did not know anything about internal Canadian politics. He was a 'hot gospeller' and was not a practical person.'[22] Finally, there was a great danger in cluttering up External Affairs with a propaganda machine, not only because of Robertson's natural antipathies toward anything smacking of propaganda (King liked him because he was 'less likely than Lester Pearson to get the Government in trouble'), but also because King's attitude toward major issues of foreign policy had become incalculable. During the war he had urged creation of an effective collective security system, but as soon as the war was over he began to retreat to his pre-war isolationism. External Affairs never knew which way he would jump.[23] On the one hand Canada's policy regarding postwar pacification of Europe was to contribute materially on a moderate scale and reduce troops; on the other, King wanted to stress Canada's positive contribution to peace in fostering good international relations. Foreign policy thus grew out of practical necessity. King believed too that emphasis should be placed in Canada's contribution to the peaceful settlement of international problems.[24]

Out of this, the functionalist approach, developed largely by Hume Wrong of External Affairs, came to dominate Canadian postwar foreign policy. In essence this meant that effective international authority in any given matter should be concentrated in bodies in which the countries mainly concerned were represented. A variation of this was a belief that the world should be bound together by a large number of different international institutions organized to deal separately with the many functions requiring international cooperation.[25]

These were ideas that Film Board propaganda had already been emphasizing. During the war the theatrical film series had helped reinforce a sense of Canadian nationhood and a national conviction that internationalism was the only way to assure peace. The films dealing with international themes, if messianic in promise, did not depart substantively from External Affairs policies. The only real trouble had been with Russian themes and *Balkan Powderkeg*. The fact remained, however, that External Affairs was an 'Establishment' body, a homogeneous band reflecting that special Canadian characteristic James Eayrs has called a meritocracy tempered by privilege, while the National Film Board's eight hundred employees included artists, socialists, and nonconformist types who were their social opposites and could never mesh easily with that department. And in spite of the prime minister's own claim that the postwar world needed better publicity, the Canadian position as practised by King was that the less said about foreign affairs, the better.[26] Thus if there was any essential criticism that could be levelled at the Film Board it was that its propaganda might have been seen as preachy. But significantly there did not seem to be many figures at External Affairs who thought much about the Film Board except that its films often contained small errors of fact. Some others thought the film agency needed closer supervision or even a good house-cleaning.

Grierson had in fact fallen victim to his own propaganda. He thought that continuation of the National Film Board was as important for Canada as it would be for his dream of using positive inspirational propaganda to promote international understanding and active citizenship. External Affairs spurned his offer and cold political reality underscored the government's attitude that in a world of power politics, public information promoting active citizenship or otherwise was, as a whole, not very significant. Years later Turnbull deflated the Grierson conception. Grierson kept his cool so well, Turnbull said, that he could fit into any scene. He never became an integral part of the establishment, yet nobody had any impression that he was an outsider.[27] To this author, he was somewhat more candid as he summarized the picture with characteristic incisiveness. From the point of view of practical politics, he said, 'Grierson had an overappreciation of his efforts; his political masters had an underappreciation which was as far below as was his above. The gap between the two was tremendous.'[28]

The Grierson strategy did not stand a chance and perhaps a unique opportunity in Canadian history slipped by. Even if the liaison with External Affairs had occurred, it is doubtful whether Canada would have continued to expound a messianic internationalist policy through the medium of film. During the war, the people at the top were probably not seeing enough film propaganda to appreciate fully the direction toward which Grierson was steering the country's information policy. There never had been a long and continuous period when members of the House or other top civil servants could see Film Board propaganda regularly. Also, film themes tended to be more eclectic than uniform. It can be assumed with some certainty that from August 1945 on, in the rapidly changing postwar world, Canada was not about to become a nation oriented toward messianic internationalism. The thinking at External Affairs was that Canada wanted to see the establishment of a world security organization in which member states had sufficient confidence that they would not embark on individual policies leading to strained relations. If the postwar world developed in such a direction, Canada should continue to cooperate closely with the United States through the Permanent Joint Board on Defence as well as in the global security organization.[29] No one seemed interested in talking about information or film policy. As for a successor to Grierson, the post of film commissioner would remain vacant for the next eighteen months. Something was amiss at the highest levels of government.

NATURAL POSTWAR CONTRACTIONS

The end of the war signalled the government's intention to reduce expenditures: one of the first areas to feel the squeeze was government information. Heeney wanted to consider the future of government information operations in general. On 23 August he proposed to change the Wartime Information Board to the Canadian Information Service. Domestic operations would be liquidated (thereby reducing expenditure by one-third) and the main emphasis would be on providing information for other countries. A month later Heeney told King that the cabinet had decided on 13 September, with the approval of Brooke Claxton, minister of national health and social welfare, and of Norman

Robertson to undertake these changes.[30] Claxton became responsible for the Canadian Information Service (including the National Film Board) and G.C. Andrew, former secretary for the Wartime Information Board, assumed the role of general manager from A.D. Dunton who soon went on to head the CBC. Dr McCann, chairman of the Film Board, announced in October the government decision that staff reductions throughout the government service were necessary. He thought the board should consider reducing its staff by two hundred. At the same time the board accepted Grierson's resignation and voted him thanks with the endorsement, 'Owing to his successful efforts, Canadian films have become more widely known and appreciated and have been an important factor in making our country better known to our own people and throughout the world.'[31]

In London that same month, Grierson learned to his disappointment that the government refused a Film Board recommendation that he receive three months' salary as a gratuity. He shrugged off what he called the 'pettifogging' of the Canadian government and continued preparing for the British government a memorandum on the future form their information services might take.

It took until November for the prime minister at last to write a formal thank-you letter to Grierson from aboard the *Queen Mary*. He was returning from a month in Britain, where while ostensibly on vacation he had been participating in talks with respect to arriving at a firm Allied strategy towards sharing the secret of the atomic bomb with the Soviet Union. He had also been discussing the question of Igor Gouzenko, a Soviet cipher clerk who had defected in Ottawa that September. He attached a letter which he had written to Grierson on 17 August, but did not send because he felt it an inadequate acknowledgment of Grierson's 10 August letter. King seemed warm and genuine in his appreciation of Grierson's effort for Canada, the National Film Board, and himself. He believed Grierson had been a faithful friend, though personal contact had been infrequent: 'Particularly have I been anxious to express to you my appreciation of the kindly interest which you have taken at all times in matters which were of special interest and concern to myself. Though my contacts with you were less frequent than I should have liked them to be, I knew that in you I had, at all times, a friend at my side and one to whom I could look for a fair interpretation of my aims and motives.'[32]

King sent the letter to the National Film Board, Ottawa. From there it found its way to Grierson in London. On 23 November, Grierson responded, writing on stationery from the Ministry of Information. Besides advising the British government on information, he was also in London to discuss with his old friend, documentary producer and Ministry of Information films adviser Basil Wright, the forming of the international documentary production company, The World Today, Inc. In the letter, he told King that he was using the opportunity to review developments in various countries of Europe. The liberated countries in particular were interested in knowing what information developments had been taking place in other countries over the past few years and he was anxious to share Canada's experience, particularly the growth of information services to rural communities in conjunction with governmental schemes of housing, health, and community planning in general. Grierson expressed his concern that no one had yet been named to replace him as film commissioner. He told King that he was willing to drop what he was doing temporarily and fly to Canada to help in the selection of a new commissioner. This was the last thing the prime minister would have wanted.

While in London that month, Grierson wrote an assessment of the Film Board for Brooke Claxton, having promised the minister this last service. It was blunt, uninhibited, and indiscreet. He lashed out at the cabinet's failure to realize what the CBC and National Film Board meant to Canada. It was a betrayal of government leadership of the nation and a betrayal of the creative workers in these organizations. Grierson praised Claxton as representative of a generation of ministers which was capable of understanding the relation of government to the educational and imaginative processes of the nation and thought Claxton might be a 'gift from the Gods after the mediocre and dreary succession of Chairmen the Prime Minister so carelessly imposed upon me.' The years of struggle with Mackinnon, LaFleche and McCann had left Grierson more cantankerous than forgiving. No ministers were his friends and Claxton was too careful politically to make reciprocal overtures.[33]

The National Film Board continued to operate well enough under McLean in his capacity as temporary commissioner. At least one person near the prime minister was blocking McLean's permanent appointment in the belief that he lacked the necessary toughness for the job. The Film Board told McLean to cut another 15 per cent off his budget. In December, Brooke Claxton suggested that *The World In Action* change its emphasis to include more direct reference to Canada. In the Commons he said that he planned to use the Film Board as it had been used, as a source of educational films, but that he believed the organization should help to bring about a growth in the tourist industry.[34] This was a come-down from the heights which the Film Board had reached in wartime. The board deferred discussion on Grierson's offer to share with them a report on film distribution in England and Europe. Something ominous was in the air, though only a few of King's closest aides knew what was brewing. The RCMP had information implicating Grierson and the Film Board in what was to become, in February 1946, the most sensational spy scandal of the decade. The Gouzenko drama would explode onto the front pages of the world's newspapers and herald the beginning of an anti-Communist witch hunt in Canada which would have repercussions over a wide area. Though less severe in intensity than its later McCarthyite American counterpart, the investigations in the aftermath of Gouzenko's evidence would destroy or tarnish a number of public careers. John Grierson was to be one among those who fell from grace. On the heels of the atom bomb, the Gouzenko spy case so shocked Mackenzie King that he became suspicious of and preoccupied with international Russian aggression until the end of his political career. As for his erstwhile propaganda chief, Grierson, King was convinced he was a communist sympathizer.

FROM RUSSIA WITH HASTE: IGOR GOUZENKO

Igor Gouzenko was a Russian cipher clerk stationed under the military attaché of the Soviet embassy in Ottawa. He decided on 6 September 1945 to defect to the West, took with him from the embassy cipher codes and a great many files, and went to the Canadian authorities with information concerning a Soviet spy ring operating in Canada. Armed with such information, he made it necessary for reluctant Canadian authorities to shield him. Norman Robertson speculated that Gouzenko defected either because he was sympathetic to Canada's effort in the war or because he was to be recalled home and to certain death. The information included the names of alleged agents, assignments, notebooks, and directives from Moscow. Some of the agents were working

The sensational September 1945 defection of Igor Gouzenko, a Russian cipher clerk in Ottawa, led to spy trials and a wave of anti-communist hysteria and cast a veil of suspicion over Grierson and the NFB. (NFB)

in government positions which made them privy to information closed to the public. Two key operatives were supposed to be in Montreal; one was in the National Research Laboratories in Ottawa and another was in External Affairs. From these revelations, King concluded that the Russians knew secret Canadian ciphers. As to the information they were collecting, it appeared as though the Russians were trying to learn about a sonar device and assess the strength of the American army and forces. Perhaps most serious of all, there was evidence that McGill University scientist Allan Nunn May, the British director of a proposed atom bomb plant to be built in Britain, gave information in the form of a uranium sample to the Russians as well as information about how to start such a plant.

Mackenzie King mulled over the ideological motivation of the agents. There was a sort of idealism in the Russian revolution which sought to get human rights for the masses of the people, he wrote in his diary. This became a religion with some and they were prepared to do anything to further that movement. He believed 'it is of course all part of a world revolution – a world communist movement to get on the part of workers a control of the government completely out of the hands of those who have privilege, power, etc.'[35]

He was horrified at the terrible consequences which might follow to Allied nations once they obtained knowledge of the affair. It could affect government, peacemaking, and possibly the world. The weight of impending doom made him feel his age. He wrote on 10 September: 'I feel very strongly, as though I should drop out of public life at once. Not attempt to go on. I can see that there is going to be nothing but embarrassment of the government from day to day and week to week. I am too weary to be able to meet situations as they arise. ...' He confided to his diary that he now saw communists everywhere, including within Canada's labour movement. 'Canada is more or less honeycombed with communist leaders who have a close association with the movement in the u.s. and all are very closely associated with the movement in Russia.' The prime minister believed there were evidences of communist tactics everywhere across Canada. 'It is all very significant and very dangerous. There is a condition of social revolution which cannot be obliterated. ... As Robertson says, the alleged abolishing of the Comintern is all nonsense. Theoretically, it may have been abolished but what we have seen shows it is in practice today as a world organization, powerfully financed and very skilfully directed.' He jumped to a rather unwarranted conclusion that Coldwell and the CCF 'have been lending themselves, unknowingly perhaps, to the spread of this old kind of communist influence.' (They were in fact almost pathologically anti-communist.) King's long career and self-image as a mediator gave him the only comfort possible at this time. He hoped 'I may be able to be an instrument in the control of powers beyond to help save a desperate situation to maintain peace now that it has at least been nominally established.'[36]

His mood became pendulum-like. Six days later he felt like a child being comforted by its mother and had visions of spiritual strength. A week after he predicted gloomily that this problem would be with him more than any other. A day after that, he saw the Canadian experience happening on a vaster scale in the United States and in the United Kingdom. That explained Russia's 'sinister' attitudes, wanting to increase power and world control. Almost three weeks later, in one of what J.W. Holmes has described as the 'impetuous extravagances of expression' which characterize his diary, he noted how strange it was that he should find himself at the very centre of the problem, having more knowledge in his possession of the Russian system of espionage and what it might affect at any moment than almost anyone living.[37]

King sent the ambassador to the United States, Lester Pearson, to see secretary of state James Byrnes and inform the Americans what was going on. King's concern was that the Gouzenko development should not destroy the arrangements for postwar settlements then being worked out by the Big Four. King wanted Pearson to get an expression of opinion from the United States government as to whether they should go ahead with the prosecution or not. Pearson thought King was hoping the Americans would say, 'Kill it in the interests of peace and the organization of the postwar world for peace; you had better forget about this for the time being or hold it in the background.' Pearson recalled years later that Byrnes was not having any of that and, while praising the Canadians' handling of the matter, asserted that it was the Canadians' responsibility and business and they could be trusted to deal with it and they should go ahead and do what they thought was best. If Pearson and King hoped the Americans would put out the fires in the interest of the wider international picture, Byrnes' remark left little doubt that the cold war was about to begin. 'Handle it your own way. I'm sure you'll do it right,' Byrnes said.[38]

Part of the whole Gouzenko drama revolved around the question of sharing the atomic bomb and establishing the direction of Canada's long-range postwar foreign policy. If in August 1945 King was a little concerned about Russia's not having been told about 'this invention,' by late October he was in Britain discussing the options with Prime Minister Attlee and ex-Prime Minister Churchill. The latter statesman had as little trust for Communists as ever (they were Jesuits without Jesus in the relationship, he said) and Attlee, if less antagonistic toward the Soviets, would go along with President Truman the following month in Washington.

King was determined to preserve what remained of cooperation and the entente between Canada and the Soviet Union. He tried to exonerate Stalin and the highest levels of the Soviet government from responsibility for what had happened. Ever the Liberal, King still found it hard to believe 'that our civilization is dominated by carnivorous animals.'[39] He had the minister of national defence, Douglas Abbott, speak on his behalf at a meeting of the Canadian-Soviet Friendship Rally a week before the Washington meeting. The speech, most probably written in consultation with External Affairs, sounded as if it had been lifted from any one of the National Film Board films on Russia:

The friendship that has grown up between Canada and the Union of Soviet States, the two great Northern Neighbours, is one which must be maintained and strengthened. Only the top of the world separates us, and that means we're next door neighbours in this modern flying age.

But our respect and admiration are founded on something more than just geographical neighbourliness. There is similarity in the vastness of our two countries. ... Our two frontiers meet at the North Pole. We have the same climate and the same resources, and we have the same problems in transportation and development. We have populations of mixed racial origins living in harmony together, and on all levels we can do much to learn from each other and to assist each other. ... In friendship, and in understanding ... lie all our hopes for the bright world of the future. ... That is why the Council for Canadian-Soviet Friendship has the warm support of the Government of Canada today. ...[40]

Good intentions notwithstanding, on 15 November the Washington declaration opposed sharing the practical application of atomic energy until such time as 'effective enforceable safeguards against its use for destructive purposes can be devised.'[41] The Gouzenko revelations had had a catalytic effect on the question of sharing the secret of the bomb. From the Washington Declaration, one can chart the permanent suspicion and distrust which would characterize non-communist and communist international relations. The cold war had begun. In one of the most bizarre twists of this historical period, King's diaries for the critical weeks 10 November to 31 December 1945 are missing and presumed lost.

For Canada and its prime minister, the tone would be noticeably less strident. War had to be avoided at all costs for fear of complete obliteration of civilization. The Department of External Affairs' Soviet experts believed that the Soviet Union would not be in a position to wage another major war in the near future and counselled that Soviet policy was defensive. The Russians would probe in hopes of acquiring more territory but they would also take care to prevent a 'hot' war from developing. Canada's policy community remained calm while the American policy community was galvanized into something close to panic.

President Truman maintained that the United States' position was to make aggression impossible anywhere and to 'contain' Russian expansionism for so long a time that it would have to modify itself. It was a policy of firmness and patience which suited both Canadians and Americans and it facilitated defence cooperation between the two allies. It also determined the direction of Canada's foreign policy.[42]

SHOCK WAVES HIT THE FILM BOARD

The shock waves of the Gouzenko drama were yet to be felt in an unaware Canada. While the RCMP began in October to verify Gouzenko's evidence, External Affairs was formulating proposals for the international control of atomic energy. Truman kept all but a handful of advisers in the American policy community in ignorance of the Soviet spy ring while he contemplated closing the door on international control. By February 1946, word was leaked out in Washington. King thought that Washington had done this so that Canada should start the enquiry and pave the way for its continuing in the United States.[43] He informed the Russians just prior to releasing the information to the public and then announced he would appoint a Royal Commission to investigate allegations of espionage in government service. The order in council creating the Royal Commission called for an investigation of 'the facts relating to and the circumstances surrounding the communication, by public officials and other persons in positions of trust, of secret and confidential information to agents of a foreign power.' The commission, also called the Taschereau-Kellock Commission, after Judges Robert Taschereau and R.L. Kellock, would feed the atmosphere of anti-communist hysteria which swept the country. King was concerned that the Royal Commission methods would result in his being held up to the world as the 'very opposite of a democrat.' It was, he said, part of the inevitable.[44] He expected too that the Soviet Union would break relations with Canada.

The sensational items the public learned about included allegations that there were agents in National Research and External Affairs and that there might be an implication of a member of Parliament. Unhappily for the National Film Board, Gouzenko produced a notebook inscribed by the Soviet embassy's assistant military attaché: 'Research Council-report on the organization and work. Freda to the professor through Grierson.' The information alleged that a particular employee, Freda Linten, who had been Grierson's secretary for six months from May to November 1944, was connected with the main spy ring. Linten, it was alleged in the ensuing investigation, was not communicating information herself, but was a 'contact' or medium through whom information was received from various agents and channelled through member of Parliament Fred Rose or by other means to the Soviet embassy.

According to the investigators' charges, Linten's work at the National Film Board was not satisfactory to Moscow and they wanted her to undertake scientific work in the National Research Council with Professor Raymond Boyer, another agent. They were to learn the chemical formulae and mode of mass production for RDX, and explosive used in National Defence weaponry, and were to communicate that information to Moscow. In the notebook mentioning Grierson, it was adduced later that Grierson was supposed to use his influence to help Linten get a new position at the National Research Council.[45] (It happened that Dr C.J. Mackenzie, president of the National Research Council, had an office next to Grierson's.) Grierson was totally ignorant of Linten's alleged connections and when the investigative commission began its queries, he was called twice to testify. The investigators hoped to prove that Linten was an agent. One Film Board employee recalled years later that she was 'annoyingly inefficient, not overly intelligent, always asking for bigger and better jobs, more money.' But the effect of the investigators' questions, purposely or otherwise, was to throw a veil of suspicion over Grierson himself. To make matters worse, there were supposedly two members of the spy ring who worked for the Wartime Information Board, albeit only after Grierson had resigned his post as general manager. Both men were officers in the Armed Forces.

Captain D.G. Lunan was connected with *Canadian Affairs* until his arrest in February 1946, and Squadron Leader F.W. Poland was taken from the RCAF in November 1944 and was put to work producing *Canada Digest* for the Wartime Information Board until his duties ended in May 1945. None the less, existing doubts and suspicions about infiltration into the information apparatus could lead to the most bizarre conclusions. John Grierson now would have to pay dearly for his employment practices at the National Film Board. Both he and McLean had shared the same attitude about employees who were 'political,' especially those who were left-wing. So long as they did not engage in active politicizing while on the job, they were free to maintain their ideological positions.[46] Traditionally a civil servant could not use the safety of his government position to pursue his political interests. Here Grierson and McLean were only following accepted government precedent. They were simply not interested in whether the employee was socialist, communist, or whatever. Hence, the composition of the staff was in the progressive tradition of left-of-centre, with perhaps a sprinkling of communists.

A distrustful Prime Minister King confided to his diary on 20 February 1946 that Grierson was still trying to reach him with regard to the appointment of a successor at the Film Board. Now that the evidence showed a link between the Russians and Grierson, previous *faux pas* became magnified in the prime minister's naturally suspicious mind. He recalled that he had stopped a wartime film which Grierson had conceived and which, had it proceeded, would have caused a terrible sensation. (He was probably thinking of *Balkan Powderkeg*.) 'I have been suspicious of his sympathies with communism, etc.,' he wrote. 'His name appears in the evidence as one who clearly was in touch with the head of the military organization here and with other Communists.'

The evidence showed that Grierson had been in contact with the leading Communist elements at the Russian Embassy. With hindsight, King wrote, 'I had always been a little concerned about what he was doing in that regard.' Now that Claxton suggested McLean as Grierson's successor, the prime minister warned Claxton on no account to allow Grierson to influence his judgment as to a successor. The whole situation at the Film Board needed looking into as there was reason to believe 'there was quite a Communist nest there.' King noted that such allegations had been reported at different times, and expected some sort of international cataclysm to follow the Gouzenko revelations. Norman Robertson wrote on behalf of Grierson to Lester Pearson: 'I am myself morally certain that he knew nothing whatever of his sometime secretary's connection with the Soviet spy ring.' He said he was sorry that Grierson felt he was suffering from the affair and noted with some irony, 'Innocence and omniscience don't easily go together and John finds it very hard to accept the fact that his secretary never told him she was sleeping with Fred Rose.'[47] Grierson's link to the affair, direct or otherwise, sealed his abandonment by the government. And McLean would remain temporary commissioner until 1947.

Reacting to the disatrous implications of the Gouzenko revelations, in March the Film Board tried to arrange regular screenings of its films for both the Privy Council and External Affairs.[48] The inability to obtain permanent screening facilities on Parliament Hill during the war years now came back to haunt the agency. Perhaps not enough members of Parliament had been seeing its films. If the Film Board was seeking vindication for having been caught in a web of guilt by association, it also seemed to be crying out that there was nothing to hide. But the prime minister was not one to change his mind easily once he came to a conclusion. He was convinced the Film Board was tainted.

The reader of King's diaries discovers that King saw much in life in terms of health and disease. To him the Gouzenko evidence was very significant – communism in Canada was a low-grade infection, a communist germ.[49] Because the personnel of the Film Board were too radical in their political views, the prime minister turned his back on them and Grierson.

As far as King was concerned, the ex-film commissioner's political undoing occurred before he was summoned by the Royal Commission in April and May of 1946. Returning from New York City, Grierson first testified on 6 April that Linten was his secretary for about a year, then, correcting himself, for about six months. E.K. Williams, counsel to the Royal Commission, then asked him to comment on evidence which implied that Linten was to use his good offices to get promoted to National Research. Grierson replied that she had asked for no offices and no services in that matter. He said, 'I merely think of her now as an ambitious girl who certainly wanted to get on in terms of the Film Board.' He said he did not know the alleged agents and contacts whom Williams had named. Grierson was becoming uncomfortable and perhaps a little testy. When asked again whether he would have used his power and/or contacts to promote Linten, he replied that such a presumption was not very considerable. Asked if he knew Colonel Zabotin, a Soviet military attaché who was the key Russian operative, he replied that he had met him once. Here the investigator probed deeper:

Q: Did you know any of the officials of the Russian Embassy at all?
A: Yes; of course I knew the Ambassadors. I am only talking of meeting people in the usual diplomatic level.
Q: Quite.
A: I knew Zheveinov, the Tass man. I liked Pavlov; he is the only person I had any kind of personal interest in. That is the boy who is still here, I think, is he, the First Counsellor?
Q: He is acting as Secretary, I think.
A: The only person I knew really was Pavlov.
Q: Just casting your mind back, can you recall any of these men intimating to you or suggesting to you that they would like to have somebody –
A: All I can say is that the Russians, as far as I am concerned, were correct.
Q: Were correct?
A: Yes. I had no reason to associate them with anything like that.
Q: Then let me put another question to you. We are trying to find answers to these things. Did you ever have an inquiry from anybody in the National Research Council as to whether Miss Linten could be used in any type of their work?
A: No. I just don't associate Linten with any National Research Council reference.
Q: Did you know a woman named Agatha Chapman?
A: No.

Q: Then it comes down to this, I take it, Mr. Grierson, that this entry which I have shown to you, Exhibit 37 [a photograph], is something that you cannot make any suggestion on that you think might be helpful to the Commission?

A: I am afraid not, sir.

Q: You cannot make any suggestion at all; is that what you mean?

A: I mean it has no reference to me that I can think of, either through Linten or directly.

Next, Commissioner Taschereau asked Grierson about the existence of study groups at the National Film Board. Grierson replied that the main group was a language group which was attempting to foster bilingualism among the employees. There were, in addition, 'study groups of all kinds,' continued Grierson, usually incidental and casual, which generally arose in connection with the work being done, often related to subjects of nutrition and health, town planning, rural economy, rural sociology, and so forth. Commissioner Kellock then questioned Grierson about a suspected professor at the Wartime Information Board. He asked Grierson if he knew anything about the professor's political ideology. The text of the testimony is worth quoting at some length. Grierson responded: 'I would call him a sentimental left ... left-wing, but sentimentally and academically so, rather than actively political.' Kellock queried further: 'Using the popular language, would you say "communist?"'

A: No. I would not think he was a member of the party.

Q: We have had a lot of evidence here –

A: That he is a member?

Q: No. I am not saying that. I just want to understand your answer. We have had a lot of evidence that people would deny being members of the party, but their views were very apparent.

A: Oh, I have had a fair amount of experience of left wing, not just here, but in England, and I would say that if I call him a sentimental leftist, he has no shade of an active political operator of the left. He has no shade and his mind is not that of a practical politician.

Q: I am not sure that I follow that, Mr. Grierson?

A: A member of the party is like a member of any other party; he is an active operator, an active politician.

Q: That may or may not be so. Would you say he was a communist sympathizer?

A: I would go no further than to say I think he was a left wing sympathizer, a friend of the Soviet Union, and so on.

Q: I have heard that phrase bandied about, but frankly, I do not know what it means.

A: A communist sympathizer? I would not put him as far as that. He is too much – he is an excellent student of Plato, to begin with, and certain matters of liberty in Plato are not so conveniently associated with the communist doctrine.

Q: What would you say about Park [another suspect at the Wartime Information Board and editor of *Current Affairs*, a fortnightly news magazine sent to the armed forces]?

A: There I would put Park very close to the very left wing. Whether he was a member of the party, I don't know.

Q: You use 'left' there in the sense of communist party?

A: Yes. There are gradations between the social democracy and communism, and it is almost a matter of high definition. I don't know whether the fellow leans to the social democrats, or to the communist.

Q: You said you would put him very close to the left, but you did not know whether he would be a member of the party, and I suppose you mean by that the communist party?

A: I have no reason to associate him with active communism.

Q: I am just trying to understand that. When you said 'party' in that connection, did you mean the communist party?

A: Yes.

Q: Then you put him pretty close to the party, although perhaps not a member of it?

A: Right.

Q: What did you know about his experience before he went to the Wartime Information Board?

A: I knew him as a lawyer in New Brunswick, a very good academic reputation, as far as I remember; a good military reputation.

Q: Did he have any military experience?

A: He came in as a captain.

Q: To you?

A: He came in from the army, yes sir.

Q: What about – is it Freda Linten or Linden?

Q: Linten.
Q: Where did she come from to you?
A: As far as I remember, she came from Montreal.
Q: And from what previous work?
A: I do remember now. I think she was in ILO [International Labour Organization].
Q: And did you re-employ her?
A: I employed her, yes.
Q: You selected her?
A: Yes, on the basis of the usual kind of application.
Q: What did you know about her at that time?
A: Except that she had a good reputation for what she was, a secretary in the ILO offices.
Q: And when she was promoted in the Film Board. I suppose you promoted her?
A: Yes.
Q: Did you know what, if any, connection she had with Fred Rose?
A: No, sir, I don't associate her with Fred Rose at all.

Here the testimony ended and the prosecution recalled him on 13 May. They were pursuing a line of questioning which, if routine, given the circumstances of the case, must have surprised Grierson for its severity, as he thought he was cooperating to the fullest extent. In testing his credibility, they implied that he had chosen Captain Park at the Wartime Information Board over another more qualified man because of Park's political leanings. Grierson denied the allegation, claiming he did not know of Park's leanings in 1943. Then the prosecution tried a direct line of attack and asked if Grierson had any objection to telling the commission his political leanings.

Q: ... First of all, are you a communist or a communistically inclined?
A: I would be delighted [to answer]. I have been a public servant now for a matter of 18 years: I was trained in the classical Whitehall school. I have been first and last a public servant, that is a civil servant. Now, that meant in the Whitehall sense that you have no party affiliations. A party should not affect one's public job, particularly in the kind of work I have done, because I have always been concerned with government information. ...

Grierson went on to state that he felt it was one's duty to press as far as possible the progressive legislation of the country but within firm and very strict rules. In developing his philosophy, he said that there were three great forces working in the world: the Catholic Church, international socialism, and liberal democracy.

I believe very strongly and very firmly that anything that is done to better the understanding of what lies behind those basic ideas in the world will represent an advance for civilization. ... In the matter of political philosophy the issue is this: those of us who have been trained and who are dyed in the wool Liberal democrats say that there cannot be any economic freedom if there is no political freedom. On the other hand, those who believe in international socialism say that there cannot be any political freedom unless there is economic freedom.

The prosecution was not impressed and queried, 'Would you say then that the effect of all that is that you are not a member of the Communist party?'

A: Oh no.
Q: That is officially. What would you say about subscribing to any of their views? Would you say that your inclinations were of the leftist variety, using your own words in connection with Park, for instance?
A: Not at all; I do not think that way. I am entirely a person who is concerned with the establishment of good international understanding. Therefore I am concerned with the floating of all ideas. I mean, I get as much from Gobineau as I get from Marx.

The commissioners were getting ready to put their final questions to Grierson. They parried a bit about the Park hiring in 1943, claiming that Grierson's knowledge of Park as a 'progressive thinker' meant that he knew Park was a communist. Grierson again denied the allegation. Commissioner Taschereau began,

There has been proved here before the Commission the existence of an astonishingly large number of communist cells masquerading as study groups. There has been proved here before the Commission that an astonishingly large number of persons working in those cells and drawing other people into them were employees of the Film Board. ...

Grierson claimed that he had no sense of this and thought that the atmosphere at the board was one of progressive, not leftist, thought. Then Investigator Williams became more pointed:

... In these Russian records we find persons named, and in almost every case it has been established that they are definitely communists or tied up with the communists, or communist sympathizers. ...

Grierson denied the allegation. But Commissioner Kellock maintained the momentum:

... Now, Mr. Grierson, all these other people being communists, the note would make sense to me if Motinov or Zabotin or whoever it was knew you as a communist –

A: Unless

Q: Just a moment until I put the proposition to you, – knew you as a communist. That would make sense to me: that Zabotin would say, 'We will get Grierson to put Freda in the National Research Council, because we know that Grierson belongs to this clan, or we know he will do it for us. ...'

Again Grierson denied the possibility of this being true and suggested that perhaps the Russians thought that Linten could manipulate her boss, Grierson, simply because he was her boss.[50] The interrogation was nearly over. Linten had disappeared and Grierson could only say that she resigned from the Film Board after being refused a raise, then vanished. His testimony was finished.

As fate would have it, Grierson addressed the International Conference of the Junior League in Quebec on the political, economic, and educational implications of the atomic bomb the very next day. Grierson's dream of world peace remained undiminished and he counselled humanity to forget atomic energy as a weapon of war and to get down solidly to the business of peace. His remarks about the Soviet Union were as incautious as his previous day's testimony. He disliked the Soviet Union's secrecy and suspicion and atmosphere of conspiracy but suggested that the West had given them reason to be secretive, suspicious, silent, and conspirational. His concluding pleas could only have been turned against him by his enemies. Any attempt to understand Russia becomes the badge of subversive activity, he admonished.

'There will be none of that science of human relationships which is to save mankind, if we frustrate and stifle the generous thoughts of our youth or by any action of church or state bar them from the fullest knowledge of the ideas operating in the world today, whether they come from Russia, Rome or from George Bernard Shaw.'[51]

A missionary never knows when or how to stop. He prepared a note on the causes of the present discontent to be sent to the government. The Royal Commission was a direct threat to three of the four free-doms for which the war had been fought – freedom from fear and free-dom of speech and of conscience. He thought it would be extremely useful if the prime minister were to restate in unmistakable terms the liberal and progressive attitudes with which he had been associated throughout his political career. If confidence were restored between Canada and the United Nations, he wrote forcefully, 'it would not be possible for the filthy insects and worms to creep out of the woodwork and reveal themselves again for their bigotry and prejudice and evil will.' If these vicious things were permitted to continue without being repudiated, he warned, there would be nothing but the growth of suspi-cion, doubt, and animosity between individuals, organizations, and communities in the state.[52] It is doubtful that Grierson ever sent this emotional appeal; it does not appear to be in the Public Archives of Canada.

The note reflected a certain exasperation with the whole episode. He had appeared as a witness with nothing to hide. He had answered the questions honestly, if too much like a schoolteacher. Perhaps he should not have tried to lecture the commission, for he had ended up being caught in an inextricable web of circumstance spun by a professional team of judges and lawyers who were pursuing their appointed task of investigating. Worse, his testimony now led to the casting of a further shadow over his public career. By King's own admission, Grierson had become suspect. Walter Turnbull has tried to modify this judgment by stating that, at most, King's associates thought he had been indiscreet and careless.[53] At best, an embarrassed King government, through minister of justice and solicitor general Louis St Laurent, offered a half-hearted word grudgingly on Grierson's behalf. Mercifully for the gov-ernment, Grierson was done and gone and soon to be forgotten. In a final insult, they refused to honour his request for reimbursement for travel costs when he came from Britain to Canada in January 1946 to maintain morale and assure the board's staff during the period of transfer.[54]

Grierson returned to New York City to nurture his most recent endeavour, The World Today, Incorporated, which he had founded in March with Stuart Legg and Raymond Spottiswoode. He had completed a distribution contract with Grant Sears, vice-president of United Artists, in which The World Today Inc. would produce thirty-nine theatrical shorts for four years dealing with world affairs, scientific and technological developments, and the world of sports, to be called *Worldwise* (on great events), *Wonderfact* (on technology), and *Venture* (on sports and outdoors). The Rank Organisation was to distribute them in Britain and Basil Wright was to join the group by organizing a film unit in London. But the shadow of suspicion followed Grierson everywhere, and the Film Board rejected his proposition and McLean's recommendation to enter into a distribution contract. The World Today never materialized.

The spin-off from the Gouzenko affair would result in the National Film Board's losing whatever goodwill Grierson and his colleagues had built up over the war years. The parliamentary opposition had enough ammunition to exploit the government's embarrassment for months and the National Film Board became a favourite target. In April, the month Grierson first testified, minister Brooke Claxton had to parry one member's charge that the National Film Board produced 'communist propaganda.' In May, it was admitted in Commons that a National Film Board circulation manager had been fired for being a 'known Communist.' In June, Claxton had to answer questions about whether the National Film Board distributed films depicting collective farming in Russia and collective Russian health services. He replied that there had been one such reference, a one-and-one-half-minute passage in *Inside Fighting Russia*, a 1942 release; otherwise the record was clean.

The Royal Commission had published three preliminary reports prior to the final excised version of the testimonies of witnesses and its findings on 27 June. July brought further attacks on the government. McLean recommended to the board that a strong defence should be prepared for the Commons debate on the budget for the misapprehension held in some quarters that Film Board personnel were too radical. In Commons, Gordon Fraser claimed that the National Film Board needed to be 'fumigated.' He was irate because the hat was passed around at the Film Board in order to obtain funds for the benefits of those accused of espionage. 'I know money was collected there, despite what may be said by any official of that department,' he claimed. Fraser was happy to see that one known Communist had been fired, and concluded, 'There are many more who should be dealt with in the same way.'[55] A week later Brooke Claxton told the National Film Board that he heard that an organized political attack was being planned on all the informational activities of the government. McLean said he welcomed a thorough investigation by a Royal Commission because the accusations of radical political leanings were groundless.[56] In Commons, the government ran into stiff opposition in its bid to expand information services. One MP argued that the information service coloured information constantly with items and points of view favourable to the administration, whose policies they were publicizing. He felt that public money should not be spent for political or propaganda purposes. Claxton tried bravely to justify the information service as a way for Canada to achieve adequate presentation abroad. He felt that this service should not be a part of the function of External Affairs and the Department of Trade and Commerce; by not being members of the diplomatic corps, members of the information service could maintain relations with members of the local press and others. He denied vehemently the existence of political propaganda in government information services since 1939 and challenged members to give him a single instance of propaganda. Fortunately, no one embarrassed him. The debate continued and only Stanley Knowles argued for the information service to do the same work at home and abroad. But the information service had drawn too much heat. Because of the great opposition to the bill, it had only one reading and died after this debate. Dan Wallace, who would become the Film Board's representative on the newly established committee to assist the Department of External Affairs in its information work abroad, summarized years later the government's attitude toward the National Film Board: they were 'upset with its pixillated free wheeling organization. The Board was a rambunctious young child getting out of hand.' The image of a left-wing staff was disturbing enough. Worse, the National Film Board had provided the opposition a perfect vehicle with which to attack the government. The organization had lacked caution and, in the wake of the Gouzenko affair, was considered generally to be a nuisance.[57] An embarrassed minister of justice, Louis

St Laurent, found himself defending Grierson that November, 'deploring the loose and ill-founded conclusions pointing to Mr. Grierson as head of the spy ring or as consciously connected with it in any way.'[58] But the momentum of events was hard to check and as the Film Board went through the natural staff reductions associated with the return of peacetime, its reputation was tarnished seriously. Happily for the government, the agency soon receded to a rather obscure part of the nation's consciousness. Television was soon to become the dominant force in national media.

REORGANIZATION AT THE FILM BOARD

Brooke Claxton wanted to make Ross McLean film commissioner in October 1946. He would not act, however, before the prime minister approved.[59] King delayed until January 1947 before making the appointment. Dr McCann replaced Claxton as chairman and oversaw more budget and staff cuts. James Beveridge became head of English production. McLean said in later years that the spy episode had probably planted doubt in Claxton's and McCann's minds about the National Film Board. McLean thought that 'misunderstanding' was the basis of the board's difficulty in Commons. Alberta reportedly began to censor Film Board films and two provincial politicians lashed out at the board's moral depravity, gangsterism, and Communist propaganda.[60]

An uncomfortable Chairman McCann had to face a cabinet discussion of Film Board staff members who had Communist tendencies late in March. Minister of agriculture J.G. Gardiner angrily named two who had been professed Communists and said his department was reconsidering its arrangements with the board. Ross McLean responded at a Film Board meeting that the allegations were wrong. The two had taken no political action since they joined the Film Board. In fact one had been with Grierson in the General Post Office Unit in England. McLean's defence was the kiss of death. McCann had had enough. The minutes of the board meeting convey only part of the passion and vitriol which permeated the air. 'The Chairman said that all of Grierson's associates were anathema,' they read. No more concise sentiment or painful admission could have been uttered. McCann stated that Grierson's difficulty was that he was too vocal. McLean must have felt abandoned. One other Film Board member, C.G. Cowan, expressed confidence in him but warned that many enemies of the Film Board or government were active. McLean retorted that he believed the Film Board's political difficulties were within the government rather than without. He insisted that the board's position was stronger than ever in the country. McCann was unimpressed. In view of the cabinet discussion about the Film Board's activities abroad, he ordered that a film which was ready for release on China should be held in abeyance. Completion of the China film (shot, incidentally, by McLean's nephew Grant McLean) should await the recommendation of the interdepartmental committee. The Film Board had planned a film programme for the coming year on international themes integrating with activities of the United Nations. All this had been in line with announced government policy. Chairman McCann thought it was a question of degree and that some interest in Canada should be developed abroad. But the unlucky Film Board was under attack from many other inside quarters. The Liberal minister of national health and welfare, Paul Martin, thought that the board's films were too expensive and could be done more cheaply by private companies,[61] while at External Affairs, Lester Pearson would finally stop circulation of the China film (called The People Between) because it implied recognition of Mao's China and that was not government policy.[62]

The natural postwar contractions and loss of theatrical distribution abroad did not improve this bleak scene. The World in Action distribution contract in the United States terminated at the end of 1945 and the several productions completed or under way (including The People Between) faced uncertain distribution. Worse, income from foreign screenings was at an all-time low, $30,000 for 1946–7. In fact the only bright spot was that, in Canada, non-theatrical circuits were drawing a respectable 600,000 a month. Various government departments were calling for films on health and welfare, agriculture, and subjects concerned with trade and industry.[63]

It is not hard to imagine how such a charged atmosphere and changed film policy obliterated totally any political inclinations which those progressives who still remained at the Film Board might have wanted to develop in their films. Political film propaganda was out – Canada Carries On turned to dealing with very mundane Canadian subjects; its first postwar release must have surprised audiences greatly by its complete digression from past themes and format. Called Music in the

Wind, its subject was the famous Casavant organs made at St Hyacinthe, Quebec. By the end of 1947 there was talk of changing the series title, since some thought the war connotation handicapped its popular appeal. With the coming of peace, *Pictorial Hometown News* and *Rural Newsreel* were no longer necessary. The *World in Action* series continued until the end of 1946, appeared irregularly thereafter, then was dropped quietly without replacement. Newsreels, including *Front Line Reports*, *Canada Communiqué*, and *Eyes Front*, were edited into a ten-minute release every two months, called *Eyewitness* and, in the French version, *Coup d'œil*. It seemed too that the internationalist themes were abandoned for themes dealing with self-reflection. In 1947 there began a new psychological series called *Mental Mechanisms*, sponsored by the Department of National Health and Welfare. Intended first for small professional audiences, these polished films were so well regarded that they were later released for general audiences. The changes which occurred were stated in the annual report of the Film Board, issued in July 1947. If, during the war, the films mirrored the urgencies of Canada at war, the films of 1946–7 were catching the image of Canada facing up to the riddles of readjustment.[64]

Substantial changes continued to occur in funding, staffing, and production. With the normal cutback to peacetime it was not surprising that there was a reduction of $200,000 for the fiscal year 1947–8. But this included an initial cut in the film commissioner's salary in 1946–7, then an additional cut of 10 per cent in 1947–8. McLean appealed the latter cut, but he did not have the support of his minister, Dr McCann, who still resented the whole communist episode and the Grierson entourage. Staff reductions continued: the staff declined from a 1945 peak of 787 to 654 in 1947. The cabinet told McCann to keep cutting and reduce annual expenditure to a million and a half dollars. From 589 in 1948, the staff fell to 540 in 1949. A depressed McLean believed that some government people had decided that film activities were merely frills. There had been twelve production units in operation in 1945; by 1948, the number was four. Production declined from 310 film subjects in 1945 to 214 the following fiscal year. Despite McLean's protests, offices in Sydney, Australia, Washington, DC, and Mexico City were closed between 1948 and 1950. At one frustrating point, a dispirited McLean said that he would try to reduce the budget to below the wartime level but that if continuous cuts were to follow the Film Board should be abolished completely.[65] There were only two encouraging aspects. The number of rural circuits operated by other bodies increased notably and there was an increase in the number of film libraries across Canada with the continued demand by rural audiences for non-theatrical subjects. McLean demonstrated in March 1948 how successful the Film Board was in fulfilling one of its chief purposes, the maintenance of national unity. Nationally, non-theatrical audiences were close to one million a month and one in twelve Canadian school children was seeing a non-theatrical Film Board film every month.[66]

The end of the war had more or less ended the special relationship between the National Film Board and the commercial film trade. During the year 1946–7 only 325 Canadian theatres made available 20 per cent of their playing time to short subjects. None the less, a respectable thirty films played to an estimated audience of two million monthly, a drop from the wartime figure of three million a month.

The Film Board was down, but not out. The cabinet did not necessarily want to turn its back completely on the use of film; they approved in late June 1947 the Cabinet Committee on External Trade Policy recommendations which had called for representation abroad by the use of films, special Film Board representation in key foreign posts, and Film Board needs with respect to external film distribution.[67]

Anything dealing with Grierson was another story. In June 1948, Grierson proposed in a letter to the Film Board to resume *World in Action* production under the auspices of Britain's Central Office of Information, where he was then working. He proposed releasing some Canadian subjects in the series. McLean supported the idea; McCann opposed both it and authorizing Grierson to use the (uncopyrighted) series title.[68]

In 1948–9 the board reflected a marked inclination toward promoting tourism. Some 130 Canadian travel films reached audiences, mostly in the United States. This included establishment of sixty-two screening points for travel films in thirty-three states, in public libraries and other educational libraries or facilities. Glum pessimists could argue that it seemed as though the National Film Board had come around full circle and was reliving the worst days of the Canadian Government Motion Picture Bureau. Then there had been little government interest in the film medium, save for travelogues, and no interest in film propaganda.

In January 1949 R.H. Winters replaced McCann as chairman of the Film Board. In May, to clear the air of distrust, McLean ended the Film Board's right to make films for the Department of National Defence until all 579 employees filled in security questionnaire forms which were to be examined by the RCMP. Meanwhile, employees of Crawley Films and Associated Screen News who received security clearance undertook such films. When the RCMP produced its list of thirty-six suspected employees, McLean did not think anyone should be removed.

He tried to defend the Film Board in a July 1949 survey prepared for the Royal Commission on National Development in the Arts, Letters and Science, established in April under Vincent Massey, now chancellor of the University of Toronto. Film Board chairman Winters was critical and dissociated himself from the survey publicly because it made specific requests for new legislation and corporate status for the film agency. Winters said that such requests were not government policy and that they represented only the opinion of some members of the National Film Board. He wanted a more thorough report of the Film Board's activities and prospects. He hired the management consultant firm of Woods, Gordon and Company to examine the Film Board's organization and business practices.

McLean too had become a target. Hollywood interests had been unequivocally opposed to his proposed scheme in December 1947 that they be forced to invest about one third of their annual profits in Canadian film productions.[69] Also, the small but vocal group of Canadian film producing companies resented what they saw as unfair Film Board competition. There were also allegations that Film Board employees were providing information to the opposition for use in preparing questions in the Commons.[70] It was painfully obvious that the government was still unhappy with its rambunctious child. J.W. Pickersgill said years later that what the Film Board lacked most was discipline. He favoured reorganization.

This was the signal for the final axe to fall. A December 1949 meeting was held by the National Film Board to discuss the renewal of McLean's term as film commissioner. After the news was released to the press, McLean learned that he had been sacked. Assistant commissioner Ralph Foster resigned in protest. The staff rallied around him and considered mass resignation, but he dissuaded them from destroying the very thing they had worked so hard to create. He could only encourage them to continue working and to do their best. McLean's unlikely successor was to be a non-film person: W. Arthur Irwin, former editor of *Maclean's* magazine, would follow him in February. The pessimistic staff expected Irwin to conduct the final scenario in the destruction and burial of the National Film Board. Yet they could not resign because it would be generally believed that those who resigned were security risks. The dilemma was whether to stay and wait to be fired as the Film Board was reduced to a cipher or quit and be branded forever a 'security risk' with no hope of obtaining employment in Canada or in the United States again.[71] Irwin looked at the RCMP list of thirty-six suspected employees and concluded that three were real security risks. Norman Robertson, now clerk of the Privy Council, selected the same three independently and they were fired quietly. None had been charged with wrongdoing, Winters explained. They had been released merely because of the absence of satisfactory evidence of trustworthiness and to proclaim their names publicly would injure their reputations and their chances of alternative employment.[72] Canada had cast a net of suspicion far and wide over its government agencies, but, ironically, the Liberals' attitude was that security risks should be given jobs in less sensitive areas so they could still feed their families and pay their mortgages.[73] The difference in cold war attitudes between Canada and the United States, where the malevolent venom of the House Committee on Un-American Activities (HUAC) was seeping into the national consciousness, should not be overlooked. Ever the moderate nation, Canada took care of potential embarrassments in the quiet light of reason and efficiency rather than in the spotlight of cameras and public hysteria.

The innuendo and suspicion were, none the less, targets too perfect for the opposition to pass up. Under the leadership of George Drew, the Progressive Conservatives launched an attack in February 1950 against the government's failure to take adequate measures to safeguard Canadian institutions from infiltration by Communist agents. Drew noted that the government, on the basis of positive information, had changed the commissioner of the Film Board and had had a house-cleaning there. When he charged that Communist activities were 'going on apace and wide open,' hyperbole lessened his credibility. In response to Drew's proposal in May to outlaw Communist activities, Prime Minister St Laurent maintained that special wartime measures were no longer required. Autonomous purges within Canada and by Canadians (like those in the labour movement) could get rid of 'these obnoxious influences.' His practical, liberal approach deflated the Conservative attack. He concluded that it was better to meet Communists and fight them above ground than it was to have them burrow underground.[74]

The directorate of the Film Board did not wish to dismantle the agency, only to supervise it more closely. They confirmed that the film commissioner should be the originator and guide of creative activity once the board laid down film policy. The whole Film Board was to take responsibility for films produced by the agency.[75]

The Woods Gordon report was presented to Robert Winters in March 1950. In describing the development of the National Film Board, the report stated that, since the Film Board had been set up as an advisory body, the assumption of production and distribution of films had not been accompanied by legislation to keep it functioning smoothly. There had been a further extension into multi-media activities like still photos, film strips, displays, and designs for posters and publications. The majority of staff had been hired on three-month renewable contracts and the lack of proper facilities (operations were conducted in ten separate buildings) hampered efficiency. The pessimists proved to be wrong, since the report was generally in favour of the National Film Board; it recommended expansion and streamlining of the organization as a business operation within the federal government. Subsequently, the National Film Act of 1939 was rewritten and discussed quietly in Commons in June; it received Royal Assent on 14 October 1950.

Irwin was not slow to inaugurate a new programme in line with cold war realities. In December 1950 he launched the 'Freedom Speaks Programme' with a statement reminiscent of Grierson in wartime: 'The basic conflict in the world today is the battle for men's minds.' The programme was to be a series of films to 'counter communist propaganda with a positive statement in effective dramatic form of the values which we as a free people believe to be basic to democratic society.' He asked for a quarter of a million dollars in development costs for films on subjects from 'the Opposition party in democracy' to 'the Canadian compromise – unity without conformity.' Included too was to be a film for Asian audiences (which one critic derided as a film to educate the natives). There was little enthusiasm from the Treasury Board and less still from the Department of Labour which said the Film

Board was three years late in its thinking: 'the battle of words for the political loyalty of men's minds is about over and we are now confronted with the definite possibilities of a shooting war to decide the issues at stake.' External Affairs liked the idea, however, and the Treasury Board appropriated the money. External Affairs wanted the programme to be developed in closest collaboration with them. A few months later it became necessary for the board to avoid the 'propagandist' taint in their films for Europe and Irwin had the title 'Freedom Programme' changed to 'International Programme.' It was evident that national crusades outside the context of a shooting war generated little sympathy. A number of films were made, then the programme disappeared gradually and quietly.[76]

Irwin had more success in 'streamlining' the Film Board. He decided to move the board out of Ottawa to a single facility in politically remote Montreal. The rationale of having a larger talent pool to draw from, cultural proximity to the 'French fact,' and the possibilities of liaison with the new medium of television and the CBC did not disguise the government's desire to keep the National Film Board far away from federal politics. The move occurred in 1956. Ironically, the Montreal site's remoteness only emphasized the Film Board's ejection into the wilderness – it was on Cote de Liesse Road in the industrial suburb of Saint Laurent, a good five miles from the centre of the city and nearly impossible to reach by public transportation. The National Film Board bore little resemblance to the missionizing agency which Grierson had created. Suffice it to say that the golden days of Grierson's and Legg's melding politics and film to predict a better tomorrow would remain but a memory as a whole new generation took the pulse of a different Canada. If the challenge of war had brought out the finest in people's ability to sacrifice and serve the community, peace seemed to take the edge off the need even to fix national priorities. Preaching to a national congregation was out, the search for a national identity was suspended. An unchallenged populace leaned back collectively into its living-room easy chairs. Television had arrived.

GRIERSON LEAVES NORTH AMERICA

As for the unsteady public career of Grierson, the shadow of doubt followed him everywhere, making it nearly impossible for him to realize his plans. He remained under a cloud of mistrust in the opinion of the FBI. Their treatment became heavy-handed and his North American plans withered and died. He had been in the United States on a visitor's visa since January 1946. In March, unknown to him, the United States ambassador to Ottawa, Ray Atherton, had written a top-secret letter to the United States secretary of state in which he had recommended that no visa of any kind be granted to Grierson until he was investigated and cleared by the FBI, in light of the Gouzenko revelations. After testimony before the Taschereau-Kellock Commission that spring, if he had been humiliated, he did not show it publicly. He addressed the American Library Association in June 1946, in Buffalo, New York, and while pressing for the increase in the use of film for education, he once again stressed the need for international cooperation between competing ideologies. He thought that librarians could help develop international understanding through education. The old optimism and faith were apparently unshakeable.

His private hopes to elevate his crusade on to the international level were high at this time, as he was being considered for a United Nations position as assistant to the secretary-general in charge of press relations. He did not suspect that FBI chief J. Edgar Hoover was applying maximum pressure in Washington to prevent his appointment. The cold war and anti-communist hysteria were just beginning to sweep the United States, with Hoover's blessing; Grierson did not get the post. By August 1946 International Film Associates ceased to be much more than an information exchange on non-theatrical film, while The World Today, Incorporated was itself beginning to sink into troubled financial waters. These developments, coupled with the difficulties of breaking into commercial distribution in the United States, meant that by the end of 1946 the whole edifice was foundering.

Meanwhile the FBI in Ottawa had been funnelling allegations directly to Hoover in Washington, corroborating stories of Grierson's fascist tendencies and Legg's suspicious activities while also confirming Grierson's communist sympathies and contacts with subversives. In February and March of 1947 the FBI made sure the State Department rejected Grierson's visa request. The story of the visa refusal appeared in the Ottawa press and opposition MP Donald Fleming, sensing the chance to score some political points, asked the government if it knew why the United States had denied Grierson his visa and whether Grierson was entitled to enter or reside in Canada. The hapless Grierson was left to dangle in the wind as the *New York Herald-Tribune* reported that he said the State Department had refused his request for a residential visa eighteen months ago without giving a reason. 'I am not a Communist and any inference of this kind is ridiculous,' he said. 'The whole thing is silly since I have been a British public servant for years.'

The absence of specific allegations only strengthened innuendo and whispering. A veil of insinuation, paranoia, and secrecy was being drawn across the length and breadth of North America. Grierson's inability to obtain a visa this second time convinced him to resign as president of The World Today, Inc. The post now passed to Stuart Legg, but only a handful of films were completed and a year later Legg returned to Britain, marking the end of the enterprise.

Little more was heard from Grierson publicly until a February 1947 announcement from Paris that he had been appointed adviser on mass media and public information problems to Dr Julian Huxley, director-general of UNESCO. As a United Nations employee he received a United States visa granting him diplomatic immunity. One Washington newspaper announced his appointment with a September story headlined 'Spy Suspect Gets UN Job.' The FBI's Hoover, chagrined that Grierson had found a way to return to the United States, persisted in trying to undermine his position. The pressure was sufficient and by February Grierson resigned as director of mass communications for UNESCO. The New York World Telegram announced in February, 'U.N. Fires Canadian Atom Spy Case Figure' and to ensure Grierson's departure, Hoover wrote to the US Attorney-General later that month that Grierson's presence in the United States was a threat to national security. The United States was having no truck with people soft on communism, especially at the United Nations. Americans took over responsibility for mass communications at UNESCO, a move Grierson described as a 'stranglehold.' He was outflanked and outgunned and soon left the United States for good. In 1948, the *New York Times* mentioned that Grierson had become controller of the films section of Britain's Central Office of Information and that he planned to make a series of documentaries depicting Britain's industrial and economic problems. Then in June 1949, another spy scandal erupted, this time in the United States, touching Grierson and burying the last of what was left of his public reputation in North America.[77]

The Americans were in the midst of ferreting out alleged subversives and, having begun with the accusation of Alger Hiss, soon plunged into a more sensational case. Authorities discovered that Judith Coplon, a former analyst in the Justice Department, had removed government documents and was having an affair with a Russian citizen. They accused her of stealing government secrets with the intent to aid a foreign power. At the same time, Hollywood began its version of a Communist witch-hunt, and on the long list of personages whom an informant had named as being Communists Frederic March's name appeared. Tied to this allegation was the fact that in September 1946, March had made a $5,000 donation to Grierson and Legg's The World Today, Inc. The informant's report charged: 'This organization is a documentary film-producing business headed by [John] Grierson and [Stuart] Legg, both of whom are subjects of investigation at New York as possible Russian espionage agents.'[78] Ironically, Grierson and Legg were already back in Britain at the Central Office of Information. In 1952 Grierson was put in charge, with John Baxter, of Group 3, the organization set up by the National Film Finance Corporation to train young directors. Then, in the mid-fifties, he returned to his native Scotland. Though discouraged with the impasse which the documentary film movement had reached, he approached Roy Thomson, the Canadian newspaper owner who had just acquired the independent television network in Scotland. Thomson let Grierson begin This Wonderful World, a programme of public and international affairs. Characteristic of the man, the title reflected Grierson's unyielding optimism and durability in a time of paranoia and cold-war hostility. The venture became a commercial success and ran for over a decade.

What Grierson had learned was that nations were not ready to forget partisan politics or sacrifice national sovereignty for a vision of international solidarity. War, either hot or cold, was the modus operandi of the world. He had wanted to 'make peace exciting' in the postwar world via the medium of film. But film was to be eclipsed by the all-pervasive medium of television with its commercial rather than ideological message. Worse for him, his entrapment in the natural snares of Canadian partisan politics shattered his idealist dream. He had not operated in Canada from a political or power base; rather, his power derived from special consideration during a national crisis. His fall from grace was living proof that though the politically strong may not always be in the right, the politically weak are invariably in the wrong.

8 | Last Words: The Grierson Legacy

By the end of the Second World War in Canada, propaganda, which had been designed to cajole populations, inspire belief, build consensus and national will, boost morale, and spell out the national purpose, seemed to have become again a suspect activity, despite Grierson's long campaign to equate it with education. His concept of education was not the liberal process of presenting fact, objection, then conclusion. It was supposed to provide a moral imperative for citizens, to stir national loyalties, to inspire self-sacrifice, to elevate the community to a higher level than self, to place cooperation above individualism and internationalism above nationalism. When Grierson had justified the equation of education with propaganda, he was reaching back to the seventeenth-century College of Propaganda, whose purpose was to educate priests for missions. Then, the purpose was to stem the rising tides of Protestant ideology, with its doctrine of individualism, and of the nascent scientific revolution. The power of the most dominant institution, the Catholic church, was to be used to control and inspire the masses by directing both creative and destructive energies. In the long run, the church lost its propaganda crusade to the nation state, which in turn raised the ideology of individualism and capitalism to a supreme virtue.

When Grierson was given the go-ahead to educate his own 'priests' for missions, he was in a peculiar way reacting against the same forces the Catholic church did battle with three centuries before. He wanted to propagandize for a higher ideal than the self and the narrow nationalism of the self-destructive nation-state. He thought an elite group of missionaries could bend the powers of the state into a useful instrument, appealing to the common sense, intelligence, and goodness of

Tom Daly learned his skills working under Stuart Legg on the NFB theatrical series. Daly became one of the principal creative talents at the Film Board. (NFB)

Postwar NFB productions veered sharply away from geopolitical themes. Here Paul Martin, minister of national health and welfare, stands on the set of *The Feeling of Hostility* (1947), one of the *Mental Mechanisms* series. (NFB)

Grierson, as he appeared to a new generation in 1964, eight years before his death. (NFB)

groups which historically had been ignored and submerged by the rhetoric of dominant institutions. His mission was a reaction both against
values of individualism and for the moral authority of the state. The
state had replaced the established church, and its secular task was to
promote collective action and responsibility for the general good. His
and his followers' reward was only the satisfaction of knowing that
service to an ideal higher and nobler than oneself is its own reward. It
was the same moral stuff that Calvin had used to oil the wheels of his
crusade. No person affiliating himself with this ideal could be bought –
with an authority derived from the God of Moses, it was authority or
power associated with awesome responsibility. As he put it years later,
quoting a British prime minister, 'Power without responsibility, all
down the ages, is the prerogative of the harlot.'[1] When he speculated on
the nature of that responsibility as teacher-motivator, he paraphrased a
French-Canadian word which was not in the dictionary. It was the verb
'imaginate.' He talked about people in education who teach the power
of 'imaginating' instead of analysing. It was their inspiration as teachers
which could open magic windows on subjects which could condition
minds and could motivate. They were part of a process of affecting the
sentiment, determining loyalties, and evoking the powers of the will to
action. The 'imaginator' was also the teacher and Grierson pronounced
that a great teacher was in his own right a great artist in the moulding
of minds.[2]

Such high-power pontification notwithstanding, why had propaganda failed to become respectable? For one thing, by 1945, after the
blood-letting of two world wars, the electronic communications revolution had pervaded and shrunk the world. Print, film, radio, and soon
television would in combination change the course of politics and
national life. If one ignores the subjective connotation usually applied
to the word 'totalitarian,' that is what governments had become during
the national emergency. They had used wartime to develop powers to
manipulate the major media to reach every level of society for their
own particular ends in order to win the war. Grierson had wanted to
extend those powers into peacetime. Liberal democracy said no. He had
been conducting what he and Stuart Legg called in 1943 a war for men's
minds, a propaganda war which employed the new techniques of mass
persuasion that had been learned in the First World War. Not surpris-
ingly, they were the same techniques which were used by the fascist

enemies who hated democracy and who believed might determined what was right. Grierson's main preoccupation was film and he wanted the documentary to be an instrument to affirm progressive democracy and to reveal truths 'in the quiet light of ordinary humanism.' If progressive democracy sounds as vague and non-controversial as motherhood, it is because Grierson purposely left his terms of reference undefined and unpolitical. As he explained it years later, 'You must always act as though you were working for the whole of Parliament.' His responsibility as film commissioner was held for the prime minister, who in turn held it for the whole nation.[3] The pious platitudes were unassailable. He believed he was orchestrating a plan of government or national management which had been in general agreed to by Parliament. He tried to make that national plan successful through information without confusing his large educational duty with the party in power.[4]

The film propaganda machine he created in Canada used the wartime context to show a young, vital, and committed Canada engaged in a mammoth undertaking on behalf of a future world at peace. The propaganda, if dependent on a background showing the swords of war, demonstrated how they would be beaten into ploughshares of peace. To the government, he was a faithful if zealous servant who inspired public faith and trust and was totally opposed to the spreading of doom and despondency, something he identified as a form of illiteracy and of non-leadership.[5] The fervour of his missionizing never diminished. In fact he believed so intensely in his self-appointed task of stirring democratic loyalties and of being the eyes of democracy that by war's end the government was ready to heed Lester Pearson's earlier admonition, 'Watch out for St. John and his disciples.'

His ideas may have been progressive and far ahead of those of the other Allied nations. He foresaw a new world order of internationalism replacing nationalism. For Canada, this was not a practical postwar dream, since the King government could not pursue inspirational platitudes in a world of power alignments not unlike earlier epochs. Grierson's messianism was intellectually unassailable, but Canada's pursuit of 'functionalism' (traditional power relationships in an all-inclusive world order) would bring it into close alignment with United States postwar foreign policy. The hot war against fascist aggression would become a cold war against communist ideology and the erstwhile Russian ally. The internationalist approach of Grierson and Legg was anachronistic in this remake of the old order. Grierson was one of the first public men to stumble as the postwar era began. His political enemies were quick to pounce and his fall from grace was rapid.

In both the *Canada Carries On* and the *World in Action* film series, Grierson and Stuart Legg had tried to promote a common faith while treating diverse themes. Those which were internally oriented often demonstrated how collective energies were bringing Canadians together as a nation, how raw materials and transportation were important cogs in the Allied war machine, and how the role of women would never again be the same in the postwar world. Those subjects which were directed toward non-parochial themes promised a postwar world in which international cooperation would prevent humanity from destroying itself. Behind that premise may have lain another less obvious quality which reflected much of the thinking of liberal left-leaning individuals in the thirties vis-à-vis the Soviet Union. That power was no longer to be treated as a pariah but as a respected member of the world community of nations. If most knew that the Soviet authorities had been ruthless in their consolidation of power, the ordinary people were to be seen like their counterparts the world over. Learning to live with the Communists reflected the progress of twentieth-century secularization. The suspension of disbelief had shifted from the religious to the political realm. Like it or not, humanity had to live with (and perhaps come to like) the former godless foe. The same thinking applied to films about vanquished Italy and, finally, a ravaged and humbled Germany. Accommodation to new political realities rather than creation of them characterized the Grierson crusade. He was only creating new loyalties to those facts. But national and international propaganda themes were two distinct species. It was one thing to coordinate internal national propaganda to lessen tension in the coal industry, but it was quite something else to preach both at home and abroad internationalism and an end to traditional power politics. Prime Minister King did not like this idealism, especially since it exposed the government's flank to opposition attack. He was more consumed with worry about how to achieve international power arrangements to avoid nuclear holocaust. Grierson's flirtation with 'controversy' was annoying rather than specifically harmful to the government policy of 'functionalism' in foreign affairs.

As he looked over the progress he had made in the war years, Grierson could feel satisfied that the documentary film as war propaganda had, with few exceptions, used images of actuality to give poetic shape and poetic effect to an important historical period when civilization was on trial. Once the trial was over, the position of the Canadian government was not unlike that of the British government in the late thirties. If some were critical of film propaganda which seemed to have become 'political,' that is, progressive and even ahead of government policy, others, probably the majority, did not think much of what Grierson had been doing because they were not very interested in the subject. Most of the government did not realize that he and Legg had been trying to steer Canada into an idealistic internationalist postwar position. Grierson had been left largely alone for over five years because he was a 'hot gospeller' and seemed to be doing some good for Canada.

At the same time, on a practical level, Grierson had conducted a low-key publicity campaign on behalf of Canada's publicly dull prime minister. There were never many references to King in the propaganda films, though not infrequent appearances in still photos did his public image no harm. But the general consent which Grierson thought was always behind him turned out to be elusive as King and the government abandoned him. He so much as admitted it in 1946 when he spoke of the degree of general sanction which does not allow forthright discussions of highly controversial problems. Those who wished to pursue controversial and difficult themes in future years, he suggested, might find sponsors less hamstrung than governments. I have tried to demonstrate how part of his failure was his inability to form permanent alliances with his political superiors. His implication by association in the sensational Gouzenko spy scandal sealed his abandonment.

It was natural that, with the end of the war, the government would reassess its information policy. The Gouzenko affair only speeded the process. President Harry Truman was driving his nation headlong into a new era of confrontation, and he expected his allies to follow him. He used the Gouzenko affair as a catalyst (along with Churchill's Fulton, Missouri speech) to achieve anti-communist unity. In the United States it served as an early curtain-raiser to McCarthyism. In Canada, despite the profound shock waves and paranoia it triggered, its long-range impact was less virulent, though unhappily for Grierson a hungry opposition, already angered at the National Film Board's free publicity for Prime Minister King, turned its attention to that agency. Revenge and the last word would be theirs. They made maximum political capital out of Gouzenko's minimal circumstantial evidence. The organization slipped into a kind of spiritual limbo. Though he was no longer in Canada, Grierson suffered disgrace. When the RCMP conducted a massive security check, the Film Board sank further into despondency. It did not seem to matter that they found no spies – the damage had already been done. The halcyon days of Grierson, the prime mover, were over. The propaganda maestro found little sympathy for internationalist ideas and brotherhood in a cold-war world.

Are there lessons to be learned from the Grierson legacy? Though I have not discussed it in the text, the Canadian experience was different from that of the United States, where the Office of War Information (the equivalent of Canada's Bureau of Public Information or Wartime Information Board) under ex-newspaperman Lowell Mellet was ridiculed for its early attempt to influence Hollywood film production. Americans demonstrated a fierce resistance to propaganda. Film director Walter Wanger wrote that Mellet's meddling was such that if Hollywood made his kind of so-called 'propaganda' they would empty the theatres. The OWI's interference, he scoffed, was based on the conviction that the American people were 'boobs.' Once Americans were in the war, they knew why they were fighting, they were not unknowing children. They resented being told, especially pedantically, that they had to make sacrifices in order to win the war. Wanger's conclusion was that audiences were unwilling to tolerate amateurish propaganda or boring movies. They wanted 'truths' to be integrated skilfully into genuine story-telling.[6]

Thus Hollywood's commitment remained, as ever, to entertainment. It began making films glamorizing the joys of military life (to stifle anti-war sentiment), then went on to explain the British and their class structure to the American public, and finally, when the United States entered the war, the films performed the role of clarification, inspiration, and entertainment. Fully 30 per cent of Hollywood's films were concerned with some aspect of the war and their success in aiding national morale had to be traced to the fact that there was a common conviction of what the war was being fought to achieve. The United States government must have been grateful for Hollywood's strong moral support. In an unusual twist on the unwritten American belief that government and private interests have little in common, by the end of the war there were five major federal departments working with the film industry in order to ensure the maximum development of overseas markets. Some might conclude that the postwar world was safer for American film markets than it was for democracy.[7]

The Frank Capra film series *Why We Fight* was an exception to Hollywood's 'hands off propaganda' attitude. This official government-sponsored series of jingo-idealistic films became part of every American soldier's basic training and in true classic documentary fashion used direct address by a narrator to confirm repeatedly why and for what Americans were fighting. They probably did much to perpetuate a belief in the Four Freedoms and good-natured liberalism.

In general, though, the United States Congress did not feel that money should be spent to bombard the American citizens with propaganda, because it feared government attempts to encourage mass communications might mean totalitarianism and an end to freedom of the press. The Congress must have been oblivious to the two Canadian theatrical series which received widespread distribution in the United States during the war years. Curiously, neither series was mentioned in Garth Jowett's *Film, The Democratic Art*, notwithstanding the National Film Board's wartime distribution figures. There is little reason to doubt that regular exposure to these films may have been changing some of the American public's attitudes to the conflict and its aftermath. During the crisis there seemed to be no opposition to Canadian-produced propaganda or fear that freedom of the press was being jeopardized, probably because both the American and Canadian governments expected the propaganda to last only until victory was achieved. With victory on the horizon in 1945, Grierson tried to preach to Hollywood the need for films to be more sensitive to their international role, especially as it concerned market domination. Few took seriously his proposal that Hollywood create an institute of international affairs for producers, directors, and writers. In the final analysis, Hollywood was not prepared to allow its product to be used as an educational tool for 'world understanding.'[8]

The lessons of the Grierson legacy start with the recognition of a series of misconceptions. Grierson probably assumed that his political masters were converted to his crusade because he had won so many battles. I have demonstrated that most treated him like an outsider who did not understand internal Canadian politics very well. He may have thought that much of his success was derived from the fact that he was a temporary, not permanent, civil servant. Canada, like most modern governments, does not encourage temporary civil servants. It prefers a permanent, rigid, and machine-like bureaucracy which is governed by unbending rules. So Grierson's position from the outset, if enviable for its freewheeling character, was always an anomalous one. He may have suffered from another misconception, believing that he had established on a permanent basis official film propaganda as an integral part of the governing process. When the government rejected his choice of heir apparent and his tentative plan to marry the National Film Board to the Department of External Affairs, it should have become obvious that no one was listening. Perhaps by then he knew that his crusade in Canada had reached a logical dead end and that he might find more success on the international level. Once he left, spiritual depression overcame the National Film Board as North America slipped into the cold war.

What Grierson seemed to miss in his assessment of Canadian politics was the fact that Canadian politicians in general did not regard the world as a part of their bailiwick, and were not known for their broad progressive attitudes toward it. It was far easier for them to put their energy into the mundane affairs of their provinces and regions. Grierson miscalculated Canada's political maturity and the rate at which the country would arrive at an internationalist view similar to his own. His ability to see politics as a long-range process leading toward international peaceful coexistence (a phrase he did not use but which describes his position) was remarkable for the time; not unexpectedly, in the short run he failed to make a significant impact in diverting Canadian politics from their regional bias. It would seem to explain in part the crusader's lack of long-term success and the failure of documentary film in Canada to become an ideological tool of change.

This leads to a last major point, the personal strength of Grierson himself. On the one hand I have demonstrated how his dynamic spirit moved people, organizations, and governments. His employees caught his infectious enthusiasm and felt that they were engaged in the job of the century. Alan Adamson, who worked doggedly for Grierson for some months after Pearl Harbor, has characterized him as 'this small, passionate, angry, caustic, militant, radical Scot, this teacher whose pedagogical secret was example, who may not in the end have been sure of what he was to exemplify, but who made the air vivid by signing it with his vitality.'[9] It was as good a description of Grierson in motion as any could be. The conclusion of Ross McLean, whose years as assistant film commissioner gave him the chance to see every facet of Grierson's character and purpose, has summed up the man and the enigma with equal verve: 'Grierson was a curious combination of a man who had respect for the conformist, yet was attached to the irreconcilable. If he was a propagandist for ideas, he was also a peculiar amalgam of irreconcilable opposites.'[10]

It may have been his major flaw. The strength of a successful movement must come from within, from its intellectual core, and, in the case of public servants, with the consent of the ruling powers. Irreconcilable opposites may seem to many to characterize twentieth-century existence, but men in government have little tolerance for opposition in their underlings, especially in a servant who publicly claims to stand an inch to the left of the party in power. It could be argued that Grierson's Canadian propaganda crusade may have been doomed long before he left for New York. The spy scandal's embarrassing circumstantial evidence only sealed its fate.

Grierson had believed that Canada's liberal democratic government would make available and encourage various media sources in times of peace to wage propaganda campaigns if their purpose was to instil in the public a faith in society, not partisan parties. But governments generally do not like to wear their hearts on their sleeves unless there is a crisis of war, or its moral equivalent. Grierson and his propagandists had employed a method which was loud and propositional, full of crescendos and repetitive in theme. Once the war was won, the method would have to change and so too would the propaganda. It was time for Canada to learn to listen to its own quiet and steady pulse. Canadian documentary film would undergo a metamorphosis in the 1950s.[11]

There is little reason to doubt Grierson's assumption that, if interest can be maintained, the documentary approach of listening to as well as speaking to the people might facilitate the democratic process and enable the millions to acquire faith in their individual systems of government and eventually a faith in a world based upon international cooperation. Perhaps documentary film could have taught working people how to make informed critical judgments on the great issues facing mankind this century. An idealist like Grierson can afford to dream, especially if he is fortunate enough to appear at a certain historical crossroad or moment of crisis, like world war. Once the crisis was over, Grierson pointed toward one road – liberal democracy chose the other, sensing that it was better to say nothing to the millions than to undo the credo of individualism and *laisser-faire* and cope with the consequences of direct government manipulation of the public's thinking and attitudes.

The governments which had employed Grierson had done so for specific ends – they wanted film propaganda to strike a responsive collective chord during the crisis of the times. It would seem that Grierson's misconception in Canada was that, once given his head, he could convert the government to his democratic crusade and convince it to respond to the needs of the citizenry with fully integrated social legislative programmes. The citizens too were to become an active element in the whole process. But his ideas were alien; social legislation was to be reluctantly doled out piecemeal, rather than presented as a coherent plan for a brave new world. If his political masters understood film propaganda and information at all, it was in terms of an assumption that information should reflect the position and belief of the ruling groups. Overall, they rejected the idea of regular political propaganda and at best they were content to address the masses infrequently by means of a one-way process. Thus would they guarantee the illusion of freedom of speech and information. As one defender of democracy (and communications specialist) described the conflict between fascism and democracy in 1942, 'In totalitarian countries the elite communicates in frankness and truth only to the elite; to the masses it communicates in terms of desired response. The distinction of democracy is that the knowing elite should communicate in frankness and truth to the masses.'[12]

Grierson's conception of communication pushed this class attitude a step further. He wanted to make democracy work by listening to the public as well as by speaking to the public. Again the sceptical might ask if Grierson was really listening to working-class Canada, say, in the same way that a publication like *Mass Observation* listened to working-class England in the pubs, community centres, and churches. His use of the Gallup Poll and Canadian Institute of Public Opinion polls at the Wartime Information Board (admittedly for non-film purposes) was and remains a dubious way to listen to the masses, though such polls may be useful to governments who wish to confirm policies. It should be remembered too that many members of the original documentary film school were Cambridge graduates who came from so-called bour- geois intellectual backgrounds. How could such people (and their Canadian counterparts) know what the working classes were feeling? Were Grierson and his students only trying to articulate what they thought the population was thinking? Such questions are not easy to answer. But the original strength of the movement lay in the fact that the filmmakers pursued Grierson's dictum, 'You must forever go where the people are.' This forced them to relate their art and intellect to the masses who comprised society, not to the groups which ruled it. The people provided the filmmakers with their subject. As late as 1969 the propaganda maestro was still cajoling and exhorting his listeners: 'The main thing is that we've got to get the man who can go and drink with the people, and drink in the right places and hear the right conversa- tions, and ask the right questions, and get the right answers,' he said. It was a matter of looking again at the whole business of reporting in depth – in dramatic depth, in and about the country and on every front.[13] Listening to him, it was as if the war was still on and his propa- ganda mission was at full throttle.

Commitment to the working man, personal honesty, absolute integ- rity, and unbridled optimism led Grierson to believe that democracy would become stronger in this century. Why could not democracies seek out and cultivate more public servants like himself? All he did was in the name of democracy. Using a lifelong talent for good timing, he had seized the opportune moments which the times had offered and believed that North America would become the successful proving ground for his theories of propaganda. It would seem that he must have been profoundly influenced by his early exposure to North America and his ideas of how North Americans got things done. Grierson acted very nearly like the cowboy out of the old West who came into town to clean things up, hung up his guns, turned in his badge, and left the townsfolk wondering just who that man was.[14] The host government could only breathe a little easier once he moved on. If the post-Second World War government could praise the citizens for having sacrificed enough to make the world safe for democracy, it was in essence the democracy of the ruling groups. The ordinary citizen was once again adrift in a sea of alienation, no closer to having a significant grasp of or input into the destiny of his 'democratic' society than before the Grierson crusade.

Was Grierson's propaganda mission an aberration? A movement needs more than strong leadership if it is to survive. Grierson's ideas made rational sense, but the successes he had were reflections of his personal charisma, not of his hosts' acceptance of or conversion to his doctrines. When they looked closely at what he and his colleagues had done, they were not overly pleased and said 'No thank you, Mr Grierson,' changing the direction of government information after he was gone, perhaps a little sorrier that he had not been kept more in check. The relatively short honeymoon of liberal democratic government and Grierson's documentary film propaganda approach ended with the close of the Second World War. Grierson and his propagandists had tried to transplant a 'foreign' value to Canada, the idea of collective community-oriented responses to the modern world; perhaps the American value of rugged individualism had already planted itself so deep within the social fabric of Canada that Grierson's idea could not take root. Canada may have come to infer, like the United States, that if the impulse for government activity in the field of communications grew stronger, the very continuance of democracy might be in danger. Besides, the era of television and the cold war would make the whole documentary approach of two-way information somewhat unfashionable. Grierson's message, 'working in the quiet light of ordinary humanism,' especially seemed hollow as liberal democracy let television assume dominance in the new age of one-way communication.

It is a truism that propaganda must reflect the aims and goals of the dominant system. Grierson's dream was to build from this point and to make film propaganda forever inspiring and an agent of change within the existing system. In hindsight, perhaps the whole crusade seems premature and, under the circumstances, resembles the proverbial cart before the horse. The dream, none the less, has been left intact to the progressives who followed in the next generations. The National Film Board of Canada is the permanent edifice he designed it to be, although it has come under attack in recent years because its sixty-million-dollar-plus annual budget, in times of fiscal restraint, is a natural target at home. And opponents in the United States found their mark when they identified recent controversial films as political propaganda by an agent of a foreign power. This is embarrassing because propaganda is no longer in the Film Board's terms of reference. Grierson's 1940 prediction that the Film Board would be the 'eyes of Canada and would, through a national use of cinema, see Canada and see it whole – its people and its purposes,' rings as true today as it did then. The film agency remains a unique experiment in a commercial world of cost effectiveness and bottom lines. It must still struggle to perpetuate its existence and prove its worthiness. The Grierson eminence remains as the Film Board continues consciously and subconsciously to interpret Canada to Canadians and to the world. His public life remains an example to those who believe that selfless devotion to a just cause is its own reward. He will always have the respect of those sympathetic to his ideas but will probably remain a dreamer to the political elites whom he sought to convert. Grierson's failure was not in his conception about what propaganda film could do, but in the questionable belief that the dominant elites in liberal democracies could be convinced to exercise their power and authority forever on behalf of the masses. His success was to establish a film tradition which others have built upon, a liberal tradition which, unafraid of controversy, still affirms and celebrates human potential and dignity.

APPENDIX

NOTES

LIST OF PRIMARY SOURCES

INDEX

Appendix

WARTIME INFORMATION BOARD   Ottawa 22nd. November 1943

Report on the W.I.B. Morale-building Programme in the
Coalmining Industry

1 Early in March the Coal Labour Supply Committee asked the W.I.B. to
  prepare a morale-building programme for the coalmining industry.
  The purpose of that programme was:
  a / To make some contribution to a reduction of absenteeism and to
  improve morale among coalminers by emphasizing the importance
  to the war effort of increased coal production
  b / To give to the miners the feeling that their efforts and contribution were being given recognition throughout the country
  c / To give to the general public some appreciation of the role of
  coalmining and the miners in the war.

2 On March 11th I submitted to the Coal Labour Supply Committee
  a programme suggesting a number of projects which might be
  attempted. Subsequent to the approval of several aspects of the programme, the Department of Labour appropriated the sum of $18,000
  for films on coalmining and $8,000 for a graphics programme.

3 Although we had recommended that an intensive survey of absenteeism in coalmining throughout Canada be undertaken as a basis for
  the morale programme, the Department of Labour did not undertake
  the survey. The absence of detailed and first-hand information on
  conditions in the coalmines was seriously felt in launching the programme.

4 Virtually all aspects of the programme have already been put into effect. In view of recent developments in the coalmines, their results may seem open to question. It must nevertheless be borne in mind that measurement of the effect of any morale programme is an extremely difficult affair. The factors responsible for work stoppages in the mines were related to matters of fundamental policy and beyond the scope of any information programme. There has been, however, considerable evidence that the programme has been well received by the coalminers and has, to some degree, served the purpose of the campaign.

5 What follows is a statement of the various projects initiated or motivated by the Industrial Morale Section of the W.I.B. No attempt is made to list them in order of their importance or time:

a / RESEARCH: As soon as approval for the programme was secured, extensive research, both in Ottawa and in the field, was begun in order to secure background data on Canadian coalmining and information as to present conditions of labour and attitudes and opinions in coalmining areas. Particularly valuable in this regard were the researches of the National Film Board staff which undertook intensive investigation in the major coalmining areas of Canada in connection with a programme of both film and still picture production. Information was also secured from the Department of Labour, the Coal Administrator's office in the Department of Munitions and Supply, the Canadian Congress of Labour, the United Mineworkers of America – Districts 18 and 26, and field correspondents.

b / FILM CIRCUITS: Arrangements were made with the National Film Board for immediate extension of the industrial film circuits, showing a monthly programme of morale and war information films, to the coalmining areas. Circuits were established in the coalmining areas as early as May, and to date, have been set up on the following 37 centres:

ALBERTA		BRITISH COLUMBIA
Cadomin	Newcastle	Cumberland
Luocar	Rosedale	Union Bay
Mountain Park	Nacmine	Nanaimo
Robb	Canmore	Natal
Mercoal	Shaughnessy	

ALBERTA

		NOVA SCOTIA
Saunders	Midlandvale	Little Bras d'Or
Nordegg	Michel	Sydney Mines
Sterco	Carbon	Glace Bay
Alexa	Drumheller	Florence
Wayne	Lethbridge	New Waterford
Blairmore		Springhill
Hillcrest		Stellarton
Bellevue		New Aberdeen
Coleman		
East Coulee		

These film circuits have been enthusiastically received both by management and workers alike.

c / FILMS: Arrangements were made with the Film Board for the production and revision of a series of films on various aspects of coalmining and the importance of coal in the war economy.

'Getting Out the Coal' and 'King Coal': These two British films, one on the importance and role of coal, and the other on labour-management co-operation in British coalmines, were revised for Canadian use and distributed through the Trade Union circuits of the National Film Board during August, September and October.

'Coalface, Canada': As soon as the programme was approved, production was started on a major film on coalmining in Canada. This film was completed this month and released in the 'Canada Carries On' series in most Canadian theatres during the week of November 15th. Special premieres were arranged in Glace Bay, N.S., and Blairmore, Alta., where most of the film was shot.

Film News Story: A newsreel story was shot in Nova Scotia on Canadian soldiers who had asked for discharge in order to return to the mines to assist in increasing coal production. This newsreel story was accepted by four or the five major American newsreel companies and exhibited in virtually all American theatres. It was described by several American newsreel editors as 'the best film story ever to come out of Canada.' It was also exhibited in practically all Canadian theatres.

d / RADIO: Arrangements were made with the C.B.C. for a series of broadcasts from the coalmining areas. These included:

'Production Front' Series: Two broadcasts on coal were included on

Allen May's 'Production Front' series – one from Sydney, N.S. on July 10th, the other from Calgary, Alta., on September 15th, on the Alberta coal fields.

'The Fighting Front' Series: On July 8th Bob Bowman broadcast on coalmining in Cape Breton from Sydney in his 'Fighting Front' series.

'Canadian Round-up': During September, the 'Canadian Round-up' series included a broadcast from Calgary on coalmining.

e / GRAPHICS PROGRAMME: Arrangements were made with the Graphics Division of the National Film Board for an extensive programme on the various aspects of coalmining. This programme included:

News Photo Release: A news photo story was released in June on the discharge of ex-miners from the army for work in the mines and on the return of ex-miners in civilian jobs to the coalmines. This story was widely published throughout the Canadian press. A similar news photo story, released for American distribution to coincide with the film news story was carried in over 4,000 newspapers in the United States.

Still Picture Page: A full page of still pictures on various aspects of coalmining throughout Canada was released for distribution throughout the Canadian press on July 10th. This page was widely reproduced across the country.

Retrogravures: Special still picture stories were prepared for release to the rotogravure sections of Canadian newspapers. A number of papers reproduced these pictures. Particularly outstanding was the 8-page rotogravure section on coalmining in the 'Montreal Standard' of July 10th.

Press & Photo Release: was prepared for distribution to Canadian papers to coincide with the premiere of the National Film Board's documentary film 'Coal Face, Canada.'

Rotogravure Wall-hangers: Forty thousand rotogravure wall-hangers depicting coalmining in Canada are now in production and will shortly be distributed, in co-operation with Provincial Departments of Education, to all schools throughout the country.

Photo-panel Displays: Twenty-four large photo-panel displays on various aspects of coalmining are being prepared and will shortly be shipped to the major coalmining centres in the country for exhibition in public buildings, libraries and trade union halls. In order to achieve maximum effectiveness, each display is being built around the coalmining activities of the particular area to which it will be shipped.

Booklets: An illustrated booklet on Canadian coalmining and the importance of coal in the war economy is being prepared for distribution throughout the industrial areas of the country. Distribution of the booklet is planned to coincide with the release of 'Coal Face Canada' for showing on the industrial film circuits.

f / LABOUR MANAGEMENT COMMITTEES: Recommendations were made to the Coal Labour Supply Committee and to the Inter-departmental Committee on Labour-Management Committees that immediate attempts be made to organize labour-management committees in the coalmines. The Inter-departmental Committee on Labour-Management Committees has already reported considerable progress in this direction.

g / INCOME TAX: Discussions were carried on by the Coal Labour Supply Committee and the Industrial Morale Section of W.I.B. with the Department of National Revenue with regard to suggested changes in the system of income-tax deductions for coalminers.

h / PRESS: Material was provided on several occasions from this office for a number of newspaper stories and articles on various phases of the coalmining situation, which subsequently appeared in Canadian newspapers and magazines.

David Petegorsky
Industrial Morale Division
WARTIME INFORMATION BOARD.

SUMMARY OF WARTIME INFORMATION BOARD SURVEYS

No.		*Some Major Themes*
1	(January 1943)	Changes due to good news, decline in divisive rumours, readiness for sacrifice
2		Attitudes to postwar Canada
3		Attitudes to war effort and further taxation
4	(February 1943)	Attitudes to wartime information and trustworthiness
5		Rumours survey
6	(March 1943)	Sense of participation in war, reactions to war budget
7		Canadian nationhood and morale questions
8	(April 1943)	Canada and Soviet Russia: needs to create atmosphere of mutually friendly postwar relations and stress the human individuals and human characteristics of the Russian system
9		State of public opinion
10	(May 1943)	Current information needs
11		
12	(June 1943)	Media problems: most effective channels?
13		Effectiveness of the war effort
14	(July 1943)	United States attitudes towards Canada
15		National pride / reactions to Sicily campaign
16		Attention to war news / reading of newspapers
17	(August 1943)	Civilian morale
18		Sacrifice: equal or unequal?
19	(September 1943)	Regional grievances
20		Anti-inflation controls
21	(October 1943)	Canadian-Russian cooperation: Canadian attitudes to postwar relations
22		Propaganda methods in Nazi Germany
23	(November 1943)	Manpower needs
24		Price and wage ceilings
25	(December 1943)	Postwar hopes
26		Where Canadians need more information

27 (January 1944)   Domestic versus world problems; Canadians concerned with former

28   Continuation of postwar controls: split opinion

29   Reconstruction and rehabilitation: the big Canadian question

30 (February 1944)   Attitudes to postwar immigration

31   French-English Canadian relations generally worse

32 (March 1944)   What is the appeal of Victory Bonds?

33   Dissatisfaction with handling of war news; national optimism leads to slackening of effort

34 (April 1944)   Few Canadians knew of or understood government *Mutual Aid* programme a year after its introduction

36 (May 1944)   Inflation: analyses of public understanding

37   Views of Germans and Japanese after the war

38 (June 1944)   Twenty topics on which Canadians want more information

39   Equal or unequal sacrifice among Canadian classes?

40   Survey of complaints against government administration

41 (July 1944)   Attitudes to postwar planning

42   Approval of price control, less support for wage control

43 (August 1944)   Where is manpower most needed?

44   Expectations for postwar employment; confidence and uncertainty

45 (September 1944)   World peace / Allied harmony?

46   UNRRA: few Canadians know of it

47 (October 1944)   Inflation – public attitudes

48   What to do with money formerly deducted as compulsory savings

49   Manpower controls in civilian work?

50 (November 1944)   How should war news be handled?

51   Winning the war and planning the peace

SEVEN-WEEK SAMPLE OF WARTIME INFORMATION BOARD
PUBLIC OPINION SUMMARY FOR WAR CABINET COMMITTEE
(Typical Summaries)

Date	Themes
10 November 1943	Optimism, Moscow, Victory Loan, coal strike, postwar pessimism, doubts that government has any real plans to prevent unemployment
17 November	Optimism, Moscow, decentralized hog production, strikes, cost of living up, wages down, victory loan, postwar fear of unemployment
24 November	Optimism, lay-offs (actual and rumoured), Japan ignored, price and wage ceilings, interest in postwar plans
1 December	Optimism declines; no German collapse expected; confidence in military leaders; farmers think war is ending (hog sales)
6 December	Decline in optimism that war will be over by Christmas; Japan still being ignored; raids on Berlin terrible but necessary; expectation of dramatic announcements from Allied meetings; desire to know postwar government plans; hog problems; children's clothing not available
14 December	Caution about early German collapse; public feels let down after sensational predictions about Teheran Conference; Prime Minister King's speech on inflation a 'masterly presentation'; majority of public behind stabilization measures; beer restrictions criticized
20 December	November optimism about war ending over; much goodwill now felt toward Russia will disappear if it fails to aid in defeating Japan; postwar plans?; controls good

The following compilation of titles and information is based upon the personal recollections of James Beveridge, Stanley Hawes, and Stuart Legg, and the published record of the National Film Board in Peter Morris' *The War Years* (Ottawa: Canadian Film Institute, 1965), 20–32.

The series *Canada Carries On* was produced under the supervision of Stuart Legg until 1942, when there were rotating producers. At the end of the war Sydney Newman became supervising producer. John Grierson and Stuart Legg produced the series *The World in Action*. Tom Daly was principal editor. Speaking of both series, James Beveridge summarized his memory of the principal architects:

It was in essence a matter of a small group, quite cohesive, with three fairly experienced British producers all masterminded by Grierson who also kept his own personal pipeline to individual young filmmakers, to jive them up and stimulate them and give them his own sense of perspective. Legg was a kind of adjutant general, a relentless cool intellect. Hawes was steady and slow and a wonderful craftsman and teacher. Meticulous. He had the greatest respect for the film medium in a physical tactile sense. [It was] respect for film as substance, as material, with its special properties and requirements. Legg was the master of 'image' – the real impact, value, and significance of an individual film image. Both of them in their different ways were terrific *teachers.*

Stuart Legg recalled a somewhat different structure. The *World in Action* unit of himself, Tom Daly, Gordon Weisenborn, and Margaret Ann Adamson (now Lady Elton) was very compact, and, having made nearly all the *Canada Carries On* issues until late 1941, made all the major *World in Action* films until 1945. A few of Hawes' films were put out under the *Canada Carries On* label from time to time, but he was not a regular producer on either series. Remembering his own role, Legg tended to minimize his very major contribution:

I was not a kind of adjutant general but a producer turning out a film a month with three permanent staff and various extra-unit technical services to help me. (Sometimes I was asked for advice by other NFB units on specific problems, but I had no general mandate.) Jim Beveridge implies that Grierson was much closer to our compact unit than he in fact was: he had countless other fish to fry at that time.

CANADA CARRIES ON

Atlantic Patrol (April 1940) 10 min; prod/ed/scr Stuart Legg
Letter From Aldershot (May 1940) 11 min; prod Stuart Legg

Home Front (June 1940) 11 min; dir Stanley Hawes

Front of Steel (July 1940) prod Stuart Legg

Squadron 992 (August 1940) revision of Crown Film Unit film

Wings of Youth (September 1940) 19 min; prod Raymond Spottiswoode; camera Roger Barlow

Britain at Bay (October 1940) UK film, Priestly?

Letter from Camp Borden (November 1940) 17 min; prod Stuart Legg; dir Raymond Spottiswoode

Un du 22ième (November 1940) prod Gerald Noxon

Children from Overseas (December 1940) prod Stuart Legg, Stanley Hawes, Ruby Grierson; Grierson's sister Ruby was lost at sea while shooting this 10-minute film aboard the *Arandora Star*

Guards of the North (January 1941) 10 min; prod Audio Pictures

Everywhere in the World (February 1941) 16 min; prod Stuart Legg

Peoples of Canada (March 1941) orig. version Gordon Sparling at Associated Screen News for NFB; later revised as 2-reel version

Battle of Brains (April 1941) 13 min; prod Stuart Legg and Tom Daly; dir Stanley Hawes

Heroes of the Atlantic (May 1941) 15 min; prod Stanley Hawes; dir and camera J.D. Davidson and Donald Fraser

Churchill's Island (June 1941) 22 min; prod/ed/scr Stuart Legg

Strategy of Metals (July 1941) 19 min; prod/ed/scr Stuart Legg

Soldiers All (August 1941) 20 min; prod Stuart Legg

Battle for Oil (September 1941) 21 min; prod Stuart Legg

A Tale of Two Cities (October 1941) 19 min; scr Graham McInnes

Warclouds in the Pacific (November 1941) 22 min; ed/scr Stuart Legg; Tom Daly compiled footage; research Margaret Ann Adamson; asst eds Gordon Weisenborn and Margaret Palmer

Wings over a Continent (December 1941) 16 min; prod Raymond Spottiswoode

This Is Blitz (January 1942) prod/ed/scr Stuart Legg; assistant Tom Daly; compilation from captured German footage

Forward Commandoes (February 1942) prod Julian Roffman?

Food – Weapon of Conquest (March 1942) 21 min; prod/ed/scr Stuart Legg; assistant Tom Daly; research, Margaret Ann Adamson

High over the Borders (April 1942) revision of film by Irving Jacoby working on contract to NFB

Geopolitik – Hitler's Plan for Europe (May 1942) prod/dir/scr Stuart Legg; assistant Tom Daly; others helping with compilation Gordon Weisenborn, Margaret Ann Adamson, Margaret Palmer (also a *World in Action* 20-min release)

Road to Tokyo (June 1942)

The Voice of Action (July 1942) 17 min; prod Raymond Spottiswoode; dir James Beveridge; Camera Boris Kauffman; asst Robert Anderson; asst camera Grant McLean

Women Are Warriors (August 1942) 14 min; dir Jane Marsh

Quebec – Path of Conquest (September 1942) 11 min; prod Raymond Spottiswoode; dir/camera F.R. Crawley

New Spirit (October 1942)

Battle of the Harvests (November 1942) 21 min; prod James Beveridge; dir Stanley Jackson; camera Dennis Gillson

Inside Fighting Canada (December 1942) prod James Beveridge; dir/ed Jane Marsh

Pincer on Axis Europe (January 1943) 20 min; prod/ed/scr Stuart Legg; assistant Tom Daly

Banshees over Canada (February 1943)

Fighting Norway (March 1943) revision of Crown Film prod from UK and some material on Norwegians training in Canada

Kill or Be Killed (*New Soldiers Are Tough*) (April 1943)

Thought for Food (May 1943) 20 min; prod Stuart Legg; dir/ed James Beveridge

Gates of Italy (June 1943) 21 min; prod/ed/scr Stuart Legg; assistant Tom Daly (also a *World in Action* release)

Trainbusters (July 1943) 13 min; prod Raymond Spottiswoode? dir Sydney Newman

Up from the Ranks (August 1943) prod Raymond Spottiswoode; dir Julian Roffman

Proudly She Marches (September 1943) dir Jane Marsh

Coal Face Canada (October 1943) scr Graham McInnes

Tomorrow's World (November 1943) prod Raymond Spottiswoode; ed/research Ernest Bornemann

Look to the North (December 1943) 22 min; prod/dir James Beveridge; camera Donald Fraser

Target Berlin (January 1944) 10 min

UNRRA – In the Wake of the Armies (March 1944) 13 min; prod/ed Guy Glover

Trans-Canada Express (April 1944) 20 min; dir/ed/camera/research
   Donald Fraser
Air Cadets (May 1944) dir/ed/scr/research Jane Marsh
Zero Hour (June 1944) 22 min; prod Stuart Legg (also a *World in
   Action* release)
Wounded in Action (July 1944) 22 min
Breakthrough (August 1944) 11 min; prod/ed James Beveridge;
   dir/photography Canadian Army Film Unit
Future for Fighters (September 1944)
Mosquito Squadron (October 1944) 11 min
Fighting Sea Fleas (November 1944) 11 min; Sydney Newman, Julian
   Roffman, and Nick Read? Canadian Navy Film Unit
Flight Six (December 1944)
Universities at War (February 1945) 11 min
Road to the Reich (March 1945) 10 min (missing from archives)
Atlantic Crossroads (April 1945) 10 min; prod Grant McLean
A Harbour Goes to France (May 1945) (missing from archives)
Headline Hunters (June 1945) 11 min; prod Julian Roffman; work of
   Canadian war correspondents based in London and Europe during
   Invasion

THE WORLD IN ACTION

Inside Fighting Russia (April, May 1942) 22 min; exec prod Stuart
   Legg; prod/ed/scr/research James Beveridge (international title
   Our Russian Ally)
Ferry Pilot (June 1942)
New Soldiers Are Tough (July 1942) 21 min
Inside Fighting China (August 1942) 22 min; possible revision of
   Joris Ivens' film *The Four Hundred Million*; prod Tom Daly?
Five Men of Australia (August 1942) revision of Australian produc-
   tion, ed Tom Daly
The Mask of Nippon (September 1942) 21 min; prod/ed/scr Stuart
   Legg; assistants Tom Daly and Gordon Weisenborn
Fighting Freighters (October 1942) 17 min
Paratroops (November 1942) prod/dir Stanley Hawes
Dover's Cliffs (December 1942)
Wings on Her Shoulder (February 1943) dir Jane Marsh
Battle Is Their Birthright (March 1943) 18 min

Road to Tokyo (January 1943) 18 min

Invasion of Europe (April 1943) 21 min

Corvette Port Arthur (May 1943) dir/scr Joris Ivens; camera John Ferno

The War for Men's Minds (June 1943) 22 min; prod/ed/scr Stuart Legg; assistants Tom Daly and Gordon Weisenborn

Letter from Overseas (July 1943)

Labour Front (August 1943) 21 min

War Birds (November 1943)

The Fighting Dutch (December 1943)

Our Northern Neighbour (January 1944) 21 min; prod/ed/scr Stuart Legg; assistant Tom Daly (international title *Russia's Foreign Policy*)

Battle of Europe (March 1944) 15 min; prod/ed/scr Stuart Legg; assistant Tom Daly

Global Air Routes (April 1944) 16 min; prod/ed/scr Stuart Legg; assistant Tom Daly

When Asia Speaks (June 1944) 15 min; prod/ed/scr Stuart Legg; assistant Tom Daly

Fortress Japan (July 1944) 22 min; prod/ed/scr Stuart Legg; assistant Tom Daly

Inside France (September 1944) 21 min; prod/ed/scr Stuart Legg; assistant Tom Daly

V-1 (December 1944) prod/ed/scr Stuart Legg; assistant Tom Daly

Balkan Powderkeg (January 1945) prod/ed/scr Stuart Legg; assistant Tom Daly (unreleased)

John Bull's Own Island (April 1945) 18 min; prod/ed/scr Stuart Legg; assistant Tom Daly

Now – The Peace (May 1945) 21 min; prod/ed/scr Stuart Legg; assistant Tom Daly

Food – Secret of the Peace (July 1945) 11 min; prod/ed/scr Stuart Legg; assistant Tom Daly

FOREIGN NON-THEATRICAL DISTRIBUTION
List of countries to which prints were shipped
(fiscal years 1943–4 and 1944–5)

Country	Prints Shipped 1943–4	Prints Shipped 1944–5
BRITISH EMPIRE		
England	400	1,270
Australia	56	62
New Zealand	–	50
Egypt	–	12
India	10	12
North Africa	–	20
South Africa	–	96
Newfoundland	–	71
Jamaica	–	20
Trinidad	–	29
TOTAL – BRITISH EMPIRE	466	1,642
EUROPE		
Belgium	–	7
France	–	62
Czechoslovakia	–	–
ASIA		
USSR	–	18
China	–	8
MEXICO AND CENTRAL AMERICA		
Mexico	26	43
Guatamala	–	1
San Salvador	–	1
Dominican Republic	–	1
Panama	–	1
SOUTH AMERICA		
Argentina	20	29
Brazil	21	29
Chile	–	22
Colombia	26	14
Cuba	–	12
Ecuador	3	4
Nicaragua	–	1
Peru	23	22
Uruguay	1	2
Venezuela	6	3
GREENLAND	–	20
TOTAL (Excluding Br. Empire and US	126	300
UNITED STATES	123	207
Puerto Rico		6
GRAND TOTAL	715	2,155

/

Notes

INTRODUCTION

1 Antonio Gramsci, *The Modern Prince and Other Writings* (New York, 1957).
2 See Bill Nichols, 'Documentary Theory and Practice,' *Screen*, 17:4 (Winter 1976–7), 34–48.
3 These fundamental attitudes toward propaganda were discussed in 1923 by an early American 'public relations' man, Edward L. Bernays. See *Crystallizing Public Opinion* (New York, 1923) and *Propaganda* (New York, 1928).

CHAPTER ONE

1 One such film can be seen in *Dreamland: A History of Early Canadian Movies 1895–1939.* Produced by CBC Television, National Film Board of Canada, Canadian Film Archives, and the commercial film industry. under the supervision of Kirwan Cox, 16 October 1974.
2 J.S. Woodsworth, *Strangers within Our Gates* (Toronto, 1909), 22–3.
3 Peter Morris, *Embattled Shadows* (Montreal, 1978), 127–58.
4 A.J.P. Taylor, *Beaverbrook* (London, 1972), 87–9.
5 Ibid., 137–8.
6 Ibid., 137–44. Also, see Tom Driberg, *Beaverbrook: A Study in Power and Frustration* (London, 1956), 125.
7 Great Britain. *Parliamentary Debates* (Commons), vol. 109, 5 August 1918, p. 958. During the debate, Jones made a pointed reference to the fact that a combination of directors of the ministry of information repre-

sented interests in banks, electric power companies, gas, railways, newspapers, rubber, insurance, iron, steel, Pullman cars, ships, and tobacco. He noted that four members of the ministry of information staff divided among themselves some fifty-four company directorships (p. 1003).

8 Public Record Office, England INF 4/1A, Official enquiries regarding propaganda during the war of 1914–18 (April 1938–June 1939, and August 1938).

9 See Arthur Marwick, *The Deluge* (London, 1965); *War and Social Change in the Twentieth Century* (London, 1974); *Britain in the Century of Total War* (London, 1968), for a discussion of the impact of total war on Britain, and J.H. Thompson, *The Harvests of War* (Toronto, 1978), chapter 2 on propaganda in Western Canada.

10 Joseph Goebbels, *The Goebbels Diaries, 1942–43*, ed. Louis P. Lochner (New York, 1948), 56.

11 Harold D. Lasswell, *Propaganda Technique in the World War* (New York, 1927), 206.

12 For a full discussion of imperial economic policy during this period, see Ian Drummond, *Imperial Economic Policy, 1917–1939* (London, 1974), 96–108.

13 Ibid., 152.

14 Sir Stephen Tallents, unpublished chapter from Tallents' autobiography which was never completed. This chapter appeared in *Journal of the University Film Association*, 20:1 (1968), 16–19.

15 James Beveridge, *John Grierson, Film Master* (New York, 1980), 132–3.

16 Grierson papers, original typescript article written for *Cinema Quarterly* (Autumn 1933).

17 John Grierson, *Grierson on Documentary*, ed. Forsyth Hardy (London, 1946), 15.

18 Beveridge, *John Grierson*, 135.

19 John Grierson, 'The Story of Documentary Film,' *The Fortnightly* (August 1939), 121–30.

20 Grierson, *Grierson on Documentary*, 124–5; 196–7; 166; 176.

21 Alan Lovell and Jim Hillier, *Studies in Documentary* (London, 1972), 18–22.

22 Grierson, *Grierson on Documentary*, 197–8. It was only in the 1960s that Marxist economists Baran and Sweezy introduced 'monopoly capitalism' to the vernacular, linking the term to a system and attitude which had no human interests to serve other than a maniacal drive for profits and

corporate immortality. See Paul A. Baran and Paul M. Sweezy, *Monopoly Capital* (New York, 1966).

23 V.I. Lenin, *On Literature and Art* (Moscow: Progress Publishers, 1967), 251. Excerpt from Clara Zetkin, 'My Recollection of Lenin' (Moscow, 1956).

24 John Vincent, *The Formation of the British Liberal Party* (New York, 1966), xiii–xvii.

25 Ronald Blumer, 'John Grierson: "I derive my faith from Moses,"' *McGill Reporter*, 1:19 (24 February 1969).

26 Grierson, *Grierson on Documentary*, 200.

27 Forsyth Hardy, *John Grierson: A Documentary Biography* (London, 1979), 80.

28 Paul Rotha, *Documentary Film* (London, 1935), p. 16.

29 Personal interview with John Grierson, 16 February 1971.

30 Personal interview with John Grierson, 10 March 1971 and Grierson, *Grierson on Documentary*, 150. A film like *Housing Problems* was a constructive prodding to 'get on' with the job of building, to which the government was already committed. See Asa Briggs, 'When You Could Buy a House for £25 Down,' *Observer Magazine* (London), 29 July 1973, pp. 23–5.

31 Elizabeth Sussex, 'The Golden Years of Grierson,' *Sight and Sound*, 41:3 (Fall, 1972), 149–53.

32 Grierson papers, undated essay.

33 Beveridge, *John Grierson*, 136.

CHAPTER TWO

1 For a more thorough discussion of the Canadian Government Motion Picture Bureau, see Peter Morris, *Embattled Shadows* (Montreal, 1978), chapter 5, 'The State and the Movies.'

2 Personal interview with Ross McLean, 5 December 1973.

3 National Film Board, 'Memorandum on the history and functions of the National Film Board,' 25 April 1947 (in possession of author).

4 Personal interview with John Grierson, 16 March 1971.

5 Public Archives of Canada (PAC), William Lyon Mackenzie King papers, memoranda and notes, 1933–9, vol. 198, O.D. Skelton to Mackenzie King, 13 January 1939.

6 Canada, *Debates of the House of Commons*, vol. 2, 7 March 1939, p. 1662.

7 Forsyth Hardy, *John Grierson: A Documentary Biography* (London, 1979), 100.

8 J.W. Pickersgill, *The Mackenzie King Record* (Toronto, 1970), 33.

9 PAC, MG26, J13, William Lyon Mackenzie King diary, 9, 11, 15, 17, 28 September; 27 October; 5, 6, 7, 8 December 1939.

10 Personal interview with Ross McLean, 5 December 1973. McLean believes that Grierson's grant for travel assignment to Canada, Australia, and New Zealand, provided by Pilgrim Trust, was funded by the Imperial Relations Trust, which in turn may have been funded by the shadow Ministry of Information.

11 PAC, King papers, correspondence (primary series) 1939, vol. 268, Grierson to Heeney, 2 November 1939.

12 PAC, King papers, correspondence (primary series), Grierson to Turnbull, 2 November 1939.

13 Personal interview with John Grierson, 14 March 1971. Grierson speculated that External Affairs was hesitant about McLean because the latter was recovering from a head injury after accidentally walking through a glass window at the League of Nations.

14 PAC, King papers, correspondence (primary series), 1940, vol. 288, Fitzgibbon to Grierson, 8 January 1940. The prime minister, who had appeared in the film, felt a 'great relief' that the film had had a warm reception. King to Pickersgill, 11 January 1940.

15 Graham McInnes, *One Man's Documentary*, unpublished manuscript deposited at National Film Board Library, Montreal 1973, pp. 10–12.

16 PAC, Cabinet War Committee, 8 December 1939.

17 John Grierson, 'Notes on Documentary by John Grierson' (marked 'private – not for circulation'), August 1943. Centre de documentation cinématographique, Bibliothèque Nationale, Montréal.

18 Raymond Fielding, *The American Newsreel, 1911–1967* (Norman, Oklahoma, 1972), 231–2. It would be interesting to know whether de Rochemont's style was influenced more by Grierson or Grierson's by *The March of Time*; perhaps there were mutual influences at work. After the war, Grierson would go into unsuccessful competition with *The March of Time*, employing his own brand of interpretive screen journalism in the documentary style.

19 PAC, External Affairs, RG 25 724W, vol. 1927, films censorship, 27 August 1940. The British government made Grierson its film censor for North America in 1940. He sent Donald Buchanan to Bermuda to receive Nazi

newsreel material seized by the Royal Navy and forward it to Ottawa where Ross McLean and Margaret Grierson, wife of John, cut out some material and released it for counter-propaganda purposes to newsreels in New York City. Other material was edited appropriately before being released. Beveridge, *John Grierson*, 141–2.

20 PAC, King diary, 19 January 1940.

21 Personal interviews with John Grierson, 14 March 1971, Ross McLean, 5 December 1973, and Walter Turnbull, 5 December 1973.

22 J.L. Granatstein, *Canada's War: The Politics of the Mackenzie King Government, 1939–45* (Toronto, 1975), 74.

23 Ibid., 92.

24 PAC, King diary, 26 March 1940.

25 PAC, King papers, correspondence (primary series), 1940, vol. 288, Michaud to Grierson, 29 May 1940; Grierson to Turnbull, 30 May 1940.

26 Ibid., Grierson to MacKinnon, 27 November 1940.

27 Forsyth Hardy, *John Grierson*, 111.

28 King papers, correspondence (primary series), 1940, vol. 288, L.W. Brockington to King, 2 December 1940.

29 PAC, Cabinet War Committee, 10 December 1940.

30 PAC, King papers, memoranda and notes series 1940–50, vol. 308, Turnbull to King, 23 January 1941.

31 PAC, King papers, correspondence (primary series), 1941, vol. 305, Grierson to MacKinnon, 11 February 1941; Grierson to Turnbull, 11 February 1941 and 30 April 1941; Turnbull to King, 1 May 1941. (Wilgress was then deputy minister at the Department of Trade and Commerce).

32 PAC, King diary, 12 May 1941.

33 Ibid., 16 May 1941.

34 PAC, Cabinet War Committee, 13 May 1941.

35 Personal interview with John Grierson, 14 March 1971.

CHAPTER THREE

1 PAC, Wartime Information Board, Claxton to King, 4 May 1941.

2 PAC, William Lyon Mackenzie King diary, 14–15 May 1941.

3 Ibid., 11 November 1942.

4 Ibid., 19 May 1941.

5 PAC, Cabinet War Committee, RG2, 7C, vol. 4, 15 October, 6, 12 November 1941.

6 *Debates of the House of Commons*, 1943, vol. 5, 13 July 1943, p. 4729.
7 PAC, External Affairs, RG25, G1, vol. 1915, draft on censorship, 20, 26 February 1942.
8 PAC, Privy Council Office, RG2, 18, vol. 15, Claxton to King, 29 May 1942.
9 *Debates of the House of Commons*, 1941, vol. 1, 20 February 1941, pp. 874–5; 13 March 1941, pp. 1510–11; vol. 4, 5 November 1941, p. 4103; 1942, vol. 1, 18 February 1942, p. 700; vol. 3, 1 June 1942, p. 2957.
10 Personal interview with Walter Turnbull, 4 January 1974.
11 PAC, Privy Council Office, RG2, 18, vol. 15, Bruce Hutchinson article, 28 February 1942.
12 PAC, Cabinet War Committee, RG2, 7C, vol. 4, 30 September 1942.
13 W.R. Young, *Making the Truth Graphic: The Canadian Government's Home Front Information Structure and Programme During World War II* (unpublished University of British Columbia PHD dissertation, 1978), 47.
14 PAC, King diary, 11 August 1942.
15 PAC, William Lyon Mackenzie King papers, correspondence (primary series) 1942, vol. 305, Grierson to Turnbull, 26 September 1942.
16 Young, *Making the Truth Graphic*, 290.
17 Ibid., 64–6.
18 PAC, Cabinet War Committee, 21 January, 3 March 1943.
19 PAC, Wartime Information Board surveys, January-May 1943.
20 Grierson to Tallents, 16 February 1943. Letter in possession of the author.
21 Grierson to Duncan McLaren, 12 March 1943 (letter in possession of the author). A practical application of these ideas was to establish personal contact with newspaper and media men across Canada. Not only did he thereby keep his finger on the pulse of the public, but he also convinced many media people of the worth of his cause.
22 Forsyth Hardy, *John Grierson: A Documentary Biography* (London, 1979), 126.
23 PAC, Wartime Information Board, 30 March 1943.
24 Ibid., monthly reports on activities.
25 PAC, King papers, memoranda and note series, vol. 376, Heeney to King, 12 July 1943.
26 PAC, Wartime Information Board, Claxton to Grierson, 2 June 1943.
27 PAC, Wartime Information Board, Grierson's speech at American Informational Meeting, 3 June 1943.

28 PAC, Wartime Information Board, note by Claxton of a conversation with Elizabeth Armstrong and Phil Coté, 28 May 1943.

29 PAC, Wartime Information Board, Claxton to Grierson, 3 July 1943.

30 These ideas for reconstruction were based on David Petegorsky's December 1942 report for the Wartime Information Board. The Film Board's chairman, L.R. Lafleche, was dubious about undertaking this responsibility, and Lester Pearson, Film Board member of the directorate, thought it should be considered later. PAC, RG 53, vol. 1, meeting of the National Film Board, 12 January 1943.

31 John Grierson, rough notes in preparation for article, 'The Shift of Power in Education,' July 1943. Centre de documentation cinématographique, Bibliothèque Nationale, Montréal.

32 PAC, Wartime Information Board, Heeney to Grierson, 23 July 1943.

33 Ibid., King to Heeney, 4 November 1943.

34 Brooke Claxton prevented one show in the series from being aired because it seemed to have strong CCF tones. Grierson tried to deflect Claxton's bluntness by agreeing that the programme contained potential but that the method of presentation left a lot to be desired. Claxton might have now felt sorry for his June 1942 declaration, 'If John Grierson is a dangerous character, it is high time we had more characters ... who do things ... without thought of the political consequences.' Young, *Making the Truth Graphic*, 99, n. 68.

35 Charles Lipton, *The Trade Union Movement of Canada, 1827–1959* (Toronto, 1973), 267–8.

36 Desmond Morton with Terry Copp, *Working People* (Ottawa, 1981), 182–3.

37 PAC, King papers, correspondence (primary series) 1943, vol. 58, Grierson to Pickersgill, 17 September 1943.

38 Ibid., Grierson to King, 6 September 1943.

39 Ibid., Grierson to King, 27 September 1943.

40 *Debates of the House of Commons*, 1943, vol. 3, 19 May 1943, p. 2819; p. 2802; vol. 2, 5 April 1943, p. 1839.

41 Ibid., vol. 5, 13 July 1943, p. 4738.

42 PAC, Cabinet War Committee, 4 August 1943.

43 PAC, King Papers, correspondence (primary series) 1943, vol. 58, Grierson to King, 9 October 1943.

44 PAC, King papers, memoranda and note series 1940–50, vol. 308, memoranda to the cabinet from Grierson, 10, 17, 24 January 1944.

45 Young, *Making the Truth Graphic*, 102–8.
46 Ibid., 297.
47 PAC, RG53, vol. 1, meeting of the National Film Board, 8 June 1943.

CHAPTER FOUR

1 Graham McInnes, *One Man's Documentary*. Unpublished manuscript deposited at the National Film Board Library, Montreal, 1973, pp. 29–30.
2 All these women spoke at the National Film Board Symposium, 'Four Days in May,' held at the National Film Board, Montreal, 6–9 May 1975, which the author attended.
3 Ernest Bornemann, 'The Documentary Film in Canada,' National Film Board of Canada. Unpublished 38-page mimeograph, 20 October 1945, in possession of the author, p. 6. (The real Charlie Gordon, Charles Campbell, contracted tuberculosis and died while working in Halifax during the war.)
4 Personal interview with Tom Daly, 13 March 1979.
5 PAC, RG53, vol. 1, meeting of the National Film Board, 9 February 1943.
6 Ibid., 11 December 1942.
7 Raymond Fielding, *The March of Time, 1935–51* (New York 1978), 87.
8 Personal interview with David Coplan, 14 October 1971.
9 National Film Board, 'The National Film Board of Canada,' September 1953, p. 9. Quoted from the *Journal of the Society of Motion Picture Engineers*, 44 (May 1945), 393–4.
10 James Beveridge, *John Grierson, Film Master* (New York, 1978), 150.
11 Personal interview with Tom Daly, 13 March 1979.
12 PAC, Privy Council Office, RG2, 18, vol. 42, Massey to King, 7 December 1942; Robertson to Grierson, 8 December 1942.
13 PAC, Privy Council Office, RG2, 18, vol. 8. King's draft of war aims, November 1939.
14 PAC, Privy Council Office, RG2, 18, vol. 20. Address to AF of L convention, 9 October 1942 by Prime Minister King.
15 PAC, External Affairs, RG25, vol. 1927, 24 December 1942.
16 PAC, RG53, vol. 1, meeting of the National Film Board, 12 January 1943.
17 Ibid., 18 July 1941.
18 *Has Anybody Here Seen Canada?* A co-production of the National Film Board of Canada and the Canadian Broadcasting Corporation, in association with the Great Canadian Moving Picture Company, 1978. See also

Kirwan Cox, 'The Grierson Files,' *Cinema Canada*, 56 (June-July 1979), 16–24.
19 PAC, RG53, vol. 1, meeting of the National Film Board, 14 April 1942.
20 Forsyth Hardy, *John Grierson: A Documentary Biography* (London, 1979), 125.
21 *Has Anybody Here Seen Canada?*

CHAPTER FIVE

1 A detailed account of National Film Board non-theatrical circuits appears in C.W. Gray's 'Movies for the People: The Story of the National Film Board's Unique Distribution System.' Unpublished monograph at the National Film Board Library, Montreal, 1973.
2 PAC, Wartime Information Board, report of the activities of the Office of the Director of Public Information from 1 April 1941 to 26 February 1942.
3 Ibid.
4 National Film Board Symposium, 'Four Days in May,' held at the National Film Board, Montreal, 6–9 May 1975, the author in attendance.
5 PAC, RG53, vol. 1, meeting of the National Film Board, 9 March 1943.
6 Chris Whynot, 'The NFB and Labour, 1945–1955,' *Journal of Canadian Studies*, 16:1 (Spring, 1981), 13–22.
7 The following films have been found in the National Film Board sound and silent film catalogues, 1941–51.
8 PAC, RG27, vol. 852, meeting of the National Film Board, 8 February 1944; Privy Council Office, RG2, 18, vol. 88, National Film Board annual report, 1944–5.

CHAPTER SIX

1 PAC, Privy Council Office, RG2, 18, vol. 17, Grierson to de Rochemont, 6 March 1942.
2 Canada. *Debates of the House of Commons*, 1942, vol. 3, 21 May 1942, p. 2620.
3 PAC, RG53, vol. 1, meeting of the National Film Board, 13 January 1942.
4 John Grierson, 'The Documentary Idea,' a letter to Basil Wright, May 1942. Document in the archives of the Centre de documentation cinématographique, Bibliothèque Nationale, Montreal.

5 PAC, RG53, vol. 1, meeting of the National Film Board, 9 February 1943.

6 PAC, Privy Council Office, RG2, 18, vol. 88, October 1941 NFB report and Ross McLean memo, 8 April 1947.

7 PAC, Privy Council Office, RG2, 18, vol. 88, National Film Board annual report, 1944–5. Grierson in fact ordered suppressed the $250,000 income from theatrical sales in 1943–4, though one can still assume that not all Film Board theatricals were reaching 5,000 theatres.

8 PAC, RG53, vol. 1, meeting of the National Film Board, Grierson to Robertson, 1 September 1942.

9 Ernest Bornemann, 'The Documentary Film in Canada,' National Film Board of Canada. Unpublished 38-page mimeograph, 20 October 1945, in possession of the author, pp. 16–20.

10 Stuart Legg interviewed in Has Anybody Here Seen Canada? A co-production of the National Film Board of Canada and the Canadian Broadcasting Corporation, in association with the Great Canadian Moving Picture Company, 1978.

11 Alan Lovell and Jim Hillier, Studies in Documentary (London, 1972), 52–79. (Timothy grew up to become a successful British surgeon.) See also Evan Cameron, 'An Analysis of A Diary for Timothy, a film by Humphrey Jennings,' Cinema Studies, 1 (Bridgewater Massachusetts, Spring, 1967).

12 PAC, Cabinet War Committee (microfilm), W-34-10, vol. 12, 26 September 1944.

13 See Irving Abella and Harold Troper, None Is Too Many: Canada and the Jews of Europe, 1933–1948 (Toronto, 1982), 72; 180; 220; 282. A somewhat embarrassed Department of External Affairs argued in 1945 that the gulf between Canadian statements of sympathy for refugees and actual commitment to their relief was so wide that it might undermine the Canadian position at the United Nations.

14 Walter Laqueur, The Terrible Secret: Suppression of the Truth about Hitler's 'Final Solution' (Boston, 1980), 9–10.

15 PAC, Privy Council Office, RG2, 18, vol. 17, 2 August 1943.

16 PAC, RG53, vol. 1, meeting of the National Film Board, 10 August 1943.

17 PAC, RG53, vol. 1, meeting of the National Film Board, 10 November 1942.

18 For feminist criticism of these and other wartime Film Board films, see Barbara Halpern Martineau, 'Before the Guerillieres: Women's Films at the NFB During World War II,' in Canadian Film Reader, ed. Seth Feldman and Joyce Nelson (Toronto, 1977), 58–66. Also, see Martineau's

'Notes for a Study of Women's History in the Media,' *Cinema Canada*, 51 (November-December, 1978), 30–4. See also the bibliography on feminist criticism in *Jump Cut*, no. 1.

19 Graham McInnes, *One Man's Documentary*. Unpublished manuscript deposited at the National Film Board Library, Montreal, 1973, pp. 129–31.

20 PAC, Privy Council Office, RG2, 18, vol. 15, digest or summaries of editorial comment for the Privy Council Office issued by the director of public information, 15–22 August 1942.

21 An interesting footnote to the Dieppe raid can be found in the King diaries in 1941, 1942, and 1944. On 20 May 1941 King wrote that defence minister Ralston said that Defence officials wanted a spectacular action by Canadian troops to encourage enlistment. The prime minister absolutely opposed the idea of raids on Europe and chastised his officials for losing all sense of values. Fifteen months later, in the wake of being released from his 'no conscription' pledge, King may have been thinking about enlistment and how a successful probe into Europe might enable him to bring in conscription without losing Quebec or forfeiting national unity. The disastrous landing at Dieppe on 19 August cost 907 dead and 1,946 prisoners from a force of 4,963. King wrote lamely in his diary on the 21st, 'It goes back I feel, above all to the time when it was felt it was necessary to have Canadians do something for a variety of reasons.' There was much to learn before another such landing could be tried and after the Allied invasion opened the long-awaited second front, he wrote, 'Clearly the martyrdom of the men of Dieppe has helped to save Britain and the countries of Europe' (13 September 1944). If he felt vindicated at last, the Dieppe fiasco was a failed event which no amount of propaganda could undo.

22 PAC, RG53, vol. 1, meeting of the National Film Board, 26 November 1942, quoting the *Boston Sunday Post* of 7 June 1942.

23 Grierson to Tallents, 16 February 1943. Letter in possession of the author.

24 James Eayrs, *In Defence of Canada* (Toronto, 1972), 322.

25 Ibid., 35.

26 Stuart Legg, interviewed in *Has Anybody Here Seen Canada?*

27 PAC, RG53, vol. 1, meeting of the National Film Board, 26 November 1942.

28 Canada. *Debates of the House of Commons*, 1944, vol. 2, 30 March 1944, p. 2018.

29 Ibid., 2020–1.

30 PAC, Privy Council Office, RG2, 18, vol. 17, 30 March 1944.
31 Forsyth Hardy, *John Grierson: A Documentary Biography* (London, 1979), 144.
32 Grierson to John Bird from Ottawa, 24 January 1944. Copy of letter in possession of the author.
33 Eayrs, *In Defence of Canada*, 139.
34 PAC, Privy Council Office, RG2, 18, vol. 88, National Film Board annual report, 1944–5.
35 C.P. Stacey, *Arms, Men and Governments: The War Policies of Canada, 1939–1945* (Ottawa, 1970), 229–30.
36 PAC, Privy Council Office, RG2, 18, vol. 17, Robertson to King, 10 January 1945.
37 PAC, Cabinet War Committee, RG2, 7C, 17 January 1945.
38 Personal interview with Ross McLean, 5 December 1973.
39 PAC, Privy Council Office, RG2, 18, vol. 17, Heeney to Robertson, 17 April 1944.
40 PAC, Privy Council Office, RG2, 18, vol. 17, R.G. Robertson to Gordon Robertson, 13 February 1945.
41 PAC, RG27, vol. 852, meeting of the National Film Board, 15 May 1945.
42 Personal interview with Tom Daly, 13 March 1979.
43 PAC, RG27, vol. 852, meeting of the National Film Board, 2 October 1945.
44 PAC, RG53, vol. 1, meeting of the National Film Board, 13 July 1943.

CHAPTER SEVEN

1 PAC, RG27, vol. 852, meeting of the National Film Board, 8 February 1944. The suppressed $250,000 conflicts with income figures on p. 169, though it proves how wide a distribution the Film Board's theatrical films enjoyed.
2 Grierson to John Bird from Ottawa, 24 January 1944. Letter in possession of the author.
3 PAC, RG27, vol. 852, meeting of the National Film Board, 11 January 1944.
4 PAC, William Lyon Mackenzie King papers, memoranda and notes series 1940–50, vol. 308, Heeney to King, 7 January 1944.
5 PAC, King papers, correspondence (primary series), 1944, vol. 78, Grierson to Turnbull, 14 March 1944.
6 PAC, RG27, vol. 852, meeting of the National Film Board, 28 March 1944.
7 Ibid., 9 May 1944.
8 Ibid., 28 September 1944.

9 Ibid., 30 October 1944.
10 Ibid., 12 December 1944.
11 Ibid., 13 February 1945.
12 Personal interview with Ross McLean, 5 December 1973.
13 PAC, RG27, vol. 852, meeting of the National Film Board, 13 February 1945.
14 Personal interview with Walter Turnbull, 4 January 1974.
15 James Eayrs, In Defence of Canada: Peacemaking and Deterrence (Toronto, 1972), 45.
16 Gazette (Montreal), 10 August 1945.
17 Personal interview with John Grierson, 14 March 1971.
18 PAC, King papers, memoranda and notes series, 1940–50, vol. 308, John Grierson, 'Outline of Policy and Future Perspectives for the Board,' 28 September 1944.
19 John Grierson, 'Searchlight on Democracy.' Written from Canada probably in the spring of 1939. Centre de documentation cinématographique, Bibliothèque Nationale, Montréal.
20 PAC King papers, correspondence (primary series) 1945, vol. 100, Grierson to King, 10 August 1945.
21 Pesonal interview with Walter Turnbull, 4 January 1974.
22 Personal interview with J.W. Pickersgill, 4 January 1974.
23 Eayrs, In Defence of Canada, 7.
24 Ibid., 185, 189, 330–1. Also see John Holmes, The Shaping of Peace: Canada and the Search for World Order, 1943–57 (Toronto, 1979), 1: 83.
25 Holmes, The Shaping of Peace, 1: 72.
26 Ibid., 97.
27 James Beveridge, John Grierson, Film Master (New York, 1978), 148.
28 Personal interview with Walter Turnbull, 4 January 1974.
29 Eayrs, In Defence of Canada, 325.
30 PAC, King papers, memoranda and notes series 1940–50, vol. 308, Heeney to King, 4, 23 August and 21 September 1945.
31 PAC, RG27, vol. 852, meeting of the National Film Board, 2 October 1945.
32 PAC, King papers, correspondence (primary series) 1945, vol. 100, King to Grierson, 8 November 1945.
33 Forsyth Hardy, John Grierson: A Documentary Biography (London, 1979), 152.
34 Canada. Debates of the House of Commons, 1945, vol. 3, 15 December 1945.
35 PAC, King diary, 7 September 1945.

36 Ibid., 10 September 1945.

37 Ibid., 11 October 1945.

38 Lester Pearson, film interview with Bernard Ostry, 8 October 1970, out-take from 'The Pearson Years,' rolls 125–6. CBC Television archives. This account differs slightly in tone and nuance from that in *Mike: The Memoirs of the Right Honourable Lester B. Pearson* (Toronto, 1975), 3: 165–6, leaving little doubt that the United States was preparing for the standoff that would become the cold war.

39 Eayrs, *In Defence of Canada*, 334.

40 Ibid., 332–3.

41 Ibid., 281.

42 Ibid., 335, 340, 343.

43 King diary, 4–5 February 1946.

44 Ibid., 13 February 1946.

45 Canada. Royal Commission, Espionage in Government Service, book 7, pp. 4110–11.

46 Personal interview with Ross McLean, 5 December 1973.

47 J.L. Granatstein, *A Man of Influence: Norman A. Robertson and Canadian Statecraft 1929–68* (Ottawa, 1981), 180.

48 PAC, Privy Council Office, RG2, 18, vol. 88. K. Greenwood to W.E. Halliday, 19 March 1946.

49 King diary, 1946, 20–1 February 1946.

50 Royal Commission, Espionage in Government Service, book 7, pp. 4112, 4114, 4115–18; book 10, pp. 5089–92, 5097–9, 5102.

51 Hardy, *Grierson*, 156–7.

52 Ibid., 157–8.

53 Personal interview with Walter Turnbull, 4 January 1974.

54 PAC, RG27, vol. 852, meeting of the National Film Board, 21 January 1947.

55 Canada. *Debates of the House of Commons*, 1946, vol. 1, 4 April 1946, p. 547; 1 May 1946, p. 1088; v. 2, 6 June 1946, p. 2224; v. 3, 11 July 1946, p. 3362.

56 PAC, RG27, vol. 852, meeting of the National Film Board, 18 July 1946.

57 Personal interview with Dan Wallace, 4 December 1973.

58 Beveridge, *John Grierson, Film Master*, 199.

59 PAC, Privy Council Office, RG2, 18, vol. 88, Claxton to Heeney, 17 October 1946; King to McLean, 10 January 1947.

60 PAC, RG27, vol. 852, meeting of the National Film Board, 18 February 1947.

61 Ibid., 25 March 1947.
62 Piers Handling, 'Censorship and Scares,' *Cinema Canada*, 56 (June-July, 1979), 25–31.
63 PAC, RG27, vol. 852, meeting of the National Film Board, 22 April 1947.
64 PAC, Privy Council Office, RG2, 18, vol. 88. Annual report of the National Film Board, pp. 1946–7.
65 Beveridge, *John Grierson, Film Master*, 140.
66 PAC, RG27, vol. 852, meeting of the National Film Board, 10 June 1948.
67 PAC, Privy Council Office, RG2, 18, vol. 88. Heeney to McCann, 26 June 1947.
68 PAC, RG27, vol. 852, meeting of the National Film Board, 10 June 1948.
69 Ibid., 1 December 1947.
70 Handling, 'Censorship and Scares,' 30.
71 Marjorie McKay, 'History of the National Film Board of Canada,' National Film Board, Montreal, 1964, p. 74.
72 Maynard Collins, 'A View from the Top: Arthur Irwin,' *Cinema Canada*, 56 (June-July 1979), 37–41.
73 J.W. Pickersgill, interview with Albert Kish in *Image Makers*, NFB-CBC production, 1981 (outtake).
74 J.W. Pickersgill, *My Years with Louis St. Laurent* (Toronto, 1975), 148–9.
75 PAC, RG27, vol. 852, meeting of the National Film Board, 1 February 1950.
76 Ibid., 6 February, 16 April, 16 July 1951.
77 Kirwan Cox, 'The Grierson Files,' *Cinema Canada*, 56 (June-July 1979), 16–24.
78 *New York Times*, 24 February 1946; 14 April 1946; 18 June 1946; 21 February 1947; 9 June 1949.

CHAPTER EIGHT

1 Grierson transcripts, interviews with John Grierson conducted by Rodrigue Chiasson and André Martin of the Canadian Radio-Television and Telecommunications Commission, February 1969 through July 1971, p. 118.
2 Ibid., 208–9.
3 Ibid., 69.
4 Zechariah Chafee, Jr, *Government and Mass Communications*, 2 vols. (Chicago, 1947), 746.
5 Grierson transcripts, 358.

6 Garth Jowett, *Film: The Democratic Art* (Boston, 1976), 309.
7 Ibid., 300; 313–14; 322.
8 John Grierson, 'Tomorrow the Movies I: Hollywood International,' *Nation*, 160: 2 (6 January 1945), 13.
9 Forsyth Hardy, *John Grierson: A Documentary Biography* (London, 1979), 123.
10 Personal interview with Ross McLean, 5 December 1973.
11 See article by Bruce Elder, 'On the Candid-Eye Movement,' in *Canadian Film Reader*, ed. Seth Feldman and Joyce Nelson (Toronto, 1977), 86–93.
12 Bernard Berelson, 'Effects of Print upon Public Opinion,' in *Print, Radio and Film in a Democracy*, ed. Douglas Waples (Chicago, 1942), 65.
13 Grierson transcripts, 256.
14 Forsyth Hardy interviewed the author on tape when in Montreal in 1976 in the presence of Ronald Blumer and Adam Symansky, and used this quote in his conclusion about Grierson in his biography.

List of Primary Sources

MANUSCRIPT COLLECTIONS

Cabinet War Committee (Wartime Information Board and National Film Board references), RG 2, 7C (microfilm), Public Archives of Canada, Ottawa

External Affairs. Films and Censorship. RG25, vols. 1915, 1919, 1927. Public Archives of Canada, Ottawa

John Grierson Collection (folios and assorted documents, uncatalogued). Centre de documentation cinématographique, Bibliothèque Nationale, Montréal

John Grierson Papers. Photocopies deposited at McGill University, Montreal

Meetings of the National Film Board. RG53, vol. 1 (1941–5) and RG27, vol. 853 (1945–51). Public Archives of Canada, Ottawa

National Film Board of Canada. RG27, vols. 848, 853, 857, 862

Privy Council Office. Wartime Information Board. Monthly Reports. RG2, 18, vols. 8, 15, 17, 20, 42, 49, 50, 52, 53, 54, 88, 110, 119, 120. Public Archives of Canada, Ottawa

Wartime Information Board. RG36/31, vols. 1, 2, 4, 8, 15. Public Archives of Canada, Ottawa

William Lyon Mackenzie King Diaries, MG26, J13, 1939–45. Public Archives of Canada, Ottawa

William Lyon Mackenzie King Papers. Primary Correspondence Series, 1939–46 (Manuscript Group 26, J1); Memoranda and Notes Series 1933–50 (MG26, J4). Public Archives of Canada, Ottawa

UNPUBLISHED MATERIALS

Bornemann, Ernest. 'The Documentary Film in Canada.' National Film Board of Canada, 20 October 1945. Mimeographed and in possession of the author

Bossin, Hye. Unpublished and unfinished manuscript and notes on the history of film in Canada, deposited at the Centre de documentation cinématographique, Bibliothèque Nationale, Montréal

Gray, C.W. 'Movies for the People. The Story of the National Film Board's Unique Distribution System.' National Film Board Library, Montreal, 1973

Grierson, John. 'The Motion Picture and the Political Power.' The Edinburgh Film Festival Celebrity Lecture, 24 August 1968, and notes on 'Media in Canada,' Fall 1969, both in possession of Eleanor Beattie

Grierson Transcripts. Interviews with John Grierson conducted by Rodrigue Chiasson and André Martin of the Canadian Radio-Television and Telecommunications Commission, February 1969 through July 1971

James, C. Rodney. 'The National Film Board of Canada: Its Task of Communication.' Unpublished PHD dissertation, Ohio State University, 1968

MacCann, Richard Dyer. 'Documentary Film and Democratic Government.' Unpublished PHD dissertation, Harvard University, January, 1951

McInnes, Graham. 'One Man's Documentary.' Unpublished manuscript deposited in the National Film Board Archives, Montreal, 1973

National Film Board of Canada. 'Memorandum on the History and Functions of the National Film Board,' 25 April 1947. Mimeographed and in possession of the author

National Film Board of Canada. 'The National Film Board of Canada,' September 1953. Mimeographed and in possession of the author

Savignac, Pierre. 'Semaine du Cinéma Canadien avec l'Office National du Film – Canada,' January, 1965. Unpublished report at the Centre de Documentation Cinématographique, Bibliothèque Nationale, Montréal

Young, W.R. 'Making the Truth Graphic: The Canadian Government's Home Front Information Structure and Programme During World War II.' Unpublished PHD dissertation, University of British Columbia, 1978

Index